# OVER-POPULATION AND ITS REMEDY

The Development of Industrial Society Series

William T. Thornton

# OVER-POPULATION AND ITS REMEDY

## n Inquiry into the Distress Prevailing among the Labouring Classes of the British Islands and into the Means of Remedying It

IRISH UNIVERSITY PRESS

Shannon Ireland

First edition London 1846

This I U P reprint is a photolithographic facsimile of the first edition and is unabridged, retaining the original printer's imprint.

© 1971 Irish University Press Shannon Ireland

*All forms of micropublishing*
© *Irish University Microforms Shannon Ireland*

ISBN 0 7165 1751 5

*T M MacGlinchey Publisher*

*Irish University Press Shannon Ireland*

PRINTED IN THE REPUBLIC OF IRELAND BY
ROBERT HOGG PRINTER TO IRISH UNIVERSITY PRESS

# The Development of Industrial Society Series

This series comprises reprints of contemporary documents and commentaries on the social, political and economic upheavals in nineteenth-century England.

England, as the first industrial nation, was also the first country to experience the tremendous social and cultural impact consequent on the alienation of people in industrialized countries from their rural ancestry. The Industrial Revolution which had begun to intensify in the mid-eighteenth century, spread swiftly from England to Europe and America. Its effects have been far-reaching: the growth of cities with their urgent social and physical problems; greater social mobility; mass education; increasingly complex administration requirements in both local and central government; the growth of democracy and the development of new theories in economics; agricultural reform and the transformation of a way of life.

While it would be pretentious to claim for a series such as this an in-depth coverage of all these aspects of the new society, the works selected range in content from *The Hungry Forties* (1904), a collection of letters by ordinary working people describing their living conditions and the effects of mechanization on their day-to-day lives, to such analytical studies as Leone Levi's *History of British Commerce* (1880) and *Wages and Earnings of the Working Classes* (1885); M. T. Sadler's *The Law of Population* (1830); John Wade's radical documentation of government corruption, *The Extraordinary Black Book* (1831); C. Edward Lester's trenchant social investigation, *The Glory and Shame of England* (1866); and many other influential books and pamphlets.

The editor's intention has been to make available important contemporary accounts, studies and records, written or compiled by men and women of integrity and scholarship whose reactions to the growth of a new kind of society are valid touchstones for today's reader. Each title (and the particular edition used) has been chosen on a twofold basis (1) its intrinsic worth as a record or commentary, and (2) its contribution to the development of an industrial society. It is hoped that this collection will help to increase our understanding of a people and an epoch.

The Editor
Irish University Press

# OVER-POPULATION

AND

## ITS REMEDY;

OR,

AN INQUIRY INTO THE EXTENT AND CAUSES

OF THE

DISTRESS PREVAILING AMONG THE LABOURING CLASSES

OF THE BRITISH ISLANDS,

AND INTO THE MEANS OF REMEDYING IT.

BY

## WILLIAM THOMAS THORNTON.

"The destruction of the poor is their poverty."
PROVERBS OF SOLOMON.

LONDON:
LONGMAN, BROWN, GREEN, AND LONGMANS,
PATERNOSTER-ROW.

1846.

LONDON:
Printed by A. SPOTTISWOODE,
New-Street-Square.

# PREFACE.

The only Preface which a work of this kind requires is an apology for the defects of its execution. Instead of pleading the claims of the poor to an earnest investigation of their distresses, one would be almost rather disposed to wonder that any other subject can be esteemed of national interest while this most momentous problem remains unsolved. The author, therefore, need take no pains to justify his choice of a subject; and he only wishes that he had equal cause to be satisfied with his treatment of it. Of his motive for writing at all, it can only be said, that "out of the abundance of the heart the mouth speaketh." With zeal for the cause he has espoused, he is amply, perhaps too amply, supplied, and he has spared no exertion to make up for the want of more sterling qualities. Perhaps, indeed, diligence was really the most indispensable requisite for his task. The volume now offered to the public has little claim to originality, and does not pretend to be the herald of any new discovery. The author's

object has been less to construct a theory of his
own, than to collect and arrange the ideas of others,
to work out their hints, to reconcile their inconsis-
tencies, and to form a regular and practicable
scheme out of their scattered and apparently incon-
gruous materials.  If he has failed in this design,
he trusts that he has at least been able to bring the
subject into a more convenient shape for discussion.
Though he may not persuade any to adopt his
sentiments, he may at least induce some to think
for themselves, and assist them in coming to conclusions of their own; and he will not esteem even
such partial success an inadequate recompence for
the labour with which his leisure has long been
occupied.

London, Dec. 1845.

# CONTENTS.

# CHAPTER III.

### EVIDENCES OF OVER-POPULATION IN SCOTLAND AND IRELAND.

# CHAPTER IV.

### CAUSES OF OVER-POPULATION IN GENERAL.

## CHAPTER V.

### CAUSES OF OVER-POPULATION IN ENGLAND.

## CHAPTER VI.

### CAUSES OF OVER-POPULATION IN SCOTLAND AND IRELAND.

## CHAPTER VII.

### REMEDIES FOR OVER-POPULATION IN ENGLAND AND WALES.

## CHAPTER VIII.

REMEDIES FOR OVER-POPULATION IN ENGLAND AND WALES —
(*continued*).

Certainty of the early Repeal of the Provision Laws. — Importance of the subsequent Conduct of Landowners in determining how Rent and the Remuneration of Labour will be affected. — Certainty of considerable Benefit to Agricultural Labourers, from the Establishment of Free Trade. — Ability of Landlords to improve their Condition forthwith. — Expediency of their preparing for the approaching Change in their

## CHAPTER IX.

REMEDIES FOR OVER-POPULATION IN SCOTLAND AND IRELAND.

## CHAPTER X.

# OVER-POPULATION,

AND

# ITS REMEDY.

---

## CHAPTER I.

DEFINITION OF THE TERM OVER-POPULATION. — IMPORTANCE
OF THE SUBJECT. — OBJECTS AND PLAN OF THE WORK.

By Over-population is to be understood, throughout
the following pages, that condition of a country
in which part of the inhabitants, although able-
bodied and capable of labour, are permanently
unable to earn a sufficiency of the necessaries of
life. A country is not necessarily overpeopled
merely because it contains a greater number of
inhabitants than its own soil can supply with food
and clothing, for the natives may nevertheless
obtain abundant supplies from abroad; and provided the supplies be adequate and regular, it
matters not from whence they come. Neither is
population always excessive where people are to
be found in a state of destitution, for this destitution may proceed solely from indolence, or from
bodily or mental infirmity. But wherever persons,
able as well as willing to work, are for many years

together unable to procure by labour a competent
subsistence, it is clear that there are too many
of them, and that the land they inhabit is over-
peopled. Further, population may be excessive
without being dense. In almost every community,
the owners of the soil, or of any considerable
amount of other property, are a minority, and many
of them must possess a greater quantity, or the
means of producing or of purchasing a greater
quantity, of food and of other necessaries than they
require for their own consumption. Few however
will be at the trouble of producing more than they
themselves can use, unless they can exchange the
surplus for something else. But many of their
countrymen have nothing to offer in exchange
save personal services, and if there be more applicants for employment than the rich are disposed
to employ, the services of all will not be accepted,
or if accepted, will be very scantily remunerated, and
either food enough for all will not be raised, or
when raised, part of it will be sent for sale to a
foreign market. In either case, the labouring class
is larger than the stock of food to which it has
access can properly maintain; and the country, however thinly inhabited it may be, and although it
may be only half cultivated, or may export provisions, is nevertheless overpeopled. It must be
observed, however, that in order to indicate over-
population, the distress of the working class must
be of long continuance, for merely temporary distress may be produced by famine, commercial
vicissitudes, or other accidents, in a country where

a livelihood may ordinarily be obtained without difficulty.

After this explanation, over-population may be shortly defined to be *a deficiency of employment for those who live by labour,* or *a redundancy of the labouring class above the number of persons that the fund applied to the remuneration of labour can maintain in comfort.* Of all the evils by which a nation can be afflicted, this is perhaps the worst. The ravages of war and pestilence are only occasional, and may be soon repaired ; a tyrant's caprice and cruelty are felt by comparatively few; and no government, however bad, which does not condemn the mass of its subjects to positive destitution, can avoid leaving them the means of considerable enjoyment. But the bulk of every community consists of persons entirely dependent on their own industry, and where these are too numerous to earn a competent subsistence for themselves and their families, competition takes place amongst them : each, in his anxiety to obtain employment, offers to accept lower wages than he requires for his comfortable maintenance, and, if the competition be sufficiently severe, will take the lowest pittance upon which life can be supported. Entire sections of the labouring class are thus reduced to extreme and almost hopeless misery. Hunger, cold, endurance of every sort of hardship, become the habitual portion of multitudes, nor are the evils of their condition limited to physical sufferings. Their moral debasement generally keeps pace with their social degradation. The desperate struggle they must maintain for existence, their cruel privations, the scenes and practices with which they must become familiar, seldom fail to harden their dispositions, and to make them deceitful, brutal, and dissolute; while the impossibility of materially benefiting themselves by any exertions of their own renders them indolent, and indolence aggravates their wretchedness. Neither has this state of things any tendency to correct itself. Whatever point population may attain, it can with equal ease at least maintain itself there, and the evils of its too great density may be not less lasting than severe.

Now, if this be the condition of the working class, it is no proof of national prosperity that the rest of the people are wealthy and civilised. A nation may be pre-eminent in power and grandeur, and equally distinguished in the arts of war and peace ; native industry and foreign commerce may supply in abundance every requisite for ease and luxury, and to these solid materials of enjoyment may be superadded all the resources of literature and science: still, if these advantages contribute only to the happiness of the few, while the many are sunk in bodily and mental destitution, the lot of such a people is any thing but an enviable one. With all their civilisation and refinement, their condition would not be ill exchanged for that of the rudest horde of wandering Tartars, whose numbers are better proportioned to their means of subsistence. The balance of happiness is apparently in favour of the latter. The conveniences of life may be almost unknown to them, and they may have scarcely a trace of intellectual culture; but if they are acquainted with few enjoyments, they are equally ignorant of the worst kinds of misery; if none can indulge in luxury, none are exposed to habitual want; to none is existence itself a prolonged penance. The distribution of national wealth is almost of as much consequence as its aggregate amount. A nation has no sense or feeling in its corporate capacity; it is its individual members that enjoy and suffer. If half of these are miserably poor, it is no consolation to them to know that their countrymen are rolling in riches. If the majority are wretched, no other epithet can properly be applied to the whole body.

To say that this description is generally applicable to the British Islands would no doubt be a gross exaggeration, but it cannot be denied that it would hold good of particular parts of them. The extreme destitution of the Irish peasantry has long been proverbial, and it now appears that a counterpart to it may be found in the Scottish highlands. Even in many English counties, the indigence of agricultural labourers, handloom weavers, and others, is such as can scarcely be paralleled out of the United Kingdom, and shows that we also are following, though happily still at some distance, in the steps of our neighbours. So much misery cannot be contemplated without awakening the intensest sympathy and the most gloomy forebodings. The constant occurrence of the topic in periodical literature, and in political discussion both in and out of parliament, the speeches, reports, and pamphlets incessantly devoted to it, evince the deep interest it excites. The present is another attempt to investigate the same engrossing subject. The first object of this essay will be, to determine how far the prevailing distress may be taken as proof of a redundant population. An endeavour will then be made to trace the circumstances in which over-population originated; and when the causes of the evil seem to have been discovered, suggestions will be offered for its correction. In the course of the inquiry, the three divisions of the kingdom will come separately under consideration, but the largest share of notice will be occupied by Great Britain. To have omitted all mention of Ireland would have been to leave the work obviously incomplete; but the reference to that unhappy island will be chiefly designed to illustrate the general principles laid down. Her distress, which has already furnished materials for so many volumes, is too deeply rooted and too complicated to admit of satisfactory examination in the few pages which can here be assigned to it.

# CHAPTER II.

It follows, from the remarks made in the preceding chapter, that the only unquestionable evidence respecting the existence of over-population,
is the condition of the labouring class; and this
cannot be ascertained satisfactorily except by reference to the remuneration of labour. It is only
when the average earnings of labourers are insufficient for their average requirements that labourers

can be safely pronounced to be too numerous.
An inquiry into the evidences of over-population
is therefore little more than an inquiry into the
wages or other reward of labour.

Unfortunately, there is infinite diversity of opinion as to what constitutes a sufficient subsistence.
No one will deny that a labourer's food, clothing,
and lodging, should be such as to maintain him
in health and strength; but it will not be so easily
settled whether he should eat meat, wear broad
cloth, and dwell in a neat cottage, or content
himself with potatoes, fustian, and a mud cabin.
Upon these points the reader will for the present
be left to form his own judgment, but it should
be clearly understood, that wages must not be
merely sufficient for the subsistence of the labourer himself. In every community there are
many persons physically disqualified for labour;
in fact, one half of mankind are so disqualified to a
certain extent by sex alone, and very young children and very old men are likewise disqualified. But
where able-bodied men can earn only a bare subsistence, feebler persons are not prevented from
maintaining themselves by physical weakness only.
They would still be unable to earn a competent
livelihood, even if they could work as well as the
rest, for their competition would then reduce the
wages of labour below the amount necessary for
subsistence. Such a state of things has already
been shown to constitute over-population. Where
population is confined within proper limits, the
earnings of those members of the labouring class

who can work, will suffice to maintain not only themselves, but also those who cannot work. The rate of wages ought to be such, as, supposing the care of maintaining the helpless members of their class to belong equally to all the able-bodied, would enable each of the latter to keep his fair proportion of dependents as well as himself. Now, even supposing that children above ten years of age, and women under sixty, can earn enough to defray their own expenses, there will still remain a vast number of persons who may be regarded as almost entirely helpless; for children under ten years of age, old women of sixty, and old men of seventy, are generally incapable of earning any thing worth mentioning. It was ascertained at the last census, that the number of such persons is, to the number of males between the ages of twenty and seventy, as 4,566,813 to 3,670,677, or as about $1\frac{1}{4}$ to 1. In England, therefore, the average earnings of an able-bodied male adult, whether married or single, ought, after supplying his own personal wants, to yield a surplus which would suffice for the subsistence of $1\frac{1}{4}$ other persons. If the average rate of wages be anywhere insufficient for this purpose, that part of the country may be considered to be overpeopled. It is, however, no sign of over-population that a man's income is too small to allow of his maintaining a more than average family. His distress in such a case proceeds from causes peculiar to himself. It does not spring from any excess of labourers, nor, strictly speaking, from the low remuneration of labour, but merely from the unusual largeness of his family, and the extreme youth or other infirmity by which an unusually large proportion of its members are disqualified from earning their own livelihood, and are rendered dependent on their parents.

The labouring population has hitherto been spoken of as if it formed only one class, but it is really divided into several, among which the rates of remuneration are far from being uniform. It might be supposed that competition would render the price of labour everywhere the same, and that the only differences in the rate of wages would arise from the superior hardship or delicacy of particular occupations. In reality, however, there are monopolies of labour as well as of other commodities. Various causes, both natural and artificial, prevent labour from flowing freely in every direction; and wherever the supply is deficient, it finds of course a better market than elsewhere. Wages, consequently, vary exceedingly in different occupations; so that, in order to represent with perfect fidelity the state of the labouring population, it would be necessary to describe each class separately. But this is neither permitted by the limits nor required by the object of this work, for the latter of which a much ruder and more hasty sketch will suffice. The working population will be treated under the separate heads of rural and urban, but many minor subdivisions, which exhibit no signs of general distress, may be altogether overlooked, and attention will be chiefly directed to agricultural and common day labourers, and to those engaged in some branches of manufacture.

Agricultural labourers claim the first notice, as well on account of the importance of their occupation, as of their forming, with the single exception of domestic servants, the most numerous class in the country. According to the census of 1841, their whole number, including women and children, in England and Wales, was 966,271; of whom 772,072 were male adults. The nature of field labour being much the same in every part of the country, it might have been expected that the earnings of agricultural labourers would likewise be everywhere pretty nearly equal; but although subject to less striking variations than wages in other departments of industry, they do really vary very materially, not only in different counties but in different parts of the same county. It may seem strange, that where wages are unusually high, they should not be immediately reduced to the common level by the migration of labourers from other quarters; but, besides that there is some foundation for Adam Smith's assertion, that " man is the least transportable species of luggage," the comparative isolation and the illiterateness of agricultural labourers prevent their knowing much of the state of affairs beyond their own neighbourhood. Moreover, until the late change in the poor-law, the laws affecting the settlement of paupers virtually almost confined the English field labourer to his native parish; and would often

have restrained him, even if so disposed, from
going elsewhere in quest of better remuneration.
It is unnecessary for the purposes of this inquiry
to examine the condition of the labourer in every
part of the country. We may confine our attention to those districts which present the most striking contrasts, and having ascertained both the
highest and the lowest degrees on the social scale
occupied by labourers, we shall be able to judge of
their general condition, and to determine in what
districts their numbers are excessive.

No other part of England seems to have a better
right than Lincolnshire to be entitled the labourer's paradise. His wages in this county, according to one account*, range from 11s. to 13s. a
week, but according to a statement made by Lord
Worsley in the House of Commons†, they are
never less than 9s. even in winter, nor less than
12s. at other seasons; while, if task-work be taken
into the account, a man's average earnings throughout the year are from 13s. to 16s. 6d. a week, to which
his wife may, at certain seasons, add 10d. or 1s. a
day by field-work. The money wages of labourers
in husbandry, however, sometimes form only part
of their income. In Lincolnshire, the practice of
allotting to them small portions of land of half
an acre in extent, at the rent customary in the
neighbourhood, to be cultivated in their spare
hours, has now become pretty general, and adds

* Reports on Employment of Women and Children in Agriculture, 1843.

† Hansard's Parl. Deb., 12th March, 1844.

greatly to their resources. Half an acre, under spade tillage, may produce on an average ten pounds worth* of potatoes and other vegetables, and will allow of a pig being kept besides, so that the average annual profit of a cultivator may be fairly estimated as high as 11*l*. Eleven pounds sterling a year are a fraction less than 4*s*. 3*d*. a week, which, added to 14*s*. of wages, will make a weekly income of 18*s*. 3*d*. altogether. In some parts of Lincolnshire, labourers are sometimes hired by the year, and at Kilstern, where this seems to be a common custom, they are said to have besides about 28*l*. a year in money, a cottage and garden rent free, " the keep of a pig in the crews in the winter, and run upon the farm in the summer," and the right to four quarters of barley and two quarters of wheat at a low price. The total income of a single man so situated may be thus estimated:

|  | £ | s. | d. |
|---|---|---|---|
| Yearly wages - - - | 28 | 0 | 0 |
| Annual value of cottage and of garden produce - - - - | 6 | 0 | 0 |
| Profit by sale of pig - - - | 1 | 0 | 0 |
| Gain by low price of corn supplied by the farmer - - - - | 2 | 10 | 0 |
|  | 37 | 10 | 0 |
| To which may be added for net produce of allotment - - - - | 10 | 0 | 0 |
| Making altogether the annual sum of - | 47 | 10 | 0 |

Or about 18*s*. 3*d*. a week.

About Kilstern agricultural labourers can afford

* Minutes of Evidence before Committee on Cottage Allotments.

to eat fresh meat almost every day; and throughout
Lincolnshire they seem to be able to do so pretty
frequently. At other times they have bacon (for
they almost always eat their pig themselves); but
their principal diet is wheaten, and sometimes
barley bread, dumplings, and potatoes; with cheese,
butter, onions, and other vegetables, and tea.

This notice of Lincolnshire requires little alteration to adapt it to the adjoining county of
Rutland, where farm-servants are similarly well
paid, and are likewise in general allotment-holders.
It may be mentioned that, both in Lincolnshire
and Rutland, the cottager frequently keeps a cow
upon his land, and gets a daily supply of milk
instead of vegetables.

Next in order, according to the social position
of the peasantry, come the three northern counties
of Northumberland, Cumberland, and Westmoreland. In the first of these the mode of hiring
farm-servants is peculiar. Some are engaged merely
by the day, in which case the wages of men are 2s.
or 2s. 3d.; but this custom is not the most common.
There being but few villages from which occasional
assistance can be obtained, farmers endeavour to
maintain upon their own lands as many persons as
they are likely to require at the busiest season.
Upon every farm there are a number of cottages,
with gardens attached, and " every man who is
engaged by the year has one of these cottages. His
family commonly find employment more or less; but
one female he is bound to have always in readiness
to answer the master's call, and to work at stipu-

lated wages, which are universally 10*d*. a day, except at harvest, when they are 1*s*. To this engagement the name of bondage is given; and such females are called bondagers, or women who work the bondage."*

The advantage of this system to the labouring class is unquestionable. The hind, as the yearly labourer is called, has a cottage and garden for himself and his family, several of whom are, in many cases, engaged by the year, as well as himself. His own wages are paid chiefly in kind; those of his sons, &c. either in money, or partly in money and partly in kind. Their average amount may be ascertained from the subjoined detailed examples, taken from Sir F. H. Doyle's Report, of the conditions entered into with their labourers by three large occupiers of land:

| *Mr. Grey.* | *Mr. Fenwick.* | *Mr. Hindmarsh.* |
|---|---|---|
| 36 bush. oats | 10 bush. wheat | 36 bush. oats |
| 24 „ barley | 30 „ oats | 24 „ barley |
| 12 „ peas | 10 „ barley | 12 „ peas |
| 3 „ wheat | 10 „ rye | 6 „ wheat |
| 3 „ rye | 10 „ peas | 1000 yards of potatoes |
| 36 to 40 bush. of potatoes | A cow's keep for the year | A cow's keep |
| 24 lbs. of wool | 800 yards of potatoes | House and garden |
| A cow's keep for the year | Cottage and garden | Coals led |
| Cottage and garden | Coals led | 5*l*. in cash. |
| Coals carrying from the pit | 3*l*. 10*s*. in cash | |
| 4*l*. in cash. | 2 bushels of barley in lieu of hens. | |

* Sir F. H. Doyle in Reports on Emp. of Women and Children in Agric., 1843. It may be worth while to mention.

A still better idea of the condition of the Northumbrian peasantry may be obtained from the annexed specimen of the half-yearly accounts between Mr. Hindmarsh and one of his hinds, and from the succeeding table, showing the sums due at the end of the half-year to several hinds on a farm in another part of Northumberland, being the surplus earnings of all the members of each family, which they had not found it necessary to call for in the course of the half-year, and had left in their master's hands till Martinmas.

*William Hindmarsh, Esq., Dr. to John Thompson.*

|  | £ | s. | d. |
|---|---|---|---|
| Jane Thompson, the bondager, 121½ days at 10d. - | 5 | 1 | 3 |
| Kate Thompson (a child), 24 harvest days at 1s. - | 1 | 4 | 0 |
| — — — 73½ days at 5d. | 1 | 10 | 7½ |
| Eliza Thompson (a younger child), 7½ days - | 0 | 1 | 9½ |
| Isabella Thompson (a dress maker at other times), 35¾ days at 1s. - - - - - | 1 | 15 | 9 |
| — — 20 harvest days at 2s. 3d. - | 2 | 5 | 0 |
| Wife, 9 harvest days - - - - | 1 | 0 | 3 |
| His old Father, 52 days - - - | 3 | 18 | 0 |
| John Thompson's half-year's cash - | 2 | 10 | 0 |
|  | £19 | 6 | 8 |

that there is nothing slavish but the sound in these terms "bondage" and "bondager." They only mark the Danish descent of the modern Northumbrians. Like the Norwegian *bonde,* and the English *husbandman* and *husband,* they are not "derived from the word *band,* or *bond,* or *bind,* synonymous with *vinculum* and its derivatives, but from the Scandinavian words, *bond, brend, bor,* synonymous with inhabiting, dwelling in, dwell. *Bonder* and *husbandmen* are the in-dwellers and householders. *Bonde* is the inhabitant, not the bondsman." — *Laing's Norway,* p. 369.

*Half-yearly Accounts of Hinds.*

| | £ | s. | d. | | £ | s. | d. |
|---|---|---|---|---|---|---|---|
| G. Cranston - | 8 | 3 | 6½ | T. Robson - - | 4 | 3 | 11 |
| A. Tunnat - - | 15 | 0 | 4¼ | J. Cranston - - | 6 | 12 | 4½ |
| J. Redpath - - | 9 | 7 | 11½ | A. Young - - | 7 | 2 | 5½ |
| S. Ewart - - | 5 | 5 | 9½ | E. Davison - - | 5 | 15 | 1 |
| A. Gray - - | 7 | 14 | 4½ | G. Chernside - - | 5 | 16 | 7 |
| A. Elliott - - | 23 | 2 | 2 | T. Middlemas - | 4 | 9 | 10½ |

T. Fullerton in debt to his master 7*l.* 9*s.* 8½*d.* He had lost a valuable cow, and his master had lent him 10*l.* to replace it.

The food of these people is, as might be presumed, composed chiefly of the articles they receive in lieu of wages, and consists of oatmeal porridge, bread made of barley and peameal mixed, potatoes, milk, and occasionally bacon. They cannot complain of deficiency in the quantity of their food. " It often happens indeed that a hind with but few in family has at the end of the year a good deal of corn to dispose of, for which his master is always willing to give him the market price." The Northumbrian peasantry are however much better fed than housed. Sir F. Doyle shrewdly remarks, that if throughout a large district cottages were held rent free, many of them would probably be unfit to live in, and Northumberland, he says, justifies the assertion. The cottages there generally contain only one room, about 17 feet long by 15 broad. The walls are of rubble, or stones embedded in mud; the floor is also mud; and the thatch, old, patched, and rotten, looks more like the top of a dunghill than of a house. There is a sketch of a group of these hovels in a little tract * by the Rev. Dr. Gilly, which shows

* Appeal on behalf of the Border Peasantry.

that they are such as no kind-hearted master would keep a cow in. It must be owned, however, that something has been done of late to wipe away this disgrace. Sir Walter Riddell and other bene-volent landlords have built ranges of comfortable cottages on their estates, and it is to be hoped that so excellent an example will soon be generally imitated.

The peasantry of Cumberland and Westmoreland ought perhaps to have been placed before those of Northumberland, for a smaller proportion of them be-long to the class of mere labourers. Heads of families are very commonly proprietors of a few acres of land which they cultivate with their own hands, procur-ing from their little freeholds not only every neces-sary article of food, but also the raw materials of clothing, which they partly manufacture themselves. These "statesmen," or "lairds," as they are called, do not aspire to luxury ; but all their wishes are amply satisfied, and few people enjoy more of hum-ble happiness. Their sons, if not required at home, enter the service of the neighbouring farmers. They are commonly hired by the half-year, for which period they are paid from 6*l.* 10*s.* to 9*l.* 10*s.*, and are lodged and boarded in their masters' houses, which they seldom leave until, through the death of some relation or neighbour, they succeed to the ownership or lease of a cottage farm. " What is called surplus labour does not here exist. Intersected in every direction by ranges of almost inaccessible and barren mountains, the population is thinly dotted over the intervening valleys," in due proportion to the facilities for cultivation and the opportunities for employment. *

These particulars may enable the reader to judge of the condition of the happiest portion of the English peasantry. Truly it presents no very captivating picture. The allotment holders of Lincolnshire and Rutland, and the yeomen of Cumberland and Westmoreland, indeed, are in a position which leaves little to be wished for, but such labourers as are entirely dependent on wages, although they may be secure from want, can scarcely be said to know any thing of comfort. Still it is something to obtain, by incessant toil, a sufficiency of the necessaries of life, and it would be well if even this modicum of good fortune were everywhere the husbandman's lot. How far otherwise is the fact we shall perceive, when, having observed him in his palmiest state, we now descend to the other extremity of the scale, and see what sort of a life he leads in the counties of Wilts and Somerset.

Dorsetshire affords an instance of the way in which the rate of wages sometimes varies at places within the same neighbourhood. If any dependence can be placed upon statements made by witnesses of the highest respectability †, which, while attracting a great deal of public attention, still remain unre-

---

* Mr. Voules' Report on Westmoreland and Cumberland, in Appendix to Second Annual Report of Poor Law Commissioners. Messrs. Bailey and Culley's Report on Northumberland, Cumberland, &c.

† See letters to Editor of " Times " newspaper, from the Hon. and Rev. Godolphin Osborne, Mr. Sheridan, and others.

futed, it is certain that in most parts of the county
the total receipts of a labouring man do not exceed
8s. a week, yet in others, in the neighbourhood of
Blandford for example, the average is represented
on equally good authority * as not less than 11s.,
exclusive of other advantages, such as the possession of a cottage either rent free, or at a reduced
rent, a potato ground rent free, and the occasional
use of his master's horses in his allotment. It is
certain, however, that this is an exception to the
rule, and that in general a field labourer cannot
one week with another earn more than 8 shillings.
A woman may earn sixpence, eight-pence, or a shilling a day, according to the season, but the employment of women in agriculture is not continuous,
and it is supposed that the earnings of a cottager's
wife throughout the year do not much exceed 50
shillings.† A man and his wife may therefore have
9s. a week, or 23l. 8s. a year, to provide for three
and a quarter persons on an average. Fifty shillings go for rent, thirty for fuel, thirty more for
soap and candles, and five pounds for clothes, leaving twelve pounds eighteen shillings a year, or about
eight-pence halfpenny a day, to buy food for the
family, that is to say, a fraction more than two-pence
halfpenny a head daily. Taking the average price

* Mr. Austin's Rep. on Emp. of Women and Children in
Agriculture.

† Dr. Kay, an Assistant Poor-Law Commissioner, made an
inquiry, in the year 1838, into the incomes of 539 families in
Norfolk and Suffolk, and found the average annual earnings of
an agricultural labourer's wife to be £2 12s. 7d.

of such bread as is used by the peasantry in the West of England to be one shilling the gallon loaf of 8lb. 11oz. and that of potatoes to be fourteen pence per bushel of 55lb., two-pence halfpenny will purchase about 29oz. of bread or 10lb. of potatoes. In Ireland, where the character of the potato may be presumed to be best understood, five pounds are considered no more than a sufficient meal for a labouring man, but it appears that two of such meals a day are as much as the Dorsetshire labourer can venture to indulge in.

It must be borne in mind, that these calculations are not intended to represent the actual condition of the Dorsetshire labourer, but rather to show what it would be if every able-bodied man had to maintain an equal proportion of the helpless members of the community. Most of the aged and orphan poor are maintained by the parish, but it must not on that account be supposed that the average number of persons for whom an agricultural labourer has to provide is less than one and a quarter, or that each person's share of the daily eightpenny-worth of food is proportionably greater. Marriages take place both much more frequently and much earlier among labourers than among people of higher rank, and their families are consequently larger than the average. Certainly the real condition of the Dorsetshire peasantry is very little, if at all, superior to the description given above. Bread and potatoes do really form the staple of their food. As for meat, most of them would not know its taste, if once or twice in the course of their lives — on the

'Squire's having a son and heir born to him, or on the young gentleman's coming of age, they were not regaled with a dinner of what the newspapers call "old English fare." Some of them contrive to have a little bacon, in the proportion, it seems, of half a pound a-week to a dozen persons, but they more commonly use fat to give the potatoes a relish, and as one of them told Mr. Austin, "they don't *always* go without cheese."

Particular stress has been laid upon the quantity and quality of food, because these are the most unerring tests of poverty. Few will stint themselves when they have the means of buying provisions, but many wear dirty ragged clothes merely because they are slovens, and every one must dwell in a hovel where no other dwellings than hovels exist. Otherwise the habitations, not less than the diet, of the Dorsetshire labourers, might be cited in proof of their extreme indigence. The cottages are generally old and decayed, and rarely contain more than three, and often only two rooms, so that grown-up persons of different sexes, fathers and daughters, brothers and sisters, are obliged to sleep in the same chamber. The walls are of mud, the floors generally of stone, but sometimes of earth, which in wet weather becomes mud, as the floors are often below the level of the ground outside. Drainage, and similar accommodations, are universally neglected, and the air is poisoned by the heaps of filth that accumulate beside the doors and windows. But though these wretched dens are doubtless as good as the Dorsetshire labourer can afford to rent, he could not choose but live in them, even if his means were greater, for the cottages in his neighbourhood are mostly of this description. As he must live near the farm on which he works, he must content himself with such lodgings as the owners of the land think proper to provide; and the condition of his dwelling, therefore, indicates chiefly the degree of the landholders' regard for their dependents, and is less certainly a proof of the inhabitant's poverty than an aggravation of his wretchedness.

Dorsetshire has lately become a byeword among the advocates of the agricultural poor, as if it exhibited the darkest picture of rural distress to be discovered in England; but in the lowest deep there is still a lower deep, as the traveller finds on passing out of this county, and entering either Wilts or Somersetshire. It has been stated, that in Dorsetshire the average rate of wages is about 8s. a-week, and there are numbers of men who have nothing besides this money payment; but still there are numerous instances of persons obtaining other advantages, which make a sensible, and sometimes important addition to their income. In Wiltshire wages are quite as low, and indeed rather lower, and the labourer seldom receives any thing additional from his master, or has any means of increasing his income, unless he has an allotment or keeps a pig. The farmers wonder how their men can live upon their earnings, and it would be wonderful indeed if the effects of insufficient food did not show themselves in the rapid deterioration of the race. Recruiting officers find a material difference in the appearance and strength of candidates from the south-western and from the north and north-midland counties, and farmers observe an equal variation in the amount of exertion which they can obtain from their men. In Wiltshire the labourer's diet consists, as in Dorsetshire, chiefly of potatoes and bread, but the proportion of the latter article is smaller, and potatoes with salt are sometimes the only food. In Somersetshire, matters are still worse. Wages are there 8s., 7s., and in some places as low as 6s. a week, without any addition, except an allowance of cyder, worth about 15d., which the labourer perhaps would be quite as well without. Allotments also are less general than in the adjoining counties. Nevertheless, as the quality of the food used in those counties cannot easily be much reduced, potatoes and bread form the chief sustenance of the cottager in Somersetshire also, though the quantity of those articles consumed by him corresponds, of course, with his inferior earnings.

From this view of the agricultural labourer's condition in the several counties in which it wears its brightest and its gloomiest aspect, a pretty correct idea may be formed regarding it throughout the rest of England. It ranges, of course, between the two extremes, being nowhere so tolerable as in Lincolnshire, and nowhere so melancholy as in Somersetshire, but nevertheless approaching in different districts to the comfort of the one or the wretchedness of the other. Thus in most parts of Yorkshire and others of the northern counties, the peasantry are little, if at all, worse off than their brethren of Northumberland. They are nearly as well fed, and they cannot be worse housed. In Kent also the rate of agricultural wages is rather above the average. Ten or twelve years ago the Kentish peasantry were among the most degraded in England, and their nearly universal dependence on the poor's rates for part of their subsistence seemed to be an unequivocal sign of over-population. The New Poor Law, however, while it threw them more upon their own resources, showed at the same time that those resources were much greater than had been supposed. Since the passing of this law the rate has not fallen, but remains at the old amount of 10s. or 12s. a-week, thus showing that previously, when so many of the poor were maintained in idleness, the funds for profitably employing them were not really wanting, but were merely misdirected.

If official reports could be implicitly trusted, the condition of the peasantry in Norfolk and Suffolk would likewise be above the average. It may really have been so until lately, at least in Norfolk, where farms are generally very large, and farmers men of considerable capital, and little disposed to drive a hard bargain with their labourers. During the last two or three years, however, the fall in the price of produce has made them anxious to diminish the expenses of cultivation, and in many instances they have tried to save by employing fewer labourers and lowering wages. Even when employment was abundant, and while wages remained at the old rate of 10s. a week, the peasantry of these two counties seldom tasted anything better than dry bread; so that, when employment was only to be had every other day, and the rate of wages fell to seven or eight shillings a week, their situation became truly deplorable.*

The peasantry of Bedfordshire and Buckingham-shire, also, are not much more to be envied than those of the west of England. These two counties are the principal seats of two manufactures — those of pillow lace and straw plat, which, twenty or thirty years ago, enabled the wives and daughters of cottagers to earn as much as their husbands and brothers. These manufactures have since fallen into decay, and are now brought so low that persons engaged in them cannot obtain a fifth part of their former earnings. The farm-labourer's seven, eight, or nine shillings a week have now become the main-stay of his family, and the smallness of their amount is only too perceptible. A recent though somewhat too highly-coloured account speaks of the cottages as being little better than pigstyes; and says, that the raggedness and filth of the inmates are surpassed nowhere but in Ireland, while their wasted forms and pale faces give them almost the appearance of people recovering from severe illness.

The Rebecca riots that took place in South Wales, in the summer of 1843, drew a large share of pub-

* See the Reports written from Norfolk and Suffolk, by the Correspondent of the "Times" newspaper, in June and July, 1844. Next to personal observation, nothing can give a better idea of the real position of the English peasantry than these most interesting letters.

lic attention to the state of the inhabitants of that quarter, where the peasantry seem to be worse off than in the worst parts of England. Seven shillings a week — the minimum of English agricultural wages — are there the maximum, and are obtained only by labourers in the employment of landowners and gentlemen farmers. Such labourers commonly have their cottages rent-free. Most of the farms, however, are small, not extending beyond 100 acres; and the poorer farmers pay their men only eight-pence, nine-pence, or, at most, a shilling a day, or sixpence or eight-pence a day with food, if, as is often the case, the men board with their masters. Coarse barley bread, flummery, and potatoes, are almost their sole food, and many of the small farmers themselves have little else except milk, cheese, and bacon. They seldom taste any other animal food.*

The general application of machinery and steam power to manufactures has caused the latter to be removed almost entirely from the country to towns, where the number of workpeople required in a large establishment is most easily procurable. One or two decaying manufactures still linger in the cottages of the poor, such as those of pillow lace and straw plat, already mentioned, in Buckingham-shire and Bedfordshire, and some others, both of the midland and western counties; and that of shirt-button making, in Dorsetshire. A good many

---

* Letters of the Welsh Correspondent of the "Times," written during the summer and autumn of 1843.

hand-loom weavers and stocking makers also reside in the villages of the manufacturing districts; and isolated factories, on a large scale, are to be found here and there in country places; but the number of persons employed in them bears too small a proportion to the mass of the rural population, and the condition of rural operatives, as far as wages are concerned, differs too slightly from that of their brethren in towns, to require more than a passing allusion to them. It may be laid down as a general rule, that, wherever agriculture is carried on in the neighbourhood of other occupations, its wages will be found nearly, if not quite, at the bottom of the scale. Almost every other business, with the solitary exception of hand-loom weaving, seems to be more disagreeable than husbandry, or to be less easily learned, or to demand greater exertion, and is consequently better paid, except when its remuneration is temporarily depressed by peculiar circumstances.

Colliers and other miners are a much more numerous and important class than rural manufacturers, but they are still less entitled to lengthened notice in this place. There is perhaps no body of men whose physical as well as moral condition is more susceptible of improvement, but, among the evils from which they suffer, scanty remuneration, the distinctive symptom of over-population, is rarely to be found. High wages are required to counterbalance the numerous hardships and inconveniences of their mode of life, and miners are always much better paid than any other unskilled

labourers in the same neighbourhood. In Staffordshire they earn from 15s. to 18s. a week; in Warwickshire, 18s. a week; in Yorkshire, 20s. to 25s.
a week; in Durham and Northumberland, 20s. to
30s. a week; in Cornwall, 40s. to 65s. a month; in
South Wales, 25s. to 60s. a week.*

Notwithstanding the generally low remuneration
of agricultural labourers, early marriages are very
prevalent amongst them, and in most cottages children are more numerous than the adult inmates.
The rural population, however, does not advance at
the rate which these facts would seem to indicate,
owing to the migration which is continually taking
place from the country to the towns. The extent
of this migration may be ascertained by a comparison of the annual reports of the Registrar-General
with the returns of the last census; from which
it appears that, in counties containing important
manufactures or numerous towns, the increase of
population between 1831 and 1841 was much
greater, and in counties chiefly agricultural much
less, than the annual excess of births over deaths,
uninfluenced by other circumstances, would have
effected. Thus, in Lancashire, the increase of
population in the ten years ending in 1841 was
330,210; and in Cheshire, 60,919; while the excess
of births (supposing it to have been the same in
each year of the series as in the last year) was only
150,150 in the former, and 28,000 in the latter.

* Report of Children's Employment Commission in Mines
and Collieries.

In particular towns the contrast is still more striking. In Liverpool and Bristol the annual deaths actually exceed the births, so that these towns are only saved from depopulation by their rural recruits, yet the first increased the number of its inhabitants in ten years by more than one-third, and the other by more than one-sixth. In Manchester the annual excess of births could only have added 19,390 to the population between 1831 and 1841; the actual increase was 68,375. The number of emigrants into Birmingham, during the same period, may in the same way be estimated at 40,000; into Leeds, at 8,000; into the metropolis, at 130,000. On the other hand, in Dorset, Somerset, and Devonshire, the actual addition to the population in the same decennial period was only 15,491, 31,802, and 39,253 respectively; although the excess of births over deaths, in the same counties, was about 20,000, 38,600, and 48,700. People cannot of course be induced to leave their birthplace and the society of their relatives and friends, and to change their habits and modes of life, except by the hope of some counterbalancing advantage; and accordingly, in most considerable towns, wages, independently of any differences in the nature of the occupation, are generally somewhat higher than in the adjoining country. It scarcely ever happens that any class of townsmen are worse paid than husbandmen, unless their wages have been depressed below their former level by peculiar causes; but an example has been very lately exhibited of such a depression, affecting the whole body of labourers in many English towns, which deserves to be particularly noticed, in order to prevent its being confounded with the ordinary condition of our urban population.

A very large proportion of the workpeople resident in English towns are engaged in manufactures. Using this term in its common and restricted, but not very easily defined sense, as distinguished from handicrafts, and as denoting only part of the processes whereby the raw produce of the earth is converted into fabrics for man's use, more than 400,000 male adults, and a still greater number of females and young persons, are so employed. A short time back the greater part of this vast multitude seemed to be sunk in the lowest depth of misery. Thousands were absolutely unable to procure employment, and might be seen standing in constrained idleness about the streets; or might be found in their dismal homes, bending over a scanty fire, their heads sunk on their breasts, and surrounded by pale emaciated beings, imploring them for food, which they knew not where to seek. Others, somewhat less wretched, were able to obtain work, but only irregularly, and at greatly reduced wages. Scarcely anywhere was there an individual wholly unaffected by the prevailing distress, and who did not perceive its presence at least in some diminution of his accustomed comforts. These expressions are no rhetorical exaggerations, introduced for the sake of effect. The subject is too serious for such trifling. They are a plain and temperate representation of the recent condition of English operatives

(the modern appellation for manufacturing labourers), and are supported, as will immediately be seen,
by the minutest and most trustworthy evidence.

In January, 1842, when misery in the manufacturing districts was at its height, the Poor Law
Commissioners thought it expedient that a searching inquiry should be instituted into the circumstances of some one town situated in those districts;
and having selected Stockport as the place which
was understood to be in the most deplorable condition, they sent there two of their assistants, to
examine into the extent, nature, and causes of the
prevailing distress. These gentlemen executed
their task with the assiduity and and ability which
have seldom been wanting in the instruments of the
Poor-Law Commission, and their Report presents
a picture of human suffering, at once so severe and
so heroically borne, as can scarcely be contemplated
without tears of mingled pity and admiration.

Stockport is one of the principal seats of the
cotton manufacture, and, five years before the
Assistant Commissioners' visit, had been in a very
flourishing condition. The weekly income of the
family of a labourer of the lowest class was then
seldom less than one pound, and not unfrequently
double or treble that amount. Between this time
and 1842, not less apparently than ten thousand
persons were thrown out of employment. Of these,
many had migrated from other parts of England,
and now returned to their own parishes. Others
voluntarily left the town, and went in search of
work elsewhere, sometimes exploring the whole of

Lancashire and Yorkshire on this errand. Those who remained behind, struggled gallantly before they applied for parochial relief: they first exhausted the little hoard accumulated in better days, and sold or pawned their furniture, eking out the money thus obtained with the earnings of occasional jobs. " They did not appear before us, " says the chairman of the Stockport Board of Guardians, "until their little savings, their household furniture, and nearly the whole of their clothing and bedding had been sold or pawned, in hopes of a change in the times. This hope has been deferred until their souls have sickened within them, and the complaints of their starving wives, and the crying of their hungry children, have driven them to the alternative of applying for relief, or of allowing their families to die from destitution." Instances occurred of persons being brought to a premature grave by the privations they thus voluntarily endured. One of these, who died within a week after the application which he was at last compelled to make to the guardians, being asked why he had not sought relief sooner, replied that he wished to go on as long as he could first, — "a very common reason" observed the commissioners' informant, "with some of the poor." Yet, notwithstanding this independence of spirit, and notwithstanding that a large portion of the population of Stockport consisted of strangers not entitled to parochial relief, the number of persons of every description who were able to claim and were compelled to accept that relief, had increased, in December, 1841, to nearly seven

thousand, one-twelfth at least of the whole population of the Union. To so large a multitude, only
scanty relief could be afforded; not more than one
shilling per head weekly. The poor rates, of course,
were increased in proportion; but the poverty of
the rate-payers created so large a number of de-
faulters, that the amount collected invariably fell
far short, not exceeding two-thirds at most, of the
sum estimated. In fact, out of 7464 rated houses
existing in the township of Stockport at the date of
the Report, 1632 were empty, and for nearly 3000
more default had occurred.

The commissioners personally visited the dwellings of several poor persons. Many of them are
expressly stated to have parted with clothing and
bedding for food, before applying to the parish.
One man had pawned his wife's wedding-ring for
eighteen-pence, and his bible for a shilling. Some
were still living by the sale of their effects, and had
not yet applied for relief. John Daniels (his name
deserves to be recorded), a silk-weaver, with a wife
and five children, having been long without work,
was obliged to apply to the parish, and obtained an
order for a month for four shillings a week in provisions. The whole of his incomings were then about
eight shillings a week. Being asked in what manner he disposed of this pittance, he said, "We make
our breakfast for seven of us of a teacupful of oatmeal made into thin porridge, together with some
bread; at dinner we have about six pounds of potatoes, with salt and bread; the tea, or supper, as
you may call it, the same as at breakfast; in the

whole about four pounds of bread daily, say eight-pence, two-pennyworth of potatoes, and two-penny-worth of oatmeal, amounting to a shilling a day for seven of us. This, and 10*d.* a week we have to pay for coals, make up the 8*s.* nearly." This man, on obtaining work, gave up of his own accord part of the allowance ordered for him by the guardians. He had received 4*s.* a week for three weeks, and when the fourth payment became due, he went to the relieving officer, and said, "I will have no more relief. I have got one warp for myself, and the prospect of another for my wife."

The cases personally inspected by the commissioners, being chiefly those in which relief was received from the parish, did not present the extreme of wretchedness. There were other families, in which, according to the chairman of the Board of Guardians, it had been ascertained that many women had "no clothes but a chemise, or wretched outer garment; no flannel petticoat, or anything fit to keep out the pinching cold of winter." The want of bedding was still more general. " A few flocks, or a little straw, spread in the corner of the room or cellar," were all that some poor creatures possessed, with "no covering but a single sheet or rug. Many had to lie together, to the number of six, seven, eight, and more, of both sexes, indiscriminately huddled together in their clothes, covered by an old sack or rug." As for the food of these miserable beings, it commonly consisted of a little oatmeal, or a few potatoes, or perhaps a little bread. " Families " said a provision dealer, "that used to buy flour, now purchase only oatmeal; they come for one or two pounds of oatmeal a day, and live upon it." A furniture broker, who was also examined by the commissioners, said, "People now bring articles of such a mean description, as they would never have thought of bringing for sale before. They offer me knives and forks, bits of old iron, anything which they have about them, and they tell me they want to raise money to buy a few potatoes with, just to carry them on another week. As for clothing, I have never seen children so badly clothed. The children come to me often with their mothers, begging their mothers to sell small articles, to get a bit of bread or a few potatoes."

A few weeks previously to the arrival of the commissioners at Stockport, a considerable sum had been raised by subscription for the relief of the poor, and a committee, composed of the principal municipal authorities, the clergy of all denominations, and some of the leading manufacturers of the place, was appointed for the management of the fund. In a circular issued by this committee, which is recommended by the commissioners to attention, "as representing the impressions of all parties in the borough respecting the extent of the distress," is the following statement. "Of 15,823 individuals inhabiting 2965 houses, lately visited under the direction of a committee appointed for the purpose, 1204 only are found to be fully employed, 2866 partially employed, and 4148 able to work, *were wholly without employment.* The remaining

7605 persons were unable to work. The average weekly income of the above 15,823 persons was 1s. 4¾d. each. The average weekly wages of those fully employed were 7s. 6¼d. each. The average weekly wages of those partially employed, 4s. 7¼d. each." *

The distress of which these are such convincing proofs was aggravated at Stockport by local causes, but it existed in a degree very little inferior in most other manufacturing towns. It was particularly severe throughout Lancashire and those parts of Yorkshire in which the cotton manufacture has its principal seat. In Manchester, there were said to be 9,000 families earning on an average only 1s. a week. In Bolton, out of 50 mills, which had formerly employed 8124 workmen, 30 mills with 5061 workpeople were standing idle or working only short time. † The weekly earnings of the bed quilt and counterpane weavers were reduced to less than one half of their amount in 1838. Those of the hand-loom weavers, though long before depressed, had fallen again from 6s. to 3s. 7½d. The destitution of the operatives and the embarrassments of their employers were shared largely by the tradesmen and handicraftsmen whose customers they had been. In Bolton a diminution of 3651l. took place in the weekly amount of wages paid in twelve trades. Out of 150 carpenters formerly earning 25s. a week each, only twenty-five remained in full work and fifteen in half work, and the number of stonemasons was reduced from 140

---

* Messrs. Power and Twistleton's Rep. on the State of the Population of Stockport, *passim*.

† Lord Kinnaird in House of Lords, 2nd June, 1842.

earning 34*s.* a week to 50 earning 10*s.* 6*d.* * Very
similar and not much more moderate were the
sufferings of the clothworkers of Yorkshire and
Wiltshire, of the silkweavers of Spitalfields and
Macclesfield, the lacemakers of Nottinghamshire,
the potters of Staffordshire, and the hardware-
makers of the same county, of Warwickshire, and
Sheffield. In the last-mentioned town, where, in
1836, there was not a single able-bodied man out of
employment, there were, in 1842, one thousand
families supported by contributions from the
trades to which they belonged, at the rate of
1*s.* 3*d.* weekly for each person, and hundreds
more were in the receipt of parish relief. † In
Leeds, 4025 families, being one fifth of the
whole population, were dependent on the poor's
rates. ‡ But it is needless to multiply examples,
for no one can have forgotten the formidable riots
that took place in the midland counties in the
summer of 1842, and which sufficiently attested
the desperate condition to which the operatives
were reduced. Almost everywhere and in almost
every manufacture the complaint of the workmen
was the same, of the difficulty of obtaining employment and of the utter impossibility of earning a
competent livelihood. If this state of things had
continued through a long series of years, no further
proof would be required that the number of operatives was excessive. But the condition of permanence was fortunately wanting. The distress

* Dr. Bowring, in House of Commons, 15th Feb. 1843.
† Mr. Ward, in House of Commons, 14th Feb. 1843.
‡ Leeds Mercury, 25th June, 1842.

did not last more than three years. Symptoms of
its approach were perceptible earlier, but its presence was not manifest till 1840, and towards the
end of 1842 it began to subside. Both previously
and subsequently to this period, the condition of
manufacturing labourers (with one or two important exceptions) was, as it still continues to be,
little less comfortable than that of great bodies of
men similarly employed has ever been. It has
been mentioned that from 20s. to 60s. a week were
the usual earnings of a labouring family in Stockport previously to the late severe distress. In
1835, the average weekly earnings of adult operatives are said to have been 16s. 6¼d. ; but from numerous examples it would seem, that single workmen of a superior order, such as spinners and
dressers, earned from 20s. to 25s. * In Manchester,
according to a table drawn up by the Chamber of
Commerce in 1832, the usual weekly wages of
male spinners were from 20s. to 25s. ; of females,
10s. to 15s.; of stretchers, 25s.; of dressers, 28s.
to 30s.; of mechanics, 24s. to 26s. ; of carders,
14s. 6d. to 17s.; of male weavers, 13s. to 16s. 10d.;
of female do., 8s. to 12s. ; of machine makers and
iron founders, 24s. to 30s. In Bradford, in 1839,
the average rate of wages in the woollen and
cotton mills, was, of men, 15s. to 35s. a week; of
women, 8s. to 15s.; and of children, 2s. 6d. to 7s.
At Sheffield, about the same time, wages varied
from 12s. to 40s. a week. At Birmingham, the
average was about 23s. 6d.; the average amount

* Stockport Commissioners' Report.

received by 76 persons employed in 32 different occupations having been 23s. * These were the rates a few years back, and they seem to be quite as high at present. In November, 1843, according to statements obtained by Mr. Cobden, female weavers in Lancashire were earning on an average from 10s. to 12s. a week, and many families employed in factories could be found earning altogether more than 2l. weekly. † Three months later, Mr. Bright, M.P. for Durham, stated, that in his own mill, employing 518 persons, the average wages of adult males were 16s. 2d., and of adult females 11s. 10d. ; and that of 51 families in his service, the average income was 35s. 9d. a week, or 92l. 19s. a year. ‡ Calico printers in Lancashire, working ten hours a day, receive from 30s. to 45s. a week, if machine printers, and if block printers can earn from 1l. to 1l. 10s. § The men employed in the Staffordshire Potteries earn from 1l. 4s. to 2l. a week, according to the sort of work they are engaged upon, and as the processes are such as admit of the employment of whole families, their united earnings are sometimes 3l. or 4l. a week. ‖ At Kidderminster, the carpet weavers earn from 1l. 10s. to 2l. 17s. a week. At Birmingham, many workmen earn from 30s. to 50s. a week, and many

* See Mr. Symons' " Arts and Artizans at Home and Abroad," 1839.

† Times, Dec. 1. 1843.

‡ Hansard's Parl. Deb., 15th March, 1844.

§ Mr. Kennedy's Rept. to Children's Employment Commissioners.

‖ Mr. Scriven's Rept. to Children's Employment Commissioners.

women, from 10s. to 14s. a week. Of 134 males
of the age of 21 and upwards, members of a provident institution, the average weekly earnings were
found to be 1l. 4s. 2d.

How far such wages as these are equal to the
maintenance of an average family, will be seen, on
reference to the subjoined Table, showing the way
in which a family of six persons do actually live,
in Manchester, upon 34s. 6d. a week. *

| | Total Expenditure of the whole Family per week. | | | Expenditure of each Individual per week. | |
|---|---|---|---|---|---|
| | £ | s. | d. | s. | d. |
| Rent - - | 0 | 5 | 0 | 0 | 10 |
| Flour - - | 0 | 5 | 10 | 0 | 11½ |
| Meat - - | 0 | 4 | 8 | 0 | 9¼ |
| Bacon - - | 0 | 0 | 4 | 0 | ¾ |
| Butter - - | 0 | 2 | 0 | 0 | 4 |
| Eggs - - | 0 | 1 | 0 | 0 | 2 |
| Milk - - | 0 | 0 | 10 | 0 | 1½ |
| Potatoes - - | 0 | 1 | 8 | 0 | 3¼ |
| Cheese - - | 0 | 0 | 9 | 0 | 1½ |
| Tea - - | 0 | 1 | 0 | 0 | 2 |
| Coffee - - | 0 | 0 | 6 | 0 | 1 |
| Sugar - - | 0 | 2 | 0 | 0 | 4 |
| Soap - - | 0 | 0 | 6 | 0 | 1 |
| Candles - | 0 | 0 | 6 | 0 | 1 |
| Salt - - | 0 | 0 | 1 | 0 | 0 |
| Coals - - | 0 | 1 | 2 | 0 | 2¼ |
| £ | 1 | 7 | 10 | 4 | 8 |

The fact of every individual here having been
able to spend a few pence a week on the super-
fluities of sugar, tea, and coffee, shows, that there

* Mr. Kennedy's Report to Children's Employment Commissioners.

can have been no want of the more indispensable articles of food, more especially as one of the family may be supposed to have been an infant, that did not consume the whole of its allowance. This particular family, it will be observed, contained more than the average number of members, while its income was, if any thing, rather below the average earnings of families engaged in manufactures, whose wages are therefore high enough to prove incontestably, that the temporary distress lately experienced by the manufacturing classes must have proceeded from other causes than their own overcrowded state. It will not, perhaps, be considered an impertinent digression, if a few pages are here employed in an attempt to point out what those causes were, before we proceed further with the proper subject of this chapter.

In the interval between the years 1829 and 1836 the condition of British manufactures may be described as one of general prosperity. In the course of this period the *quantity* of native produce and manufactures exported from the United Kingdom, was increased by very nearly one-third, and though this vast increase is in a great measure attributed to the increased cheapness of the goods, and does not imply a corresponding increase in the *value* of the exports, the latter also advanced very materially ; viz., from 38,271,597*l.* in 1830, to 47,372,270*l.* in 1835. The extension here denoted was experienced chiefly by the cotton and woollen manufactures, but, as will be shown by the subjoined Table, it was experienced in a greater or less degree by every important branch of industry.

Declared Value of BRITISH and IRISH PRODUCE and MANUFACTURES Exported from the UNITED KINGDOM in each of the Years from 1830 to 1843, inclusive.

| Years. | All sorts from the United Kingdom. | Cotton Manufactures: Hosiery, Lace, Small Wares, Twist, and Yarn. | Woollen ditto. | Linen ditto. | Silk Manufactures. | Earthenware. | Hardware and Cutlery. | Iron and Steel, Wrought and Cast. | Brass and Copper Manufactures. |
|---|---|---|---|---|---|---|---|---|---|
| 1830 | 38,271,597 | 19,428,664 | 4,851,097 | 2,066,424 | 521,010 | 442,193 | 1,412,107 | 1,078,523 | 867,344 |
| 1831 | 37,164,372 | 17,257,204 | 5,739,714 | 2,448,686 | 578,874 | 461,090 | 1,622,429 | 1,123,372 | 803,124 |
| 1832 | 36,450,594 | 17,398,392 | 5,479,866 | 1,783,432 | 529,990 | 490,787 | 1,434,431 | 1,190,748 | 916,563 |
| 1833 | 39,667,347 | 19,659,672 | 6,535,853 | 2,199,441 | 740,294 | 478,515 | 1,408,453 | 1,425,723 | 883,241 |
| 1834 | 41,649,191 | 20,502,423 | 5,975,657 | 2,605,837 | 637,013 | 492,724 | 1,484,681 | 1,485,414 | 961,606 |
| 1835 | 47,372,270 | 22,128,384 | 7,145,826 | 3,208,778 | 973,786 | 539,990 | 1,831,766 | 1,640,939 | 1,093,949 |
| 1836 | 53,368,572 | 24,632,058 | 7,994,807 | 3,645,097 | 917,822 | 837,774 | 2,270,630 | 2,340,207 | 1,072,002 |
| 1837 | 42,070,744 | 20,596,123 | 4,993,117 | 2,613,051 | 503,673 | 563,237 | 1,460,808 | 2,009,259 | 1,166,277 |
| 1838 | 50,060,970 | 24,147,726 | 6,157,813 | 3,566,435 | 777,280 | 651,344 | 1,498,327 | 2,535,692 | 1,221,732 |
| 1839 | 53,233,580 | 24,550,375 | 6,694,965 | 4,233,452 | 868,113 | 771,173 | 1,828,521 | 2,719,824 | 1,280,506 |
| 1840 | 51,406,430 | 24,668,618 | 5,780,810 | 4,128,964 | 792,648 | 573,184 | 1,349,137 | 2,524,859 | 1,450,464 |
| 1841 | 51,634,623 | 23,499,478 | 6,300,821 | 4,320,021 | 788,894 | 600,759 | 1,623,961 | 2,877,278 | 1,523,744 |
| 1842 | 47,381,023 | 21,679,348 | 5,822,350 | 3,372,300 | 590,189 | 555,430 | 1,398,487 | 2,457,717 | 1,810,742 |

Altogether, an addition of more than nine millions sterling was made, in the short space of six years, to the amount annually obtained by the sale of British exports, and after deducting the value of the increased quantity of materials contained in those goods, the largest portion of this sum would still remain to be added to the fund annually distributed amongst labourers and their employers. A corresponding accession to the income of the manufacturers was made in the home market, where the consumption of British goods was extended at least as much as abroad. The aggregate income of the manufacturing classes might however be augmented, without benefit to either the workmen or their masters, if their numbers and the capital invested in their business were disproportionately increased at the same time. The *rates* of wages and profits might then be lower, though the total amounts were higher than before. It is certain, indeed, that this was not the case with wages at the time spoken of, for the wages of operatives in the years immediately preceding 1836, were, if anything, rather higher than they had been for many years previously. But it must be acknowledged that complaints were prevalent at that time of reduced profits in several important branches of industry, particularly in the cotton manufacture, the most important of all, owing, as was supposed, partly to the excessive investment of capital, and partly to foreign competition. These complaints were made by persons of such high authority, that it would be presumptuous flatly to deny their accuracy; but it may be permitted to remark, that the continued influx of capital into the cotton manufacture, notwithstanding the asserted decrease of profit, shows that profits in that business were at least as high as in any other, and that, as foreign competition did not prevent the exportation of British goods from increasing with extraordinary rapidity, it could not have exactly reduced profits, though it doubtless had its effect in preventing them from rising so high as they otherwise might have done. At all events, profits were high enough to induce the masters not only to continue, but greatly to extend, their transactions; and this, coupled with the full employment and adequate remuneration of the workmen, may be accepted as sufficient proof of the reality of the asserted prosperity of the whole manufacturing body. Until 1836, too, this prosperity seemed to be, and indeed was, based on a sound foundation, but in that year an important change took place in this respect.

Of the whole foreign commerce of Great Britain, very nearly one-fifth is, or at least till lately was, carried on with the United States of America; and it need scarcely be remarked, that when two countries are so closely connected, no important movement can take place in one without its consequences being more or less felt in the other. The people of the United States possess every requisite for the growth of their wealth and power — immense unoccupied tracts of fertile soil, an extensive coast, numerous navigable rivers, free institutions, and an enterprising spirit; and their actual progress has

been without example in the history of nations.
Their prosperity, however, is not unchequered, but
is liable to severe disturbance from neglect of so
obvious a precaution as that of securing a good and
stable pecuniary currency, and of guarding against
its depreciation by the over-issue of paper-money.
We, in England, have had no great cause to pride
ourselves on our prudence in this respect, but our
omissions, deplorable as their consequences have
frequently been, have been far surpassed in recklessness by the Americans. Among the latter, not
only is every set of men at liberty to establish a
joint-stock bank, and to issue notes payable on
demand, without the wealth and character, or even
the names, of the issuers being known, and without
any security being taken for the real existence of
the bank's declared capital : the shareholders are
not even held responsible for the whole debts of
the bank, but only for an amount equal to their
shares of stock, or of some fixed multiple thereof.
Needy adventurers are thus enabled to become
partners in a bank, and bankers, even when men
of property, are tempted to engage in the most
hazardous speculations, for which a few reams of
silver paper made into notes furnish ample resources, and to discount bills and make advances or
loans with careless prodigality. As their notes,
while current, possess all the qualities of money,
and as the value of money, like the value of all
other commodities, is, *cæteris paribus*, inversely as
the quantity in the market, these operations of the
bankers frequently render the currency redundant,

and depreciate its value. Prices rise in proportion; speculators make, or seem about to make, large profits; their good fortune tempts others to imitate them; fresh advances are obtained from the banks; prices rise still higher; activity pervades every department of trade. Suddenly this pleasing picture is overcast. With the price of other articles, the price of the precious metals rises also; the foreign exchanges become adverse, and gold and silver coins are eagerly sought after, to be melted down or exported. Notes are returned to the banks to be exchanged for specie: many of the banks are probably unable to meet this demand, and even the most substantial cannot do so without contracting their issues, and by refusing the usual discounts and other accommodation to their customers, placing both the latter and themselves in danger of ruin. But, instead of a longer description, it will be sufficient, in order to show the disastrous results of the American system of banking, to state this one fact: — that between the years 1811 and 1830, no fewer than 195 banks became altogether bankrupt, independently of a much greater number that stopped for a while and afterwards resumed payments.* It is not easy to exaggerate the wide-spread ruin that must have accompanied these failures.

During the greater part of this period there existed one banking establishment, " the Bank of the United States," of undoubted solidity, with a large paid up capital, and branches in all parts of

---

* Macculloch's Com. Dict., art. "Bank."

the Union, where its notes being readily accepted, served in some measure to restrain the operations of the other banks. But, in 1836, the charter of this national establishment expired, and President Jackson, for no other conceivable reason than perhaps to show that the science of government, like all other sciences, can only be acquired by study, refusing to renew it, the United States' Bank ceased to exist as such, and became a mere provincial bank, with a sphere of action confined within the limits of Pennsylvania. In the other states a number of joint-stock banks immediately sprang up to supply its place; so that between June, 1834, and January, 1836, the whole number in the Union increased from 506 to 713. Other circumstances concurring at the same time to excite a spirit of commercial speculation, the activity of the American banks increased still more than their number, and in the two years ending with the 1st January, 1836, the value of the bank-notes in circulation increased from $95,000,000 to $140,000,000, and the loans and discounts of the banks from $324,000,000 to $457,000,000.*

This excessive issue of paper-money originated, as was just observed, in a spirit of commercial excitement, but aggravated the cause from whence it sprang, and was itself aggravated in return. Its first effect was a rise of prices, and this led to trading speculations, more particularly in foreign goods, which, having become dearer in the American

* Macculloch's Com. Dict., art. "Bank."

market, while their price in the producing countries remained unchanged, seemed to promise extraordinary profits. Unlimited orders for goods were accordingly sent to foreign countries, and more particularly to Great Britain, where an increased demand for native manufactures had already sprung up from a different cause. The harvests in England, in 1834 and the two following years, were so unusually productive, that the average price of corn during that period was only 44s. 8d. per quarter, or less than it had been in any previous year since 1786, or for nearly half a century. The only class that can suffer from a plentiful harvest is the farmers, who, though they have more corn to sell, may not be able to obtain so large a sum for their whole stock; but, with this exception, every member of the community, from the prince to the ploughman, has reason to rejoice in the low price of food. Every one, having less to pay for food, has more money to spend in other things; and it has been proved by experience that the difference in the sums laid out by the labouring classes in dress, &c. in cheap and dear years, has more effect upon the welfare of the manufacturers than almost any other cause whatever. Owing then to this increase of both the home and foreign demand, our manufacturers in 1836 found their profits advancing rapidly, and they naturally strove to maintain and enlarge their shares of so lucrative a business, while other persons were equally eager to obtain admission into it. Ample means for both purposes were unhappily procurable from the joint-stock banks, which were then not very much better regulated in England than in America; and which, between September, 1834, and September, 1837, increased in number about one half, while their issues in the same period increased from less than two to not quite four millions sterling. Mills, factories, and furnaces sprang up in every direction; and in the single county of Lancaster, new steam engines, of the aggregate power of about 7000 horses, were set up in the course of 1835 and 1836. The resident inhabitants of the manufacturing districts were found to be too few to perform all the work offered to them; and agricultural labourers, attracted by the hope of high wages, were brought to their assistance from every corner of the kingdom. With the exception of the farmers, who were depressed by the low price of their produce, the whole nation seemed never to have been in a more thriving state; but it was not long before the inevitable reverse took place.

The first blow was received from America, where the insane proceedings of the banks led to a reaction, and to a demand for specie which they were unable to satisfy; so that by May, 1837, every bank in the United States, without, it is believed, a single exception, was compelled to stop payment. The excessive importation of foreign goods into the American market must, of itself, have occasioned a fall in their price that would have proved ruinous to many speculators; but when to this was added the total annihilation of paper-money and of credit consequent upon the stoppage of the banks, the

ruin became nearly universal.   The whole commercial community might be described, without
very gross exaggeration, as in a state of bank-
ruptcy.   Of course, this state of things extended
its influence to England.   The merchants there
were in many instances ruined by the failure of
their American debtors, and the losses of the merchants were shared largely by the manufacturers.
The latter, however, were not so much injured by
their actual losses as by the diminished demand for
their goods; for, owing chiefly to the commercial
revulsion in the United States, the value of British
exports to foreign countries fell, in 1837, to more
than eleven millions sterling below its amount in
the preceding year.   Nevertheless, the production
of manufactured goods in Great Britain does not
seem to have experienced a check for a very considerable time.   The manufacturers in general probably fancied that the depression of trade would be
of short duration, and did not immediately perceive
the necessity of contracting their operations; and
those among them who had established themselves
with borrowed capital, saw no other chance of
meeting their engagements than by extending their
business as much as possible.   Every manufacture
consequently continued to be carried on with unabated activity; and as the number of factories,
&c. had been largely increased in 1835 and 1836,
the quantity of goods produced, instead of falling
off in proportion to the diminished demand, seems
even to have gone on increasing.   This abundance
of goods lowered their price, and their low price

caused the consumption of them in foreign countries to be so largely augmented, that, in 1838 and the three succeeding years, the average annual value of British exports became nearly as great as it had been in 1836, and much greater than it had been in 1835. This increased exportation was not indeed beneficial to the master manufacturers, for it was occasioned by prices so low as to leave little or no profit on capital; but, as long as it lasted, it kept the operatives in full employment, and prevented them from feeling very sensibly the distress of their employers. But it was impossible for the latter to continue this course long, and their difficulties were augmented by the scanty harvests of 1838-41, which, raising the price of food in England by one-half above its price in 1835-6, reduced in a corresponding degree the home demand for their goods. Their resources gradually decreased, and as prices still remained depressed, many of them in the course of 1841 were compelled to withdraw from business, and most of those who remained could only work " short time," that is, fewer days in the week and fewer hours in the day. Thousands of working people were then thrown out of employment, and that severe distress began to pervade the whole class, of which an attempt has been made by a few examples to convey some faint idea.

It has been shown that this distress was only temporary, and that the ordinary condition of manufacturing operatives is very far from being one of privation. Handicraftsmen are in general equally well off. Journeymen tailors seldom earn less than

18s. a week, or shoemakers less than 15s., while, in London, those who work by the piece earn half as much again, and the wages of carpenters, sawyers, bricklayers, masons, painters, plasterers, slaters, and blacksmiths range between 18s. and 40s. a week. The position of operatives and handicraftsmen, however, affords no clue to that of other portions of the labouring population of towns. The skill, only to be acquired by long practice, which is required in all handicrafts, and in most manufacturing processes, and still more the great number of workmen needed to carry on an extensive business, enable them to combine successfully against their masters, and to raise their wages much higher than free competition would permit. The fear of their deserting him in a body, and the impossibility of readily supplying the places of so many skilled labourers, frequently compel a master to acquiesce in the unreasonable demands of his men, who are thus enabled not only to dictate, within certain limits, the rate of wages and the hours of labour, but to forbid the employment of persons of whom they disapprove, or the engagement of a greater number of apprentices than they may think it prudent to admit to a knowledge of their art. Suitable arrangements are made for the exercise of this power. In almost every trade in the kingdom the journeymen are formed into local associations, which are governed by laws and officers of their own. In some instances, all the workmen in a place engaged in a particular business assemble, and appoint their office-bearers by a majority of votes; in others, the several factories, or the

" houses of call" at which the workmen meet, send
delegates, who afterwards select four or five of
themselves to form a ruling council.  But, however
appointed, this committee is invested with absolute
authority, which it often exercises in a most despo-
tic manner.  It directs at its pleasure all the movements of the association; it decides according to
its own judgment when a " strike" or cessation of
work shall take place, and its edict is immediately
obeyed by all to whom it is addressed.  These forthwith, though often very reluctantly, abandon their
occupation, compelled to do so, both by regard for
the oath administered to them on joining the association, and by fear of persecution and of personal
violence, or even death, which is not unfrequently
inflicted on refractory workmen by the emissaries
of the ruling council.   In this state of constrained
idleness they are maintained for a while by means
of a fund to which every member of the association
contributes, until either this fund fails, and they
are compelled to accept their master's terms, or
until he, on the other hand, is compelled to accept
theirs, to escape the loss and ruin consequent upon
a continued stoppage of his business.   One condition upon which they almost always insist is, that
none but members of their association shall be employed by their masters; and to check the excessive
influx of new members, a heavy pecuniary fine
(amounting frequently to 5l. or more) is imposed
on all persons, whether skilled workmen or apprentices, obtaining admission into the society.*   By

* Reports of Committee on Combinations of Workmen, 1838.

such means as these wages are often raised very considerably above their natural level, and one necessary result is, that the rates of wages in different occupations vary exceedingly, and quite independently of any difference of skill to be exerted or of hardship to be borne. This is the case even among manufacturing operatives. While cotton-spinners have been earning from 20s. to 30s. a-week, power-loom weavers have obtained only 14s. or 15s.; and though handloom weavers of silk, linen, and woollen often earn 16s. or 18s., handloom weavers of cotton have for years been unable to obtain more than 7s. a-week. The difference here, it is true, arises partly from inferiority of skill or strength on the part of the worse-paid workman, but partly also merely from his inability to obtain admission into the better-paid occupation.

The condition of handloom weavers, it should be observed, has been depressed, in consequence of improvements in machinery, and other circumstances peculiar to them, so that, notwithstanding their great number, and the large proportion which they bear to the whole class of manufacturing operatives, they cannot be taken as fair examples of that class. Handloom weavers of cotton have not of late, even in comparatively prosperous times, and when fully employed, been able to earn more than 6s. or 7s. a week on an average, so that, without reference to their recent still deeper depression, they may be safely pronounced to be in as pitiable a situation as any portion of the whole population of the country, whether urban or rural. But, with this, and one or two other exceptions, operatives and handicraftsmen are generally in a position very superior to that of other labourers in towns, that is to say, of porters, spademen, &c., who have no particular qualification for any pursuit, but are ready to turn their hands to any thing requiring merely muscular strength and ordinary ingenuity. Yet even these, in the metropolis and other great towns, commonly earn from 10s. to 18s. a week. In London, labourers in the docks, whose condition may be regarded as representing pretty faithfully that of unskilled labourers in general, get from 15s. to 18s. In Manchester, porters get 14s. or 15s. a week; packers, 1l., and common day labourers from 10s. to 15s. Ten shillings a week, indeed, seem to be the lowest rate at which out-of-door labourers are ever paid in English towns, and in general their wages are a shilling or two higher. Upon the highest of these wages it is not impossible to support a family pretty comfortably, and even the lowest, however inadequate for comfort, are, as we discovered in our survey of the agricultural districts, considerably more than are absolutely necessary for existence. It might reasonably be thought, therefore, that where they were prevalent there could not be any surplus labour, as otherwise they would probably be reduced still lower by the keen competition of the unemployed. Such an inference would not be strictly correct. The occupations carried on in towns are not, for the most part, such as to require the engagement of many unskilled labourers by the same employer.

Most masters have probably only two or three such workmen in their service, and entertaining for them the personal regard commonly springing from familiar intercourse, they are not eager to avail themselves of an opportunity to lower their wages. Masters who employ a greater number of men are proportionably wealthy, and they also are restrained by shame, or by a better motive, from taking advantage of the distresses of the poor. Thus there may be persons absolutely unable to obtain employment in a place, where those who are employed are in the receipt of tolerable wages. An example of this is the destitution in the midst of London, to which public attention has of late been so strongly drawn. It has been discovered that " fifty or sixty persons of both sexes and of all ages, have become dwellers in the parks, with no other shelter at night than what the trees and hollows in the embankments afford." * Into two asylums in the city, opened for the purpose of affording a night's lodging to houseless wanderers, 9840 persons were admitted in the first three months of 1843. † In the neighbourhood of the docks, at the eastern end of the metropolis, "hundreds of poor men may be seen before daybreak in the winter, waiting for the opening of the gates, in the hope of obtaining a day's work, and when the youngest and strongest and those best known have been taken, hundreds still may be seen returning, sick at heart, to their

* Times, Oct. 11th, 1843.
† Id. Dec. 22nd, 1843.

destitute families." *   These poor creatures would
doubtless joyfully accept a smaller remuneration
than that obtained by their more fortunate competitors, but, for the causes mentioned above, it
would be impossible for them to obtain work even
on such terms.

These causes, however, could only be of temporary operation, and could not long protect wages
from the natural effects of competition in a town,
in which part of the able-bodied inhabitants were
in a state of permanent destitution.   But there is
no reason to suppose that this is the condition of
any part of the able-bodied population permanently
settled in London.   This metropolis did indeed
suffer, although in a lesser degree, from the distress that lately invaded so many other parts of
the kingdom.   Many of its inhabitants, doubtless,
experienced unusual difficulty in gaining a livelihood, but the difficulty was greatly increased,
if it was not entirely produced, by the influx of
strangers from the country, and it is among the
latter that the scenes just alluded to have generally occurred.   A large proportion of the miserable
denizens of the parks are country girls, brought
up to town by their seducers, and then turned
adrift ; and the rest are chiefly foreign refugees
and other strangers.   Out of the thousands admitted into the asylums for the houseless poor,
not more than a few hundreds belong to
parishes in London, the remainder being labourers

* Letter from rector of Whitechapel, Times, Nov. 30th,
1843.

and others from the provinces, who, being thrown out of employment at home, have wandered up to the capital, in hopes of meeting with better fortune there. Most of the disappointed applicants for employment in the docks are expressly said to be emigrants from the country, and from Ireland. The presence of these hapless wanderers in London merely shows how desperate must have been their condition in their native districts, and proves nothing with respect to labourers long resident in London. Among the latter, though cases of individual distress are not wanting, it is certainly rare to find a man of good character, and in good health, who is prevented from obtaining a decent subsistence by inability to procure employment.

In large provincial towns, the facility of obtaining employment is probably much the same as in London, but the remuneration of unskilled labour is generally rather lower. In Manchester, for example, a common day labourer, though sometimes earning 15s. a week, is perhaps as frequently obliged to content himself with 10s. This last sum would not go farther towards the support of a family in a town than in the country; but a town labourer, if married, has a considerable advantage in the earnings of his wife, who can often gain a much larger sum in various ways than she could possibly do in farm labour. A woman's wages, however, though a material accession to her husband's income, would seldom, unless she were regularly employed in a factory, suffice to maintain her if she lived alone; and women having no male associate and entirely self-dependent, are consequently liable to great privation. London contains many such. Several melancholy examples have lately been brought to light, of wretched females working eighteen hours daily at shirtmaking or other similar occupations, and earning only 4s. a week ; but these examples, distressing as they are, are unimportant as symptoms of excessive population, the only purpose for which they can properly be cited here. Wherever men are able to earn something more than their own subsistence, a bare subsistence at least may generally be obtained by all who can undertake the same employment, and the destitution of females must proceed less from inability to obtain work than from inability to perform it — less from the excess of their numbers than from the defect of their strength. The occupations suitable for women may be overstocked and consequently ill paid ; but there are other employments not unduly crowded, in which, if women could work like men, they might gain a livelihood. It is not indispensable to the well-being of society that women in general should be able to maintain themselves in comfort by their own unassisted exertions. This it is not in their power to do at any stage in the progress of society. The female frame is not adapted to severe exertion, and the occupations for which it is suited are not very extensive, so that women are obviously intended by nature to be partly dependent for support on the other sex. All that is requisite is, that a woman's earnings, together with those of her husband or other male relative, should be sufficient for the maintenance of an average family, and this seems to be the case in most English towns.

Similar observations are suggested by the condition of part of the children engaged in the various manual occupations carried on in this country. The tender and sometimes literally infantine age at which they are set to work, the prolonged toil they are generally made to undergo, and the cruelty they are often exposed to, all lead to the conclusion that nothing but stern necessity, or the most heartless selfishness, could induce their parents to consign them to so miserable a doom. At the same time, the insignificant trifle which the little sufferers earn by their premature exertions, is frequently insufficient to purchase even the merest necessaries of life. In the workshops of Birmingham and Wolverhampton, in the potteries of Staffordshire, and among the lace-makers every where, there are numerous instances of boys and girls under ten years of age, working ten, twelve, nay even sixteen or eighteen hours a day, yet clothed in rags, without shoes or stockings, even in winter, and complaining that they "never get meat," that they "seldom get bread," that "potatoes and salt" are their usual food, that they often go without a dinner, that they "never get enough to eat." *
Here is a foul ulcer, that cannot be neglected without danger to the whole body politic ; here is a

* Appendix to Second Report of Children's Employment Commission.

picture of woe, to stimulate the philanthropist's
ardour, and to dash with bitterness the cup of the
rich man's enjoyment; yet even here is no certain
sign of excessive population. That, unless the
children are orphans, their parents have either
larger families than their own earnings can maintain, or are more brutally indifferent than wild
beasts to the welfare of their offspring, is evident
enough; and it is likewise manifest that the children are unable to earn a competent livelihood for
themselves. But there is no proof that the parents
have not wages sufficient for the support of an
average family, or that the children would not be
able to procure their own subsistence, if they had
the strength of adults. There may be abundant
employment for able-bodied labourers, and the
destitution of these children, like that of the females
mentioned in a preceding paragraph, may proceed,
not from their excessive number, but from their
physical weakness.

The particulars stated in this chapter are, as the
writer is well aware, exceedingly few and meagre,
and much more likely to excite than to gratify
curiosity respecting the condition of the labouring
class. They may perhaps, however, be regarded as
sufficient for the special purpose for which they are
adduced; and it seems unnecessary to fatigue the
reader with farther details of the same kind. The
general conclusion to be drawn from them is, that
although almost every where throughout the country population presses hard on its proper limits,
and has even overstepped them in many places, it

has not exceeded them very considerably, except in a few districts. Seven or eight shillings a week are certainly not sufficient for the proper maintenance of an average * family, and where, as in some of the rural districts of Wales, Somersetshire, Wiltshire, and Dorsetshire, these are a man's usual earnings, it is evident that people who suffer so much from mutual competition must be too numerous. But in most English counties the joint wages of an agricultural couple are seldom less than 12s. a week. They are, as has been seen, a good deal higher in many places, and a considerable accession of income may be derived from a garden or allotment of land, the keep of a pig, &c. Now, though the bare sum of twelve shillings a week would be a feeble barrier against want, fourteen might perhaps suffice to procure every thing absolutely necessary for a married couple with the average number of helpless dependents. The food supplied to paupers in some rural workhouses, though abundantly sufficient for health and strength, as any one who has seen the consumers will allow, and very superior, both in quality and quantity, to what most independent labourers use, does not, on an average of men, women, and children, cost more than 2s. 6d. a head weekly. Provisions for workhouses being obtained in large quantities, and by contract, from the lowest bidder, are from 20 to 30 per cent. cheaper than

* By an average family, is meant such a family as was described on page 9., consisting of a man, his wife, and $1\frac{1}{4}$ helpless dependents. Children able to earn their own livelihood are not included.

they would otherwise be; but after allowing for this difference, 10$s$. a week should still apparently suffice to purchase wholesome food for $3\frac{1}{4}$ persons, leaving 4$s$. a week to pay for rent, clothes, fuel, and sundries. If there be no comfort here, yet neither is there a manifest deficiency of the positive necessaries of life; and where these are so nearly within every one's reach, over-population may have commenced, but cannot have made much progress. It is true that the weekly pittance just mentioned would scarcely procure even necessaries, without better management than is often seen in a labourer's cottage, and that, however judiciously expended, it could only give the cottager and his family the same fare as the inmates of a well-regulated workhouse. This, though it would generally be an important step in advance, would not be improvement enough to satisfy a philanthropist. One would wish that the poorest man should be able to indulge occasionally in inexpensive luxuries; that he should be able to attend a little to appearance in his dress and dwelling; that he should have leisure both for self-culture and for recreation; and above all, that his own earnings should suffice for the support of his wife and young children, so that the former might generally remain at home to look after domestic affairs, and the latter go to school, instead of spending the day in field-labour for the sake of a few halfpence. But the consideration of the means by which the cottager's position may be thus far elevated, belongs more properly to a subsequent chapter. At present it is sufficient to have shown his actual condition.

The misery existing in towns is greater, both in
amount and degree, than that which the country
can exhibit; but the excessive populousness which
it indicates does not properly belong altogether to
the towns in which it is found. Misery is not indeed a sign of over-population at all, unless it proceed from the scanty remuneration of labour. The
inhabitants of a town are not necessarily too numerous, that is to say, there are not necessarily more
of them than can obtain employment, merely because many live in underground cellars or close
rooms in narrow courts, amid heaps of filth and
pestilential exhalations. It is not impossible that
the dwellers in such places may be earning high
wages, or might be doing so if they did not prefer
a life of thieving or prostitution to one of honest
industry. But if their vocation require them to
live in a town, they must needs live in such lodgings as the town affords, and must put up with the
best they can obtain, even though they may be rich
enough to pay for better in other situations. If
the only ones they can procure are ill-ventilated,
undrained, unprovided with water, where cleanliness is impossible, they must perforce live in dirt,
and they will soon be able to do so without repug-
nance, for there seems to be nothing to which one
becomes so quickly accustomed. Their filthy, disgusting habits and modes of life may prove, then,
not that the town is over-peopled, but only that it
is ill-planned, ill-built, and ill-provided with accommodation for its poorer inhabitants. Unquestionably there is in most considerable towns a vast deal

of misery not attributable to this cause. Hundreds of able-bodied men are commonly to be found in some of them, vainly striving to earn a competent subsistence by their labour. A large proportion of that very numerous class, the hand-loom weavers, are in this predicament. The sufferings of these particular operatives, indeed, may be in some measure self-inflicted, since they cling to the occupation in which they have been brought up, when they might apparently earn rather higher wages by doing the work of common out-door labourers. But, as the latter are in general not at all too highly paid, increased competition would reduce their wages below the amount required for a decent subsistence. Hand-loom weavers, therefore, could not maintain themselves properly, although they might somewhat improve their condition, by engaging in unskilled labour; and, as this is always the last resource, their distress may be pronounced to be a perfectly unequivocal symptom of over-population. The same remark applies to one or two other classes of manufacturing operatives, whose occupation, like that of the hand-loom weavers, has been partially superseded, owing to the adoption of machinery, changes of fashion, or other causes. Such operatives are, however, confined to certain localities; and in towns in which they are not present, there are seldom any able-bodied men of known good character unable to procure a tolerable livelihood. Few remain long out of work, except strangers from the country or from Ireland, who certainly have often to endure very cruel privations. But it is obvious that these cannot be immediately included among the residents of a place which they have merely visited in quest of employment, and their destitution only demonstrates the extreme redundance of population in the districts from which they have migrated.

It would serve no useful purpose to attempt to estimate the numerical amount of the excessive population of England. Nothing more than conjecture is possible on such a point; and, even if certainty could be attained, the idea conveyed to the mind of the intensity of the evil would not be so clear as that which may be formed from an examination of its effects upon the condition of the people. It must be observed, however, that in countries in which there is a legal provision for the relief of the destitute, the social condition of the labouring class cannot always be inferred with perfect accuracy merely from the average rate of a labourer's earnings, for this rate may then be prevented from falling so low as it would otherwise be reduced by competition. A labourer, who, in default of every other resource, is secure of a comfortable subsistence from the poor's rate, may venture to refuse to work for wages which he does not consider adequate, and the earnings of all those who work may be tolerably high, while a considerable number of able-bodied men are out of employment, and supported by public charity. It is evident that these men should be added to whatever might be supposed on other grounds to be the

excess of population, and it is of importance therefore that their number should be ascertained.  The
whole number of paupers, in-door and out-door,
relieved in 585 Unions in England and Wales, in
the year ending with Lady-day, 1844, was, of in-
door, 195,220 ; and of out-door, 1,054,462 : altogether, 1,249,682 ; of whom, 431,484 were what
are called " able-bodied" adults of both sexes, and
one half of this last number, or 215,742, may be
presumed to have been male adults.  But we
should form a very exaggerated notion of the
extent of pauperism, if we supposed that these
numbers were constantly in the receipt of relief.
The whole amount expended upon paupers, during
the year, was 4,370,171*l*. ; from which, about
938,467*l*. must be deducted for the expenses of
establishments, salaries, &c. ; leaving 3,431,704*l*.
for the purchase of food and clothing.*  The
average cost of these articles for an inmate of a
workhouse is about 2*s*. 6*d*. a week, or 6*l*. 10*s*. a
year; so that 3,431,704*l*. sterling would suffice for
the constant maintenance, during a year, of only
527,954 ; of whom, according to the proportions
stated above, considerably less than one-fifth, or
about ninety thousand, might be adult males.
When it is considered that the workhouse test is
applied to only a small portion of the whole number
of applicants for relief, and that other paupers are
permitted to remain in their own homes without
being subjected to any peculiarly distasteful con-

* App. B. to Eleventh Annual Report of Poor Law Commissioners.

ditions, it may be inferred pretty confidently that few abstained from demanding parochial assistance who stood very urgently in need of it, and that the amount of relief administered yearly corresponds pretty closely with the amount of absolute destitution.

If this destitution, and the other symptoms of a redundant population in England, are less extensive than previously to inquiry might have been supposed, there is so far reason for congratulation, but none for apathy, or continued neglect of a disease which is wholly incompatible with national prosperity. It is only in the early stages that over-population can be treated with very sanguine hopes of success. After it has been suffered to make much progress, it is, if not incurable, yet, of all political disorders, the one most difficult of cure. There is none, either, which, in circumstances favourable to its growth, advances with such rapid strides towards a crisis. Little more than one generation has been required to make Ireland what she is; and as short a period might probably, in similar circumstances, suffice to convert England into an Ireland of human misery and degradation.

# CHAPTER III.

IF the published returns of what has been called
official pauperism furnished any clue to the general
condition of the Scottish people, the inference
thence deducible would not be unpleasing. In the
years 1835, 1836, and 1837, the average annual
number of paupers in Scotland, permanently or

occasionally assisted by the parish authorities, was 79,429, or about 3¼ per cent. of the whole population, and the average sum annually expended on their relief was only 155,121*l.*, which, at the rate of 2*s.* 6*d.* weekly per head, would suffice for the constant maintenance of only 23,864 persons, or less than one per cent. of the population.* In England the paupers annually relieved are, on an average, rather more than 9 per cent. of the population, and the sum annually expended upon their subsistence would suffice for the constant maintenance of nearly 4 per cent. of the population. But if even in England, where every native who really requires parish relief is able to obtain it on application, there is yet a considerable amount of unrelieved distress, still more it may be thought must this be the case in the northern part of the island, where relief cannot be legally demanded, except by the aged and impotent, and where it is rarely extended to the able-bodied, except in sickness. Even for the former class, the provision made is almost every where inadequate, and in many places only nominal. The law, or at any rate the practice in Scotland, does not require parishes to be assessed for the support of their poor, but only authorises an assessment when sufficient funds are not forthcoming from other sources, the collections made in the churches being chiefly depended upon. Up to the middle of the last century, these and other voluntary contributions were found sufficient for the

* Rep. of Committee of General Assembly on Management of Poor in Scotland.

maintenance of the poor throughout Scotland; and
though assessments have since become pretty common, they are still unknown in nearly three-fourths
of the whole number of parishes, containing more
than one-half of the whole population of the country. They are least used where they are most
required, viz. in the Highlands, where the congre-
gations are so poor that little is collected in the
churches, and where frequently not more than 5*l.*
or 6*l.* are contributed annually for distribution
among fifty or sixty paupers.

In reality, there is a great deal of distress in
Scotland, not less perhaps in proportion to the population than in England, but it is more confined
to particular localities, and is unfelt in a large portion of the country. It exists chiefly in the Highlands and Islands, and in towns. In the Lowlands agricultural labourers are in general better
off than the same class amongst us. Such as are
engaged by the day, indeed, very seldom receive
more than 12*s.* a-week, and more commonly only
9*s.* or 10*s.*, but the number of those who are entirely
dependent on their wages is not great. Day-labourers have almost always gardens or kailyards
attached to their cottages, and are often permitted
to raise a few potatoes for their own use on the
lands of the neighbouring farmers. Several of
them too, though the number has greatly diminished
of late years, are crofters, or occupants of small
farms of three or four acres, and these enjoy a large
share of comfort. The great body of farm servants,
however, are hired by the year, and if unmarried,

are lodged and boarded by their masters, and receive besides from 10*l.* to 16*l.* a-year, with which they have only to find their clothes. Formerly they resided in the farm-house, and this is still the prevailing custom; but of late years they have, in many instances, been removed to a bothy or out-house adjoining, where, though the cost of their maintenance may be the same, they are excluded from the methodical arrangements and humanising influences which contribute to their welfare when they are admitted into their master's family. Whether in the bothy or the farm-house, their diet consists principally of meal, potatoes, fish, milk, cheese, and butter, but they are occasionally treated with butcher's meat, and many unconsidered trifles, — " crumbs" from their master's table, frequently fall to their share simply because they are on the spot to receive them. Yearly labourers, when married, live rent-free in houses on the farm, which have usually small gardens attached to them : a cow is kept for them, or an allowance in milk or money is made instead, and their wages are about 8*l.* or 10*l.* a-year, besides six or seven bolls of oatmeal, and a quantity of potatoes and fuel. With these means, thrift and foresight enable them to live happily enough, and the ingle still burns as brightly in their humble dwellings, and the Saturday night passes as cheerfully, as in the time of Ferguson and Burns.* Farm-servants engaged by the year are less exposed than they otherwise would be to be thrown out of

* Poor Law Inquiry (Scotland) 1844, Appendices 2. 4. Mr. Symons' Report on Hand-Loom Weavers, pp. 17, 18.

employment, and even day-labourers are seldom in want of work, except for a short time in the depth of winter.

This description of the peasantry of the Lowlands may not be altogether inapplicable to those of most Highland districts south of the Caledonian canal, but it bears no resemblance to the condition of the people in any of the more northern counties, with the single exception of Caithness. In all but the one last mentioned, hinds engaged by the year are seldom paid more than two-thirds of what they would receive in the south, and few of them are fortunate enough to obtain regular employment. Farm servants, however, form only a small proportion of the peasantry, a much greater number being crofters, or tenants of small pieces of ground, from which they derive almost their whole subsistence. Most of them live very miserably. The soil is so poor, and rents in some instances so exorbitant, that occupiers of four or five acres can do little more than maintain themselves, yet it is their aid alone that saves their still poorer brethren from starvation. This is true even of Sutherland, which is commonly represented as a highly improved county, and in which a signal change for the better is said to have taken place in the character and habits of the people.* Recent inquiry has discovered that even there, in districts once famous for fine men and gallant soldiers, the inhabitants have degenerated into a meagre and stunted race. In the healthiest situations, on hill sides fronting the

* Macculloch, Stat. Acct. of British Empire, vol. i. p. 315.

sea, the faces of their famished children are as thin and pale as they could be in the foul atmosphere of a London alley.* Still more deplorable are the scenes exhibited in the western Highlands, especially on the coasts and in the adjoining islands. A large population has there been assembled, so ill provided with any means of support, that during part of almost every year from 45,000 to 80,000 † of them are in a state of destitution, and entirely dependent upon charity. Many of the heads of families hold crofts from four to seven acres in extent, but these, notwithstanding their small size, and the extreme barrenness of the soil, have often two, three, and sometimes even four families upon them. One estate in the Hebrides, the nominal rent of which is only 5200*l.* a-year, is divided into 1108 crofts, and is supposed to have more than 8300 persons living upon it. In another instance a rental of 1814*l.* is payable (for little is really paid) by 365 crofters, and the whole population of the estate is estimated at more than 2300.‡ In Cromarty 1500 persons are settled upon an estate let nominally for 750*l.*, but paying not more than half that sum.§ The island of Rum is at present occupied by a single tenant, whose family and servants, altogether about fifty persons, are now the only inhabitants besides himself, and are living very comfortably; but in order to enable them to do so, it

* Times Newspaper, June 7th, 1845.
† Report of Highland Emigration Committee, 1841.
‡ Id., Mr. Bowie's Evidence.
§ Id., Mr. Scott's Evidence.

was thought necessary that a former population of about 500 should emigrate. It is supposed that one half of the population might with advantage be spared from the island of Skye, two-fifths from Tyree, and 17 or 18 per cent. from Mull.

Some few persons in these parts may obtain occasional and short-lived employment in the kelp manufacture or in fishing, and some of the crofters keep a cow or one or two sheep, where there is common land for pasture. Otherwise, they have no certain resource but their plots of ground, the present produce of which, even if held rent-free, would often be insufficient for their subsistence.

Of course, they live most wretchedly. Potatoes are the usual food, for oatmeal is considered a luxury, to be reserved for high days and holidays, but even potatoes are not raised in sufficient abundance. The year's stock is generally exhausted before the succeeding crop is ripe, and the poor are then often in a most desperate condition, for the Poor Law is a dead letter in the north of Scotland, and the want of a legal provision for the necessitous is but ill supplied by the spontaneous contributions of the landowners. Among the latter are to be found a few, distinguished by liberality to their distressed tenantry. The late Duchess-Countess, and proprietress-general, of Sutherland, was in the habit of distributing many thousands of pounds every winter among the poor of that county. Sir George Sinclair, of Caithness, among many other acts of benevolence, distributes 130 pecks of meal monthly among as many poor people of the parish in which he resides. In 1837, Lord Macdonald sent supplies to the famished inhabitants of Skye, to the value of 2,000*l.*, though the rents of his estates in that island were, at the same time so much in arrear, as scarcely in some districts to pay the salaries of the clergy, and other public expenses. Two years before, Mr. Hay Mackenzie, a landowner in Cromarty, distributed about 200*l.* worth of oatmeal among the tenantry of an estate from which he was receiving less than 480*l.* of rent. The Highland lairds, in general, however, are not remarkable for their generosity to their inferiors, and the principal part of the assistance which the poor receive, is derived from persons almost as poor as themselves. * In spite of every aid, there are cases every year of families living for a time almost entirely on shellfish picked up on the shore, with a little water-gruel at night, without either bread, or potatoes, or meal of any kind, except the little of which their gruel is made.

Further evidence of the over-population of these districts can scarcely be required, or it might be sought in the large towns to which, in Scotland, as in England, emigrants are always flocking from the country, in the hope of bettering their condition. In Glasgow, there are nearly 30,000 poor Highlanders, most of them living in a state of misery, which shows how dreadful must have been the privations to which such misery is pre-

* Report of Highland Emigration Committee, Mr. Scott's Evidence.

ferred. Such of them as are able-bodied obtain employment without much difficulty *, and may not perhaps, have much reason to complain of deficiency of the first requisites of life; but the quarter they inhabit is described † as inclosing a larger amount of filth, crime, misery, and disease, than could have been supposed to exist in one spot in any civilised country. It consists of long lanes, called " wynds," so narrow, that a cart could scarcely pass through them, opening upon " closes," or courts, about 15 or 20 feet square, round which the houses, mostly three stories high, are built, and in the centre of which is a dunghill. The houses are occupied indiscriminately by labourers of the lowest class, thieves, and prostitutes, and every apartment is filled with a promiscuous crowd of men and women, all in the most revolting state of filth. Amid such scenes and such companions as these, thousands of the most intelligent of the Highlanders are content to take refuge, for it is precisely those who are best educated and best informed that are most impatient of the penury they have to endure at home.

The inhabitants of the Glasgow wynds and closes may be likened to those of the Liverpool cellars, or to those of the worst parts of Leeds, and of St. Giles' and Bethnal Green in London; and every other class of the Scottish urban labouring population may likewise be delineated with the same

* Report of Highland Emigration Committee, Evidence of Rev. Dr. Macleod.

† Mr. Symons' Report to Hand-loom Weavers' Commission.

touches (more darkened, however,) which have been used in describing the corresponding class in English towns. Manufacturing operatives are in pretty much the same position in both countries. Those of Scotland shared even more largely than their southern brethren in the distress of 1840—2, when Paisley in particular exhibited scenes of woe far surpassing any thing that has been related of Bolton or Stockport. In ordinary times, however, they are generally highly paid, the only considerable exception being the hand-loom weavers in cotton, comprising probably not less than 30,000 families, among whom the average wages of a male adult are certainly under 7s. a-week. Artisans are paid highly, though not quite so highly as in England, and with wages ranging from 16s. to 26s. a-week, ought to be able to live in comfort, and to guard against distress arising from sickness or temporary loss of work. The wages of day-labourers are from 10s. to 12s. a-week. They are kept down by the Irish and Highlanders, with whom the large towns, particularly those near the western coast, are crowded; but it does not appear that the influx of these immigrants very much exceeds the demand for them. In Glasgow, at least, where they are most numerous, they are said to arrive nearly in proportion as they are wanted, and seldom to remain long without employment. The most severe distress experienced in the Scottish towns is probably that of desolate women, and of orphans or children, whose parents are only anxious to rid themselves of an useless burden, and force them to pick up a

living as they can.   In Glasgow especially, the sufferings of these poor creatures are such as cannot
be paralleled elsewhere in Great Britain; but, dreadful as they are, they cannot, for reasons already
stated, be regarded as signs of over-population.
Other causes of human wretchedness are rife in
Scottish towns, but this particular evil, though it
certainly exists, does not seem to have reached to
a very great height in any of them, or to have
spread greatly beyond the districts and islands in
the north and west, which we have lately been
considering.   We must now proceed to a country
where this description must be reversed, where
over-population is the almost universal rule, and
where a small tract with developed resources duly
proportioned to the number of its inhabitants is a
rare exception.

| | Total Area. Square Miles. | Cultivated Land, including Plantations, Square Miles. | Cultivated Land. | Site of Towns. | Uncultivated Land. | Water. | Total Area. | Rural Population. | Civic Population. | Total Population. | Population per Square Mile of whole Area |
|---|---|---|---|---|---|---|---|---|---|---|---|
| | | | Acres. | | | | | | | | |
| ENGLAND.... | 50,387 | 40,050 | 25,632,000 | Reckoned as Uncultivated Land. | 6,615,680 | } * | 32,2 .7,680 | 6,120,094 | 8,875,044 | 14,995,138 | 297 |
| WALES....... | 7,425 | 4,870 | 3,117,000 | | 1,635,000 | | 4,752,000 | 453,872 | 457,731 | 911,603 | 122 |
| SCOTLAND.... | 29,600 | 7,880 | 5,043,450 | | 13,900,550 | † | 18,944,000 | 764,687 | 1,855,497 | 2,620,184 | 88 |
| Leinster  ... | 7,619 | 6,370 | 4,077,132 | 15,569 | 731,886 | 51,624 | 4,876,211 | 1,531,106 | 442,625 | 1,973,731 | 259 |
| Munster  ... | 9,475 | 6,257 | 4, 05,028 | 14,693 | 1,893,477 | 151,381 | 6,064,579 | 2,009,220 | 386,941 | 2,596,161 | 253 |
| Ulster......... | 8,555 | 5,448 | 3,487,322 | 8,790 | 1,764,370 | 214,956 | 5,475,438 | 2,160,698 | 225,675 | 2,386,373 | 27) |
| Connaught . | 6,862 | 3,545 | 2,269,300 | 3,877 | 1,906,002 | 212,864 | 4,392,043 | 1,338,635 | 80,224 | 1,418,859 | 207 |
| IRELAND...... | 32,512 | 21,623 | 13,838,782 | 42,929 | 6,295,735 | 630,825 | 20,808,271 | 7,039,659 | 1,135,465 | 8,175,124 | 251 |

\* Included in the space reckoned as uncultivated land.
† Omitted from the calculation.

The difficulties of an inquiry into the state of the labouring classes in Ireland have of late been very greatly lessened by the Commissioners employed to take the Irish census in 1841. The extraordinary pains and minuteness with which these gentlemen executed their task, render their Report the most successful attempt that has ever been made at the classification of an entire nation; and some of the results obtained by them are so important, and bear so strongly on the subject before us, that it will be useful to exhibit them in this place in a tabular form, accompanied, for the sake of comparison, by some corresponding particulars respecting the other divisions of the United Kingdom.

A glance at this Table will be sufficient to show how strikingly, in many respects, the condition of

| Rural Population per Sq. Mile of Cultivated Land. | No. of Families chiefly employed in Agriculture. | No. of Families chiefly employed in Manufacture and Trade. | No. of Families otherwise employed. | Total Number of Families. | No. of Farms above One Acre. | No. of Farms between One and Five Acres. | No. of Farms between One and Fifteen Acres. | Total No. of Male* Adults engaged in Agriculture. | Farmers and Graziers. | Ploughmen, Herdsmen, Agricultural Servants, & Labourers. | Total Number of Male Adults. |
|---|---|---|---|---|---|---|---|---|---|---|---|
| 152 | ... | ... | ... | ... | ... | ... | ... | 919,221 | 194,596 | 724,625 | 3,893,748 |
| 93 | ... | ... | ... | ... | ... | ... | ... | 79,254 | 31,807 | 47,447 | 233,427 |
| 97 | ... | ... | ... | ... | ... | ... | ... | 160,282 | 50,732 | 109,550 | 630,328 |
| 240 | 214,046 | 92,692 | 55,396 | 362,134 | 133,220 | 49,152 | 94,747 | 344,243 | 80,761 | 263,565 | 581,944 |
| 321 | 292,983 | 78,989 | 43,182 | 415,154 | 162,386 | 57,028 | 118,348 | 492,308 | 125,159 | 367,159 | 699,211 |
| 396 | 267,799 | 141,801 | 30,205 | 439,805 | 234,499 | 100,817 | 199,809 | 424,202 | 167,046 | 257,175 | 661,028 |
| 377 | 199,360 | 38,534 | 17,800 | 255,694 | 155,204 | 99,918 | 145,139 | 318,247 | 80,130 | 238,151 | 399,712 |
| 325 | 974,188 | 352,016 | 146,583 | 1,472,787 | 685,309 | 306,915 | 558,043 | 1,579,000 | 453,096 | 1,126,050 | 2,341,895 |

* Male Adults.

t is necessary to mention, that in this Table the limit of age assigned to adults engaged in agriculture, is ṇe same for Great Britain as for Ireland; all persons fifteen years old or upwards being included in the case, while in the former only those of twenty or upwards are reckoned as adults.

Ireland contrasts with that of Great Britain, and particularly of England. Contrary perhaps to the common opinion, population is somewhat less dense than in England; that is to say, the number of persons to the square mile is smaller; but although less dense, it is very much more redundant. Over-population, as has been already shown, depends on the proportion which the inhabitants of a country bear, not to the quantity of food which that country produces, or is capable of producing, but to the amount of employment which it affords, or to the means possessed by labourers of purchasing or otherwise procuring food. But it is only in rural districts, where the inhabitants are chiefly employed in agriculture, that the amount of employment has any connexion with the extent of surface. In towns it is quite independent of this circumstance. Now, in Ireland, rural districts are much more thickly peopled than in England. The rural inhabitants are there nearly seven-eighths of the whole population, instead of considerably less than one-half, as in England; the families chiefly employed in agriculture are more than five-eighths of the whole number, instead of about one-fourth part, and the male adults employed as farmers or as labourers in husbandry, are more than two-thirds of the whole number, instead of less than one-fourth. Nor is it only these relative proportions that are greater; the absolute numbers of country residents, and of persons and families engaged in agriculture, are likewise larger in Ireland than in England. Yet the quantity of arable land is not very much less than

twice as great in the latter country as in the former;
and it might be suspected that while in the one
only about 760,000* were engaged in the tillage of
25,632,000 acres, 13,838,782 acres in the other
could not afford sufficient employment for 974,188
families. Such a suspicion would not indeed be
necessarily correct. English agriculture would be
exceedingly benefited by the application to it of at
least double the actual quantity of labour, and the
agricultural population of Ireland is not at all
beyond what is absolutely requisite for the tillage,
in the completest and most productive manner, of
the portion of that island actually under cultivation.
In order, however, to afford full employment and a
competent livelihood to the multitude of husbandmen settled upon it, the cultivated land of Ireland
ought either to be divided pretty equally amongst
them all, so as to make every family occupiers of a
portion of ground sufficient for their maintenance,
or such as occupied more than their shares ought
to be men of capital and enterprise, able and willing
to make the best use of their land. Neither of
these positions is the real one. It is true that in
Ireland land is in general very much subdivided, so
that out of a total number of 685,309 farms†,

* At the census of 1831, the number of families in England
chiefly employed in agriculture was computed to be 761,348.
The Census Commissioners of 1841 contented themselves with
ascertaining the number of persons in Great Britain, without
attempting, like the Irish Commissioners, to divide them into
families.

† Exclusive of holdings of less than one acre.

nearly one-half are between one and five acres in extent, and nearly five-sixths are between one and fifteen acres. But, great as is the number of small occupiers, the labourers without any land at all, or with nothing but small garden plots, are far more numerous.

Besides, not only can few or none of the occupiers of less than fifteen acres have any occasion to hire labourers, but most of them, after tilling their own fields, have a good deal of spare time, in which they would be very glad to be hired themselves. Of larger farmers there are only 127,266, and these, with few exceptions, are too poor to hire more assistance than is absolutely necessary to prevent their fields from lying waste, and too ignorant and spiritless to adopt a better style of culture if they had the means. It may be inferred, from a knowledge of these circumstances, that there cannot be any thing like regular employment for so many as a million and a half of agricultural labourers (the number of male adults wholly or in part dependent upon wages), and that most of them must be generally out of work, and exceedingly ill paid when employed. It may be further suspected, that their wretchedness is not confined to themselves ; but that, if they cannot obtain work, they endeavour to obtain land, and that their competition, by extravagantly raising the rent of land, reduces the petty farmers nearly to a level with themselves. It may likewise seem probable that they flock in multitudes into the towns, and prevent the price of labour there, when not protected by the combination of the workmen, from rising much, if at all, higher than in the country. These conclusions might suggest themselves to any one who was aware of the proportions in which the Irish nation is divided into its various classes, and of the small amount of capital invested in agriculture. Of their perfect correctness the proofs are manifold; but it would be almost a mockery to set about formally proving the truth of what every body knows perfectly well. Both the misery of Ireland, and the over-population which it indicates, are universally acknowledged; and if any evidence on the subject is now brought forward, it is intended rather to give some idea of the extent than to demonstrate the existence of such notorious evils.

The following sketch of the general condition of the peasantry is extracted from the Second Report of the Irish Railway Commissioners, whose statements, though not free from inaccuracy, are well deserving of attention:—

" Population is most crowded and numerous in the counties of Armagh, Monaghan, and in parts of the counties of Antrim and Down. Diminishing in density, but still furnishing a large proportion to the square mile, the population extends over the counties of Longford, Westmeath, King's, Queen's, Kilkenny, Carlow, and Wexford; and thence a large mass, second only to the northern portion, spreads over the southern counties of Tipperary, Limerick, and parts of Cork and Waterford. Beyond the Shannon lies a district very thickly peopled, and the parts of Roscommon, Leitrim,

&c., adjacent to the river, have nearly the same proportion of inhabitants. These four divisions of the population differ in social condition, in habits, character, and even in personal appearance, more than the narrow limits of their location within the same country would lead us to expect. The northern portion are better lodged, clothed, and fed than the others : the wages of labour are higher, being on an average about one shilling a day, and their food consists chiefly of meal, potatoes, and milk. They are a frugal, industrious, and intelligent race, inhabiting a district for the most part inferior in natural fertility to the southern portion of Ireland ; but cultivating it better, and paying higher rents in proportion to the quality of the land, notwithstanding the higher rate of wages.

" In the southern districts we find a population whose condition is in every respect inferior to that of the northern ; their habitations are worse ; their food inferior, consisting at best of potatoes and milk, without meal; the wages of labour are found reduced from 1s. to 8d. a day ; yet the peasantry are a robust, active, and athletic race, capable of great exertion, often exposed to great privations, ignorant, but eager for instruction, and readily trained under judicious management to habits of order and steady industry.

" The population of the midland districts does not differ materially in condition from that of the south ; but the inhabitants of the western districts are decidedly inferior to both in condition and appearance. Their food consists of the potato alone, without meal, and in most cases without milk; their cabins are wretched hovels; their beds straw; the wages of labour are reduced to the lowest point — upon an average not more than 6*d*. per day. Poverty and misery have deprived them of all energy; labour brings no adequate return; and every motive to exertion is destroyed. Agriculture is in the rudest and lowest state. The substantial farmer, employing labourers, and cultivating his land according to the improved modes of modern husbandry, is rarely to be found amongst them. The country is covered with small occupiers, and swarms with an indigent and wretched population. It is true that some landed proprietors have made great exertions to introduce a better system of agriculture, and to improve the condition of their immediate tenants, and a few of the lesser proprietors have made humble attempts to imitate them; but the great mass of the population exhibits a state of poverty bordering on destitution.

" These distinctions as to the usual diet of agricultural labourers in the different parts of Ireland are strictly applicable to those only who have regular employment. When they are out of work, which is the case in many places during three or four months of the year, the line is not so easily perceived. Then a reduction in the quantity as well as in the quality of their food takes place ; but still, though on a diminished scale, their relative local degrees of comfort or of plenty are maintained nearly according to the above classification. In no extremity of privation or distress have the peasantry of the northern counties approached to a level with those of the west; while Leinster and the greater part of the south, though sometimes reduced to the lowest condition, retain generally, even in the most calamitous periods, a shade of superiority. There are districts, indeed, in every quarter of the land, where, through peculiarities of situation or other causes, distress falls with an equal pressure upon all; but such exceptions are rare, and so limited in extent as scarcely to qualify the foregoing observations." *

It is very remarkable that the northern province of Ulster, in which the peasantry are here correctly represented as being so much better off than in the rest of Ireland, is nevertheless much the most thickly peopled of the four great divisions of the island; and has likewise the largest rural population, both absolutely, and relatively to the extent of arable land. It also contains a greater number of agricultural families than any other province, except Munster; and, although more than half of the cultivators are occupiers of land, the class of mere labourers is likewise more numerous than in Connaught, and almost as numerous as in Leinster. The explanation of this anomaly is to be found partly in the difference in the tenure of land, and partly in the fact that, of the rural population, a large portion is engaged in manufactures (particularly in the linen manufacture), which are diffused over the face of the country, and carried on in the

* Irish Railway Comm. 2d Report, pp. 5, 6.

cottages of the peasantry; and that most of the so-called agricultural families are partially employed in the same manner. There is thus more employment for the people in proportion to their number in Ulster than in other parts of Ireland, and population, though more dense, is less excessive.

The prosperity of Ulster, however, is only comparative; and even there employment is deficient and population redundant. In its most flourishing counties, Armagh, Down, and Antrim, where the traveller from the south or west is most struck with the improved appearance of the cottages and their inhabitants, the agricultural labourer in many places cannot earn his shilling a day oftener than three days in the week on an average throughout the year. In winter, from December to March, he has scarcely any thing to do; but at that season, nevertheless, he is often best provided with food, as it is not unusual for him to rent a bit of potato land from a farmer, which he pays for with labour, and the produce of which maintains him in the winter months. His hardest time is in summer, from May or June till August, when he is again out of work, and has, besides, pretty well exhausted his stock of potatoes; and then, unless he migrates to England or Scotland for the harvest, his only resource is the mendicancy of his wife and children; for he himself can seldom be compelled to beg by the cruellest privations. These remarks apply with increased force to the remaining counties of Ulster, in some of which the peasantry are also suffering in consequence of the gradual retirement

of the linen manufacture from the country to the
towns. This, among other causes, has contributed
to the depression of the rural inhabitants in Monaghan and Londonderry; but the most wretched
county of the whole province is Donegal. " Nothing can exceed," says Mr. Nicholls, " the miserable appearance of the cottages there, always teem-
ing with an excessive population." The people are
intelligent enough to perceive the sources of their
distress. They admit that they are too numerous,
"too thick upon the land;" that they are " eating
each others' heads off." But what can they do ?
They can only "live on," subsisting on shell-fish
or weeds when their potatoes fail, and begging
when no more shell-fish or weeds can be found,
always hoping " that times may mend, and that
their landlords, sooner or later, will do something
for them."*

Throughout Leinster, agricultural labourers
have scarcely any work, except in the spring and
autumn quarters; during the other six months of
the year, the greater part of them are thrown almost completely out of employment. This statement was made at almost every place entered by
the Commissioners appointed in 1834 to inquire
into the condition of the poor in Ireland, although
one parish in every barony in each of the counties
of Carlow, Kildare, Longford, Westmeath, and
Wexford was visited. At one place in Carlow, at

* Poor Inquiry (Ireland) App. A. to First Report, pp. 455—
474.; also, Mr. Nicholls' Second Report on Establishment of a
Poor Law for Ireland, pp. 81, 82.

least 500 men were said to be out of work, of
whom " many did not get two days of it in a
month." At another, out of fifty who applied to
the parish priest for recommendations, only ten succeeded in getting work. In Kildare, said one witness,
" if you are not noted as a good labourer, in the
busiest time of the year you may be left in the
streets for a month together without any one ask-
ing what brought you there." In a parish in
Longford, it was declared that there was not employment for a fourth part of the labourers between the months of September and March, and
again from the beginning of June to the middle or
end of August. In a parish in Westmeath, it was
agreed on all hands that one half of the labourers
were out of work great part of the year, and the
witnesses only differed as to whether it was for
two, three, or six months. As wages in Leinster
are never more than 10$d.$ a day in the busiest season, it is evident that a labourer can lay by nothing
for the time when he will be out of work, and it
may naturally be asked how he then contrives to
live. In winter he is comparatively comfortable,
for he has just dug up his crop of potatoes. He
has usually a bit of land of about a rood in extent,
which he sometimes holds on condition of manur-
ing it, but for which he is much more frequently
obliged to pay a most extravagant rent, seldom at
a lower rate than 3$l.$, and generally, if the land be
let to him manured, as high as 7$l.$ per acre. From
this conacre, as it is called, he may get nine barrels,
each containing forty-two stone of potatoes, on

which he may make shift to maintain himself till spring, when employment begins. But in May or June he is again out of work; his potatoes have been long since eaten, and melancholy are the expedients to which he is then reduced. Perhaps he may get some food on credit from the farmers, and although he always has to pay 20 or 30 per cent. for it above the market price, he thinks himself lucky, because he hopes that his creditor will employ him in order to ensure payment of his debt. But credit is now much less easily obtained than formerly. " Faith," said a man at Rathangan, in Kildare, " there's but little chance of our paying it back." Sometimes the women and children beg, but seldom in their own neighbourhood, for the sense of shame is most acute, in spite of all their wretchedness. Sometimes the children linger near the better sort of dwellings, not begging, but " with hunger in their looks, and evidently waiting to be asked." Their mute appeal is often successful, and sometimes obtains a few potatoes, even from persons who keep none back for themselves. But this resource is very precarious, and when it fails, or when a family disdains to resort to it, they gather " pressagh," a weed something like Scotch kale, which grows amidst the corn, and upon this and boiled nettles they frequently live for days together. Pressagh is exceedingly unwholesome, and is observed to give a yellow colour, something like its own, to those who eat it; but necessity has no law, and when the poor creatures are warned of the hurtful nature of their food, they

ask, " What can we do ? — can we starve ? If this
would kill us, we should have been dead long since,
for many's the time we have put up with worse."
When weeds disgust or are unobtainable, the starving poor try to " kill the hunger with water," or
to " stifle " it by lying in bed all day. Throughout
the evidence collected by the Commissioners are
instances of persons who had repeatedly remained
without food for twenty-four or forty-eight hours;
and it is mentioned, that when in the idle season a
man is fortunate enough to get a job, it is common
for the farmer to give him his wages in the morning, in order that he may buy food for breakfast,
and so gain strength to do his work. Men with
less powers of endurance than the rest sometimes
eat up their seed potatoes, and with them their
only means of subsistence during the ensuing winter, or they grub up the young roots in June or
July, when they are no bigger than marbles, and as
unfit for food from their quality as their size.*

This description of Leinster only requires that
some of its features should be a little heightened,
in order to make it equally applicable to Munster.
The agricultural population is considerably larger
in the latter province, and competition is keener
both for employment and land. The smallest
cabin lets for 30s. a year, and the rent of conacre
land ranges from 4l. to 10l. an acre. This term, it
may be proper to repeat, is given to the slips of
land which in most parts of Ireland are hired by

* First Report of Irish Poor Inquiry Commissioners, App.
A., pp. 393—415.

agricultural labourers, for the purpose of being planted with potatoes. They are commonly held under one of the *larger* farmers, that is to say, a farmer occupying upwards of forty acres, and the same piece of land is seldom underlet in this manner for more than one season at a time. The conditions of tenure are various. Sometimes, as was mentioned in the account of Leinster, the labourer pays the rent in manure. When a man's family is able to collect a heap of manure, any farmer will "turn it out" upon as much of his land as it will cover, taking care to spread it very thickly, and will permit the labourer to take from it a crop of potatoes. The quantity of land manured in this way varies from less than one-eighth to three-eighths of an acre, scarcely any labourer being able to manure half an acre. Sometimes, the conacre is paid for in labour. A farmer with more than forty acres of land must have at least one labourer permanently in his service. The man's nominal wages are about 6*d*. or 6½*d*. a day, but he seldom really receives any money. He obtains from the farmer a cabin for which he is charged 27*s*. or 30*s*. a year, an acre or an acre and a quarter of manured land, at about 4*l*. an acre, and generally grass for one sheep, valued at 10*s*. It takes him about 250 days to work out these sums at the stipulated rate, and then, if he is lucky enough to get a job, he may earn a few shillings for himself. Otherwise his crop of potatoes, the wool of his sheep, and his pig and fowls if he happen to keep any, are his sole means of support. A man living in this way, under a farmer that has good land, is supposed to be sure of having potatoes enough for the whole year; but if the land be poor, he has not enough, and is always in want when summer comes round. Most farmers are poor, and unable to manure the land. Of course, very few labourers are so fortunate as to have a permanent engagement of this kind, and if they neither have it, nor yet are owners of a dungheap, they must pay for their conacre (if they hire one) in hard cash, and at the extravagant rate already mentioned. Competition is so keen, that almost any rent that is asked will be offered, and lest the tenant should be unable to pay it, he is not suffered to remove his crop until he has either paid or given security for payment. His chief means of raising the requisite sum are the sale of his pig, and the wages he can pick up by migrating at harvest time to the neighbouring counties, or to England, or by occasional jobs at home. The last, however, is a most precarious and scanty resource : in two parishes in the county of Cork, one containing 250 and the other 240 labourers, dependent on occasional employment, exclusive of labourers in permanent employment, it was found upon inquiry that the average quantity of work afforded to each man was only sufficient for three months in the year in the former place, and for four months in the latter. How then do these men live ? They dig up their potatoes long before they are ripe, eat pressagh or corn kale, and lie in bed all day " for the hunger," like their brethren of Leinster, and have it seems somewhat less compunction in sending out their

wives and children to beg.   Want of food impairs
their strength and shortens their lives, so that a
man becomes unfit for work before sixty, and starvation sometimes kills them outright.

People who have scarcely ever enough to eat
cannot be expected to have much money to spare
for clothes.   The most fortunate Munster labourer
scarcely ever buys two articles of dress in the
same year.  He gets a hat one year, a coat the next,
a pair of breeches the next, and a hat has been
known to last a man twelve years.   The clothes
become rags long before their term of service is
expired, and their owner is not only ashamed to
attend chapel, but in severe weather is sometimes
obliged to leave his work because he can no longer
bear the cold, half-naked.   Some of the witnesses
examined by the " Poor Inquiry " Commissioners,
described their tattered appearance with that
strange humour that always sparkles through an
Irishman's misery.   One man speaking of his
children said, " They have so many wings and
flutter about so, that if they go out on a windy
day, a smart blast would hoist them over the ditch."
The dwellings of the Munster peasantry are as bad
as their clothes.   An ordinary cabin is about twenty
feet long and twelve broad, with walls of stone or
mud, and is sometimes divided into two apartments,
but never contains a second story.   The floor is
simply the ground upon which the cabin is built
made tolerably level, the roof is of straw and often
lets in the rain, and there is no ceiling nor any
covering on the rafters in the inside except soot.

Every cabin has a rude chimney, and many have a pane or two of glass to let in light, but some have only a square hole, which is stuffed with straw at night and in cold weather. Half of the cabins contain no bedstead, but their inmates lie on straw spread out on the ground, without blankets or any other covering except the clothes they wear in the day-time.

Notwithstanding their deplorable condition, the Munster peasantry meet with little compassion from the gentry. The Kerry landlords, indeed, according to the evidence of a most respectable witness, say, the poor are " damned well off." It will be only poetical justice if hereafter they become *similarly* well off themselves. The landlords are not even content with doing nothing for the relief of the poor; they aggravate their distress by their short-sighted rapacity. Taking advantage of the competition for land, they raise rents nearly twice as high as they ought to be; and though the farmer does not and cannot pay all that he promises, so much is extorted from him that he is left in a condition little better than that of the common labourer. Tenants of considerable farms are obliged to work themselves, and to make their sons help them, instead of hiring men; or, if they do hire labourers, are obliged to screw down their wages as low as possible. They sometimes leave their potatoes undug for a long while for want of money to pay for labourers. Few can bear the expense of properly cultivating their land, or can either manure it sufficiently or observe a due rotation of crops. They are driven into over-cropping, anxious only to obtain the largest return during the current season, and quite regardless of permanent improvements. The soil is thus every year deteriorated, fences are broken down, and houses allowed to fall into a state of dilapidation. An anecdote related by the Poor Inquiry Commissioners is very significant of the depressed condition of the farmers. A labouring man, who was complaining that it was not worth while to sell his pig on account of the low price at the time, was asked why he did not kill it. He replied with a smile, " The farmer I live with holds forty acres of land, and he has not killed a pig these three years." When such is the state of the larger landholders, it need scarcely be said that the mere cottiers, the tenants of from one to ten acres, are in a most desperate plight. In fact, they are only nominally superior to the labourers, and they are continually falling into the exact position of the latter, when, as happens to numbers of them every year, they are dispossessed of their little holdings.*

It may be thought that in Munster misery must have reached its extreme, and that it is impossible for the peasantry to be worse off anywhere: but whoever really entertains this opinion has evidently not extended his observation to Connaught. Still more melancholy scenes await him there. It should, however, be observed, that the descriptions here given of the four Irish provinces are only in-

* Irish Poor Inquiry, App. A. to First Report, pp. 415—455.

tended to represent their general condition, and must not be understood as denying that within the limits of each exist considerable districts, of which a much more pleasing picture might be drawn. In every province there are counties which may be favourably contrasted with the rest. In Leinster, for example, Louth will bear a comparison with the best parts of Ulster, and in Munster the aspect of Limerick and Tipperary is a shade less dark than that of Cork or Kerry. So also in Connaught there are varieties of wretchedness. Roscommon, Sligo, and Galway are not perhaps in a much worse state than the worst parts of Munster, while the whole world can scarcely furnish a parallel to the desperate condition of Mayo. The cultivated land of this county swarms with an agricultural population, of which the portion entirely dependent on the wages of labour may almost be said to be without any resource whatever. Land is so minutely divided, that out of about 46,000 farms 44,000 are under fifteen acres, and are held by men too poor to employ any hands but their own. Nevertheless, there are 67,000 males of fifteen years and upwards calling themselves labourers in husbandry, by which they mean that they are ready to take work if any one will give it, though few among them are lucky enough to get employment one day in four. In some extensive parishes there is literally no demand for labour whatever; every tenant tilling his own ground without assistance, and men who have no ground trusting to Providence. Most of the labourers, however, have a small piece of ground, which they commonly hire from the small farmers, sometimes, though rarely, on condition of working a certain number of days, or of placing on the land a certain quantity of manure, and sometimes on condition of paying a money rent. If they cannot obtain land in this way, they take possession of part of the waste, which constitutes nearly two-thirds of the county of Mayo, and this they are allowed to hold rent free for a year or two, or until, by reclaiming it, they have made it worth paying rent for. As soon as they have planted their potatoes, they leave their own village, and either alone, or in company with their wives and children, roam through the surrounding country. As soon as they get a few miles from home they begin to beg, for it is only in their own neighbourhood and among their own acquaintances that they are ashamed to do so, and thus an interchange of beggars takes place among the different parishes. Some of them cross over to England for the harvest; but comparatively few of the mere labourers are able to do this, for want of the few shillings required for the expenses of the journey. Even those who reach our island often fail to obtain work, and return as poor as they went, after suffering severe hardships, and frequently destroying their health by sleeping in the open air at night and in all weathers. If, however, by any means they can contrive to scrape together money enough to redeem their potatoes, that is to say, to pay the rent of the land, if any be due, and also the price of the seed, which is generally obtained on credit, they return home in the autumn, and subsist during the winter upon the produce of their slip of land; otherwise the crop is seized by their creditors, and their only resource during the winter is to beg from people almost as poor as themselves. The labourers, however, are scarcely so much to be pitied as some of the class immediately above them, the farmers of from one to five acres. These men are reducéd nearly to the same shifts as the labourers in order to pay their rent, and migrate like them, during the summer, to other parts of Ireland or to England. If they fail in their object, and are obliged to abandon their crops to the landlords, they are rendered as completely destitute as the labourers, and will not stoop to the same means to relieve their distress. They are, for the most part, too proud to beg from their neighbours; and if the latter, suspecting their wants, did not voluntarily assist them, they might perish with hunger. The Irish peasantry are indeed ever ready to help each other: the few who have enough for themselves, seldom eat without sending something to their famishing friends; and a man who did not offer part of his meal to the neighbour that happened to come in when the potatoes were boiled, would be scouted as a churl. Still this mutual generosity, where all are so poor, can at best only relieve distress by extending it, and must leave a vast amount of distress untouched. There is no season of the year in which the Connaught peasantry are properly supplied with food. It has been already mentioned, that their ordinary diet differs from that in use in

other parts of Ireland by consisting only of potatoes without the addition either of meal or milk;
but even the potatoes are generally of inferior
quality. Those most commonly planted in Connaught are called " lumpers," which require less
manure and produce more abundantly than other
sorts, but furnish a soft, watery food, equally un-
palatable and unwholesome, upon which even pigs
do not thrive. The texture, in fact, is more that of
a turnip than of a potato. Where " lumpers "
are the only food in plentiful seasons, it need
scarcely be said, that in times of scarcity the
potatoes which ought to be reserved for seed are
eaten, even by farmers; that potatoes are dug up
while still " so small that only hunger could see
them;" that noxious weeds are also used as food,
and that, in short, resort is had to all the reckless
expedients spoken of in the account of Leinster
and Munster. A practice peculiar to Connaught is
that of bleeding the cows, of which the landholders,
having a range of mountainous waste, generally
possess one. The owners of cows must be far removed above the level of the poorest, yet even they
consent thus seriously to injure the animals which
form the most valuable part of their property, for
the sake of the scanty nourishment contained in the
blood. But far more desperate means are sometimes adopted to allay the pangs of hunger. In
1831 a cargo of potatoes arrived at a sea-port in
Mayo, which, when the hatches were opened, were
found to be so much decayed, and to give out such
a stench, that they were thrown overboard as unfit

for use. Upon this the people crowded to the beach and plunged up to the middle in the water to gather them, although the rottenness might be seen oozing through the bags in which they were carried away. Numbers became sick from using them, and many, even of the fowls that eat them, died. In summer, when dearth both of employment and provisions is always greatest, men may be seen " lying in the ditches with weakness, and I have seen them," said one of the witnesses examined by the Poor Inquiry Commissioners, " working on the bog, when they could not throw the third sod from mere hunger and weakness." " If," said another, " you were taking your notes here in summer, you would ask us no questions ; you would tell by the lankness of a man's jaws how much food he had in his house." It may seem as needless as it is painful to accumulate evidences of the misery of these poor creatures. " A fountain of ink," to use the words of one of themselves, " would be spent before all the tale would be written." Yet the picture would be incomplete without some notice of their habitations and clothing, as well as of their food. The former cannot be better described than in the words of an intelligent foreigner, who thus expresses his astonishment at the first sight of some Connaught cabins : —

" In the west of Ireland there are districts where a man may imagine himself in a wilderness abandoned by mankind, — where nothing is to be seen but rocks, bogs, and brushwood, and where wild beasts alone may be supposed capable of housing.

All at once, however, on closer inspection, little green patches like potato fields are seen scattered here and there amid the rocks, and a stranger is tempted to go nearer and examine them. Let him look where he is going, however, or he may make a false step; the earth may give way under his feet and he may fall into — what? into an abyss, a cavern, a bog? No, into a hut, — into a human dwelling-place, whose existence he had overlooked, because the roof on one side was level with the ground, and nearly of the same consistency. If the traveller draw back his foot in time, and look around, he will find the place filled with a multitude of similar huts, all swarming with life. — I remember," says the same writer in another place, " when I saw the poor Lettes in Livonia, I used to pity them for having to live in huts built of the unhewn logs of trees, the crevices being stopped up with moss. I pitied them on account of their low doors, and their diminutive windows; and gladly would I have arranged their chimneys for them in a more suitable manner. Well, Heaven pardon my ignorance! — A wooden house, with moss to stop up the crevices, would be a palace in the wild regions of Ireland. Paddy's cabin is built of earth — one shovel-full over the other, with a few stones mingled here and there, till the wall is high enough. But perhaps the roof is thatched, or covered with bark? Ay, indeed! A few sods of grass cut from a neighbouring bog are his only thatch. Well, but a window or two at least, if it be only a pane of glass fixed in the wall? or the bladder of some animal, or a piece of talc, as may often be seen in a Wallachian hut. What idle luxury were this! There are thousands of cabins in which not a trace of a window is to be seen; nothing but a little square hole in front, which doubles the duty of door, window, and chimney: light, smoke, pigs, and children, all must pass in and out by the same aperture."*

The furniture of these cabins is quite in keeping with their external appearance. Kohl says, that when the coach stopped, he used to get down to inspect the inside of the houses, but he could often see enough without leaving his seat, for at times he could "study the interior economy of the establishment through the holes in the roof — the broken plates in the kitchen, the potato kettle on the hearth, the heap of damp straw for a bed in one corner, and the pigsty in another."

In a parish containing a population of 10,553, it was found by the Roman Catholic clergyman of the place, on a careful examination, that there were altogether 400 beds, so that, allowing three persons on an average to each bed, 9553 must have lain on straw at the best; — and from a similar calculation of the number of bedsteads, it further appeared that 7070 persons were lying on the floors of damp cabins. In a village within the same parish, of 45 families, comprising 206 persons, there were ascertained to be just 39 blankets. In another parish, containing 1648 families, there were found to be 388 families with two blankets each, 1011

* Ireland, by J. G. Kohl.

with one blanket each, and 299 with no blankets at all. What is called a blanket is, moreover, frequently nothing more than a bundle of rags, for the same article has been known to last a family for seventeen years, and is generally in constant use both night and day, many a mother having little other clothing. When beds and bed clothes are wanting, straw is the most usual substitute for both, but even straw must be carefully husbanded. " The straw we lie on," said one of the Mayo cottiers, " was given us by some neighbours in charity; we do not change it; we do not part with it all; but as it wastes away, the neighbours give us a wisp to add to it." When straw cannot be procured, the poor " pull the rushes that grow on the sandbanks by the roots, and spread them as a bed for themselves, just as they would do for pigs."

With respect to dress, the poorest of the Connaught peasantry remain for years together without buying an article of it. In one parish there were found to be more than 3000 persons who had bought nothing worth speaking of for five years. The men make desperate efforts to procure " a breeches," and, chiefly by the help of other people's cast-off rags, they do generally contrive to screen —not to cover their nakedness; but their wives would not be decent enough to go out begging without wrapping an old sheet or blanket round them, and the children are often without even this apology for clothing. " There's a son of mine," said a man, pointing to a half-naked boy about twelve years old, in a man's coat all rags, dangling and trailing about him; " he never wore a trousers, he never had one; it's a borrowed coat he has on him now; you see he has nothing else but a shirt: that shirt is the only stitch of clothing he has of his own. In cold weather, he must keep close to the house unless he runs from one house to another; or as he gets a borrowed coat, or a sheet to roll about him, he may run from village to village." This plan of borrowing is not of course confined to the children. The labourers who appeared to give evidence before the Commissioners were without shoes or stockings, and their other clothes were mere rags, leaving them every where open to the weather. Yet, even of these rags part were borrowed for the occasion. One of the men declared, that the shapeless piece of felt which he wore instead of a hat was not his own, and that for three weeks he had been unable to work for want of some protection against the cold. Small landholders paying 3l., 4l., or 5l. rent, are sometimes so destitute of clothes, that they cannot go to market without borrowing a coat from one person. a waistcoat from another, and a pair of trousers from a third. A farmer of eight acres, who was present when this last statement was made, said " I lent my coat yesterday to a neighbour, taking his sack of oats to Westport." When people go to confess, the man who is first discharged by the priest lends his coat to his neighbour, that the latter may go in also : and the women do the like, and change not only their cloak but their gown.*

* App. A. to First Report of Poor Inquiry Commission, pp. 355—393.

The points of distinction between the rural and urban inhabitants of Ireland are observable only among a small portion of the latter. With the exception of the capital, and five or six other seaports, and of the few places which depend chiefly on manufactures, Irish towns in general have rather the appearance of overgrown villages. Little trade of any kind is carried on in them, and the mass of the labourers are agricultural, differing from their rural brethren only in the place of their residence. Wages may be a trifle higher than in the country, owing to the somewhat superior condition of the employers of labour in towns, which renders them more ashamed to drive too hard a bargain with their servants; but this is an advantage by which few are benefited. The supply of labourers is so much beyond the demand, that numbers of them may almost always be seen standing idle in the streets, waiting for the chance of being hired; and it often happens, that out of a hundred collected in this manner in the morning, not more than ten are missing by sunset. Several of the little inland towns have been well described in a few words by that cleverest of sketchers, Mr. Thackeray. At Kilkullen, near Naas, " few people were to be seen, except a crowd round a meal shop, where meal is distributed once a-week by the neighbouring gentry." It was market day when he passed through Carlow, but the " parcel of wretched rags and trifles exposed for sale," only reminded him of the primitive articles which, as travellers tell us, "change hands in a town of African huts and traders on the

banks of the Quorra." At a posting-place called
Ballyhale, in Kilkenny, "a dirty, old, contented,
decrepit idler was lolling in the sun, and hundreds
of the population of the dirty, old, decrepit, contented place, were employed in the like way." At
Bandonbridge he " looked along one side of the
houses in the long street through which he went, to
see if there was a window without a broken pane
of glass," but declares on his conscience, that every
single window had *three* broken panes. It was
market day there too, and "in a little, miserable,
old market-house, a few women were selling butter-
milk, bullocks' hearts, liver, and such-like scraps of
meat." At Bantry, " the main street was thronged
as usual with blue-cloaked women carrying on their
eager trade of butter-milk and green apples, but
with the exception of this street and the quay, with
their white-washed and slated houses, it is a town
of cabins. The wretchedness of some of them is
quite curious. As for drawing them, it was in vain
to try; one might as well make a sketch of a
bundle of rags. An ordinary pig-sty in England is
really more comfortable. Most of them were not
six feet long or five feet high, built of stones
huddled together, a hole being left for the people
to creep in at — a ruined thatch to keep out some
little portion of the rain. A Hottentot kraal has
more comforts in it: even to write of the place
makes one unhappy, and the words more slow." *

Some of the manufacturing towns, most of which

* Irish Sketch Book.

are situated in the province of Ulster, are the only ones in which the mass of the inhabitants can be said to exist in any thing like comfort. By far the most considerable of these is Belfast, which contains twenty mills for spinning linen yarn, employing nearly 7000 persons, and several factories for the weaving of linen cloth, employing about 1000 persons, besides numerous manufactories of articles of minor importance. The operatives are in general pretty well paid; spinners get about a pound a-week, and linen weavers, whose business has suffered little from the invasion of power-looms, from 8s. to 12s. a-week. The wages of mechanics are nearly as high as in England, and common day-labourers earn on an average 7s. 6d. a-week. These last wages would certainly not suffice for the decent maintenance of a family in England; and although provisions are much cheaper in Ireland, it is probably only in accordance with Irish ideas that the diet of Belfast labourers is said to be " good, and their dress and demeanour respectable." There is pretty constant employment for able-bodied men of all classes throughout the year.* Some considerable manufactures were formerly carried on in Dublin, but these have now in a great measure disappeared, and there is far from sufficient employment for the indigent crowds ever flocking into the capital. The poorest quarters of the city consequently present a

---

* Appendix C. to First Report of Irish Poor Inquiry Commissioners; Appendix N. to Second Report of Children's Employment Commission; also, M'Culloch's Geograph. Dict., art. " Belfast."

most melancholy appearance, and their inhabitants
are evidently engaged in a constant struggle for
existence. The wretchedness of Dublin is, however,
greatly surpassed in one or two other sea-ports.
In Cork, although the rate of wages for common
labourers is a shilling a-day, the scarcity of employment is such that few or none earn more than
five or six shillings a-week. It is supposed that
about 20,000 persons of both sexes and all ages
live from hand to mouth, having only casual employment, and that 6000 more may be termed
destitute in the strictest sense of the word. In
Limerick, with a smaller population, there is a
larger amount of destitution: ten thousand of the
inhabitants are supposed to be dependent on acci-
dent for subsistence. The sufferings of these poor
people, so far as they consist of want of food and
clothing, are altogether the effects of their poverty;
but that part of their wretchedness which is produced by deficient house accommodation is shared
almost equally by highly-paid handicraftsmen and
artisans. The *Ghetto*, or vile quarter, — that assemblage of narrow, dark, noisome lanes and courts, in
which, though crime makes its den, honest industry
must often make its home for want of shelter elsewhere, is not likely to be wanting in Irish towns,
when there is scarcely a considerable town in Great
Britain in which it may not be discovered lying
unsuspectedly close beside the haunts of wealth
and pleasure. The lower classes of the urban
population of Ireland are lodged still worse, if possible, than the occupants of the cellars of Liverpool

and the closes of Glasgow. In the old town of Limerick families of eight or nine persons inhabit single rooms not more than four yards square, into which the rain pours through the roof, and the wind rushes through the broken windows.* One sixth of the population are thus lodged. In Cork, says Mr. Thackeray, after mentioning the loneliness of the "respectable" portion of the city, "there are quarters swarming with life, but of such a frightful kind as no pen need care to describe; alleys where the odours and rags and darkness are so hideous, that one runs frightened away from them. In some of them, they say, not the policeman, only the priest, can penetrate." † As, however, the defective house accommodation of the lower classes does not always proceed altogether from their poverty, it is unnecessary to dilate upon the subject at present, further than to mention a remarkable fact, ascertained at the last census, viz. that above a million of families, not much less than five-sixths of the whole nation, are living either in mud huts or in single rooms of larger houses. Independently of this, sufficient specimens of other kinds of misery have been given to serve as illustrations of the extent to which over-population has proceeded in Ireland.‡

---

* Appendix C. to Third Report of Irish Poor Inquiry Commission, part i. p. 87.

† Irish Sketch Book, vol. i. p. 136.

‡ Report of Irish Census Commissioners, p. 16.

Part of the evidence from which the preceding particulars have been taken was collected in the year 1835, when there was no legal provision for the Irish poor. Since then a poor law has been applied to Ireland; the whole country has been divided into Unions, and 112 workhouses have been built, into which 71,217 paupers were admitted in the course of the year 1844. It is not probable, however, that these measures can have sensibly diminished the immense mass of destitution existing beyond the walls of the workhouses : indeed, we have the positive testimony of recent tourists that they have not done so*, and at any rate they cannot have diminished the over-population which that misery indicated, for the necessity of relieving destitution by charity is as unequivocal a sign of over-population as destitution itself. The inference drawn from the evidence in question is therefore as applicable to the present as to any former period.†

* In 1842, Mr. Thackeray, passing through the county of Cork, found many of the potato gardens half dug up in the first week of August, nearly three months before the potato is ripe or at full growth, and while winter was still three months away. — *Irish Sketch Book*, vol. i. p. 175.

† In explanation of the absence of quotations from the evidence collected by the Irish Land Commissioners of 1844, it may be proper to mention, that this chapter was written some months before that evidence was published. It would certainly have been desirable to appeal to the latest authorities on Irish wretchedness ; but the omission to do so is of the less consequence, as the description given by the Commissioners of 1835, which has been chiefly followed in the text, is amply corroborated by all their successors.

# CHAPTER IV.

CAUSES OF OVER-POPULATION IN GENERAL.

Decrease in the Demand for Labour. — Excessive Augmentation of the Numbers of a Community. — Propensity of Mankind to multiply too rapidly. — Motives for restraining this Propensity. — Influence of such Motives upon People in easy Circumstances. — Their utter Inefficacy among the very poor. — Tendency of Misery to promote Population. — Illustrations of the Theory proposed. — Structure of Society among pastoral Nations. — Gradual Conversion of the Poor of such Communities into agricultural Serfs. — Physical well-being of Serfs. — Transformation of them into free Peasant Proprietors. — Prosperity of the Peasantry of Germany. — Esthonia. — Holland. — Belgium. — Sketch of the Progress of Society in the Netherlands. — State of the Norwegian and Swiss Peasantry. — Causes and Antiquity of their Prosperity. — Explanation of the Pauperism existing in Continental Towns. — Past and present Condition of the People in Poland and France. — Wretchedness of the labouring Class in Southern Italy. — Happiness of the Peasantry in Tuscany and Lombardy.

A PERMANENT deficiency of employment for the labouring class, which has been shown to be the state of things indicated by the term Over-population, does not always proceed from an increase in the number of labourers, but may also originate in a diminished demand for labour. If an important part of the business carried on in any country be abandoned, or contracted within narrower limits, or removed to a foreign soil, or even to a new situation within the same territory, or if machinery be largely substituted for human labour, a number of persons may be thrown out of work who may possibly never again be able to obtain adequate occupation. Such a country will have become over-peopled in consequence merely of the diminution of employment. The population which formerly was not too large to maintain itself in comfort will have become excessive, although it may not have increased in the smallest degree.

Some few places in Great Britain have been rendered too populous in this manner, the manufactures formerly carried on in them having been removed to a distance, or old industrial processes having been superseded by improved methods. Although, however, this has been the case in some few instances, it has by no means been so generally throughout the country, in which, when we consider the vast extension of agriculture, as well as of manufactures, of late years, we cannot doubt, that in spite of the adoption of machinery in almost every branch of industry, there must be a greater aggregate demand for human labour at this than at any previous period. As therefore the total amount of employment has increased, its deficiency could not have been constantly becoming more manifest, unless the number of work-people had increased still more than the quantity of work, so that in order to account for the over-population of this island, it will be principally necessary to discover the causes of the excessive increase of the people.

If in the wantonness of disputation the most obvious truths were not sometimes stoutly contested, it would be superfluous to demonstrate that mankind, like all other animals, have both the power of increasing beyond the means of comfortable subsistence, and also a strong propensity to exercise that power. If the means of subsistence could be supplied in unlimited abundance, and provided no cause of extraordinary mortality were in operation, a community could evidently double itself in a short period, (repeated experience has shown that twenty-five years at most would suffice for the purpose,) and unless the people were deaf to the dictates of nature, it is certain that their numbers would be doubled accordingly. They would also continue to all eternity to be doubled at intervals of the same length, if the means of subsistence continued to increase in the same proportion : population, in short, would go on for ever increasing by geometrical progression if sufficient means of subsistence were procurable. But the means of subsistence are far from unlimited. Those of the whole human race cannot at most exceed what the whole earth is capable of yielding, and those of every community are in like manner bounded by the limits of the territory which it inhabits, or with which it has intercourse. In reality, they are much more closely contracted, for, owing to the unequal division of land, to vicious legislation, want of agricultural skill, and other causes, no country is ever permitted to yield a tithe of the annual produce which might be drawn from its soil, and even in the quantity which is actually obtained, persons with no other property than their labour must not hope to share, unless they can get employment. The means of subsistence of this class of persons are consequently only proportionate to the amount of employment for them, and are subject to limits which, though capable of very great expansion, are reached at a very early stage of society, and begin to press as soon as they are reached. But although the means of subsistence be thus limited, the people dependent upon them may still continue for a while to increase in number; and it is clear that they will continue to increase up to the utmost number that can possibly be kept alive, unless they either restrain their natural inclination to marriage, or practise vices or habits unfavourable to the growth of population, or unless they are kept down by the frequent occurrence of war, sickness, or some other destructive agency. Unless one or other of these causes operates with sufficient force, population must advance until many members of the society are unable to procure a sufficiency of the necessaries of life, and until want, or the diseases engendered by want, produce a mortality which prevents it from advancing further. These propositions, which, except in the mode of expression, are almost identical with the first principles of Malthus's theory, are so self-evident, that notwithstanding the prevalent fashion to oppose every opinion maintained by that writer, it seems sufficient to state them simply without adding a syllable in their support.

But in order to account for the over-populousness of any particular place or region, it is not sufficient to show that population has everywhere a tendency to become excessive unless the propensity by which it is impelled be restrained or counteracted. Strong as the propensity is, there must be some influence strong enough to control it, or, in spite of the ravages of war, pestilence, and infanticide, the earth would long ago have been over-peopled, and all the inhabitants of almost every country would be suffering from want. This is really the condition of the labouring class in some parts of the world, but it is so of the labouring class only, and even that class is in most countries more or less raised above want, while in some it is abundantly supplied with all necessaries. This plenty, however, would evidently not be lasting, if the people exerted unrestrainedly their powers of self-multiplication; and it is necessary to ascertain what motive prevents their indulging their natural inclination to marriage, and why the same motive is not equally effectual everywhere.

Among people possessing freedom of action, the motive can be no other than fear of the consequences frequently resulting from an imprudent match. It is foreseen that the care of a family may require the sacrifice of some habitual comforts; or may render it impossible to retain, after marriage, the same social position as was previously occupied. This last consideration is perhaps the strongest of all: at least, it acts where others are little felt. Lovers, who have no anxiety about the welfare of children that may never be born, and who would be content to make some sacrifice for the sake of enjoying each other's company, may be unwilling to disqualify themselves for associating with their present equals. Even if their means be sufficient to procure for them in abundance every necessary and substantial comfort, they may yet hesitate to marry, unless they can keep up the outward appearance required in the circle in which they are accustomed to move. These dissuasives from marriage are so powerful among the higher classes, that, as has been well remarked, if the world were inhabited only by people of property, it would probably soon become depopulated by natural failure of the species. They have somewhat less influence in inferior conditions of life, not so much because they are less felt (for a peasant is probably as anxious as a lord to retain the respect of his acquaintance, and whatever other advantages he may possess), as because, in the middle and lower ranks, social advantages are less irrecoverably forfeited by an imprudent match. A duke's son, who marries with only a younger son's portion, can scarcely hope ever again to be able to live in the style in which he has been brought up; but the son of a merchant or a farmer, though his means be at present small, may not unreasonably expect to be one day as well off as his father. Though weakened, however, the prudential considerations just alluded to are still very effectual in every con-

dition of life, except in those which are so low that
it is impossible to sink much beneath them. In
these they are absolutely inoperative. A half-
starved wretch, who has only rags to wear, and a
ruined mud-hovel to sleep in, knows that he cannot
be more despised, though he may be more pitied, if
the holes in his cheeks and coat, and in the roof
of his shed, become twice as wide as at present.
Neither is the absence of shame on account of his
outward appearance supplied, as might be expected,
by increased dread of the more real ills of poverty.
On the contrary, it seems that the more wretched
a man is, the more heedless he is about increasing
his misery. If he were in easy circumstances, he
would be reluctant to risk any of his comforts; but
a very poor man may have no comforts to lose. If
his means be barely sufficient to appease the cravings
of nature, without affording him any positive gratification, he may think that, being already so badly
off, he cannot become much worse; and that it is
not worth while to practise present self-denial, from
the dread of a slight increase of future privation.*
He might possibly be disposed to postpone the
indulgence of his inclinations, if there were a
chance of his condition improving; but, if he have
no such hope, the present opportunity may seem as
unobjectionable as any that is ever likely to occur.
He may even persuade himself that it will be for

---

* This argument has been briefly summed up in one of Dr.
Johnson's memorable sayings : — " A man is poor — he thinks,
I cannot be worse, so I'll e'en take Peggy." — *Croker's Boswell*,
vol. ii. p. 103.

his advantage to marry early, that his sons may be able to assist him in his old age, when he would otherwise be altogether destitute. He may reason in this manner, if he think at all; but it is more likely that his misfortunes will have rendered him inconsiderate and reckless. With so gloomy a prospect before him, he may prefer to close his eyes upon the future, and, caring only for the present moment, he may snatch at any means of alleviating his sorrows, without calculating the cost. Be this as it may, it is certain that the prudential considerations which constitute the only voluntary restraint on marriage, and which sometimes exercise even an excessive influence amongst the rich, are absolutely powerless amongst the very poor. It has been frequently observed, that very wealthy families seldom attain a great antiquity, but generally become extinct in a few generations * : whereas, when the lower classes of a community are subject to severe permanent distress, their numbers almost invariably increase to the utmost extent which the means of subsistence will permit.

Misery, the inevitable effect and symptom of over-population, thus seems to be likewise its principal promoter. It seems, indeed, to be the only circumstance which occasions an excessive increase in the numbers of a community, except when people are placed in situations in which, being unable to estimate correctly the amount of employment, they over-rate their means of subsistence; or, when

---

* See examples of this, cited in support of a very different theory, in Mr. Doubleday's work on Population.

some political arrangement, such as a charitable provision for the poor, encourages them to get families around them which they cannot themselves maintain. With these exceptions it will, I think, be found that, wherever population has received an undue impulse, the people have first been rendered reckless by privation. A few illustrations shall now be offered in support of this opinion, and an attempt shall be made to show, by examples, first, that when a people are placed in possession of plenty, they generally continue to enjoy it until something occurs to occasion an absolute diminution of the total amount of their resources ; and, secondly, that when by any cause they are reduced to want, their want is almost invariably aggravated by the increase of their numbers.

Among wandering, at least among pastoral tribes, war, epidemic diseases, the frequent barrenness of women, and the extraordinary mortality of children, seem to keep down the numbers of the people sufficiently, without requiring them to place any restraint on their connubial inclinations. All travellers agree that these inclinations are freely indulged, and their statements respecting the honour in which marriage is held, and the general desire for children, are confirmed by the evidence of Scripture with respect to the primitive Israelites, and that of Tacitus with respect to the ancient Germans. Yet it seems probable that the numbers of a pastoral tribe are scarcely ever more than duly proportionate to the average means of subsistence. They are indeed, at times grievously thinned by famine, but this seems to be the effect of accidental and temporary causes, such as drought, or the loss of cattle by disease or depredation, or the improvidence of the people, which prevents them from properly husbanding their resources. It is clear that they do not suffer habitually from scarcity of food, or slavery would not be so common amongst them, but the poorer freemen would hire themselves out to the rich. Neither would there be any necessity for a lover to purchase his bride from her parents, according to the present practice. A father would be glad to get his daughter off his hands if she were merely a burthen to him; but he sets a price upon her, because, in providing her suitor with a wife, he is at the same time depriving himself of a valuable servant.

But although over-population be an evil unknown to pastoral nations, it will be very useful to inquire into the condition of the lower classes in such communities; for most civilised nations are descended from pastoral ancestors, and many of them still feel the effects of the social relations which existed among their rude progenitors. There can be little doubt that shepherds or herdsmen were the first occupiers of almost every country, for independently of other arguments in favour of that opinion, the rapid migrations of vast multitudes from one side of the globe to the other, which are known to have taken place in early times, could only have been effected by people who possessed in their cattle perambulatory magazines of provisions. Now the structure of society among pastoral nations depends very greatly on the natural features of the territories they inhabit. If these be of very small extent, very barren, or much divided by mountains, large rivers, or other barriers, the tribes, or collections of families living together, must necessarily be small for want of pasture, and the same cause will prevent any individual from acquiring very great numbers of cattle, and from very greatly surpassing his companions in wealth or power. There can be no great inequality of rank, but every freeman, when emancipated from parental control, will acknowledge no authority save that of the assembled heads of the community. The chief will hold a merely honorary office; he will be unable to do anything in peace or war without the consent of the other heads of families, for the latter, by combining amongst themselves, could easily resist his commands. Such appears to be the state of society in the deserts of Arabia, and in some nearly equally sterile tracts inhabited by Turcomans, to the east of the Caspian Sea. If on the other hand there be abundance of good pasture, a tribe may attain a very considerable size, and the cattle of a single proprietor may be counted by thousands and tens of thousands. Such an one may be raised by a concurrence of fortunate circumstances far above his neighbours in wealth and power, and may become their chief in reality as well as in name. Successful wars with other tribes may extend his dominion, and increase the disparity between himself and his subjects, until his authority becomes altogether absolute. Such is the history of Gen-

ghis Khan, Tamerlane, and other potentates who have
succeeded in reducing all the wandering hordes of
Tartary under their sway. Even if no individual
be able to exalt himself in this manner, and if there
be a considerable body of rich herdsmen, pretty
nearly on a level, the existence of such an aristocracy is equally fatal to the liberty of their
inferiors. Every rich man must maintain a number
of dependents, captives taken in war, or poor clansmen of his own, to look after his cattle. These
retainers have no law but their master's will, and
they are ever ready to assist him in any act of
oppression. A man of small property has therefore no security, except in the protection of some
superior, to whom he yields an obedience more or
less implicit, according to the disparity in their
respective means.

Experience shows, in opposition to the fashionable
theory, that there is no necessary transition from a
pastoral to an agricultural life, and that some
peculiar causes are required to produce a change of
this kind. If, however, a wandering tribe does
become stationary, a wealthy herdsman preserves
his supremacy over all the land on which the cattle
of himself and his followers have been accustomed
to graze. Part of the land is appropriated by such
of his dependents as possess flocks of their own,
but these continue to acknowledge their allegiance
to their lord, and become in fact his vassals. As
for his more immediate retainers, the servants fed
and clothed by his bounty, they are placed on the
domains which he takes into his own possession,

and generally till their master's ground, as they formerly tended his flocks. Their subjection to him becomes if possible still more complete than before, for their distribution over the land, and consequent separation from each other, and their attachment to the soil, deprive them of the mutual support, and of the facilities for escape, which they possessed when dwelling in a camp. It was in this manner that the mass of the wandering Goths and Scythians of antiquity degenerated into Russian and German serfs, as completely at their master's disposal as the rest of his live stock. Such probably was already the condition of the peasantry of Gaul and Spain, when those countries were annexed to the Roman Empire; and if it underwent any change during the period of Roman domination, it was certainly restored by the barbarians who overran the Roman provinces.

Although, however, a serf may hold both life and property by no other tenure than the permission of his lord, and may be altogether without protection from any outrage which the latter may choose to offer, he may not suffer from a scarcity of the necessaries of life, but, as far as his mere bodily wants are concerned, may be in a very tolerable, and even comfortable situation. His lord may, if he please, deprive him entirely of the fruits of his labour; but, in a thinly-peopled country, in which manufactures have made little progress, and foreign commerce is unknown, a great landholder would be only encumbered by larger contributions of raw produce than his household could consume. The quantity he requires may be much less than the whole produce of his estate, and when the cultivators have supplied sufficient for his wants, they will probably be allowed to retain the remainder of their crops for their own use, and may be enabled both to feed and clothe themselves well. If the country remain in an uncivilised state, the rents of the peasantry may continue for ages without any sensible augmentation, and the same families may be left undisturbed in the possession of their respective holdings, from the absence of any motive for ejecting them. In process of time, customs become confounded with rights, so that at length it would be looked upon as a piece of injustice to demand increased contri-butions from a serf, or to oust him from his land, as long as the old rate was punctually paid. If, while this was the state of feeling, an influential middle class were to grow up, or if the Crown should be desirous of curbing the power of the nobles, the rights of the peasantry would be more boldly asserted, and more generally recognised, until at length they were formally established by law. Several examples of this have taken place within the last half-century, during which the peasantry of Austria, Prussia, and the Russian provinces on the Baltic, have been raised from prædial slavery to the condition of freemen and proprietors of the lands occupied by their ancestors, on condition of annually paying to the lord of the manor certain fixed amounts of labour or produce. The present position of these en-

franchised serfs is, in general, a very enviable one.
Before their emancipation, they were well supplied
with all necessaries, — not less abundantly, it may
be presumed, than the serfs of the present day on
large estates in Russia, who are lodged in substantial, roomy, well-warmed huts, are clothed in thick
dresses of sheep-skin, drugget and flannel, have
as much rye-bread, eggs, salt-fish, lard, bacon, and
green vegetables as they can eat, and feast on fresh
meat on every holiday.  The fear of losing these
good things, probably sufficed to prevent them
from marrying without ample security for their
continued enjoyment, or the authority of the landlord, naturally indisposed to permit his estate to be
over-run with beggars, may possibly have been in-
terposed to check improvident matches.  By one
cause or other population was confined within
moderate bounds, so that, at the abolition of serfdom,
every peasant was placed in possession of a piece of
land, always sufficient for his maintenance, and
often of considerable extent.  The prudence arising
from the possession of property then became
strengthened, and produced proportionate effects.
Population has certainly advanced, but less rapidly
than the means of subsistence, and the condition
of the peasantry has been decidedly ameliorated
since they were freed from their feudal chains.

Thus, throughout Germany, the peasantry are
exceedingly industrious; they labour busily early
and late, but they feel that they are labouring for
themselves, and their toil is rewarded by the substantial comforts they enjoy.  They have, it is

true, little refinement in their notions or habits. The women are often set upon the hardest tasks, while the men sit at their ease smoking, and the dirt and odours of their habitations are intolerable to eyes and ears of any delicacy ; but these evils are borne only because they are unfelt : such wants as the people are sensible of are all abundantly satisfied. " Every man has his house, his orchard, his road-side trees, so hung with fruit that he is obliged to prop them all ways, or they would be torn to pieces. He has his corn-plot, his plot for mangel-wurzel, for hemp and so on," his cattle, sheep, and swine. His house is strong and well built, generally of stone, and though gloomy and slovenly within, made warm and comfortable by a large iron stove : it is, moreover, furnished with all needful utensils, and is particularly well stocked with bedding and homespun clothing. The peasant's dress is commonly a long coat, and cocked or hollow-sided hat, and in winter he wraps himself in a huge blue cloak with a fur collar, and a cape reaching to his middle. His usual fare is coarse but nourishing ; he indulges freely in the cheap luxuries of beer and tobacco, and on Sundays and holydays he feasts at a pic-nic or a public-house, and whirls away his care in a gay waltz.[*]

The enfranchised serfs of Estonia, whose emancipation dates only from 1828, possess the elements of happiness in greater abundance than their German brethren, but do not understand so well how

* Howitt's Rural and Domestic Life of Germany, pp. 40—56.

to turn them to account. They occupy farms, frequently as much as twenty or twenty-five acres in extent, for which they pay rent "in the shape of so many days' labour, man and horse, per week, upon the lord's fields," besides "certain contributions of corn, and of a calf, a goose, so many fowls or eggs, and so many bundles of flax." After satisfying the landlord's claim, by far the greater part of the produce remains for the farmer, who has no one to blame but himself if all his bodily wants are not plentifully supplied. The nature of his diet may be in some measure inferred from the list of articles which make up his rent. He dresses himself in sheep skins, or in a long coat coming down to his heels, made of undyed wool, and wears on his feet sandals of untanned cow's hide; but to show that it is not poverty that prevents his getting better clothes, he displays rows of silver buttons down the breast of his holyday suit. His house is commonly a one-storied erection, built of roughly squared logs, and occupying as much space as an English old-fashioned farm-house, with a double wall on the entrance side, separated by a passage of about six feet wide, which greatly tends both to warmth in winter, and coolness in summer. This passage is shared by pigs with the farmer's children, and horses and cattle also dwell under the same roof; but the apartments especially appropriated to the family, though dark and smoky, offer nothing to disgust even the fastidious eyes of an English lady, and are furnished with a stove and other necessary furniture.* Finally, scarcely any Estonian is so poor as not to keep at least one horse to draw his sledge.

The Germans and Estonians are descendants of serfs, but there are three or four countries in Europe whose inhabitants have inherited equal advantages from ancestors who never lost their freedom. The peasantry of the Netherlands, for instance, are in general at least as well off as those of Germany. In the kingdom of Holland, indeed, the class of small proprietors is less numerous. The farms there are generally of considerable size, seldom less than 50 acres in extent, and often very much larger, and are cultivated in a great measure by hired labourers. These are paid at the rate of about 20$d$. a day, if without food, but farm servants generally board and lodge with their master, and eat at the same table with his family. In that case their food consists chiefly of wheat and rye bread, potatoes, turnips, French beans, bacon, fresh and salt beef, and pancakes of buck-wheat flour and bacon: the money wages which they receive in addition range from 5$l$. to 12$l$. 10$s$. a year. Such earnings, even in a country next to England in dearness, are sufficient to show that the labour market is not overstocked, and all travellers agree in bearing witness to the apparent comfort of the lower classes of the Dutch people. The neatness and cleanliness of their dwellings, and the superabundance of their clothing, are proverbial. Not

* Letters from the Baltic, Letter 9.

a house nor a fence is to be seen out of repair, nor a garden that is not carefully cultivated. One meets with no ragged or dirty persons, nor with any drunken men, and the sight of a beggar is equally rare.* In Belgium the money wages of agricultural labourers are not perhaps more than half as high as in Holland†, but the difference is compensated by the greater cheapness of all necessaries, and cannot be of much consequence to servants who board with their masters, as almost all of them do. Those in the employment of the better class of Flemish farmers, " dine in a plentiful and orderly manner with the farmer and his family at the same table, which is covered with a clean cloth, and well supplied with spoons, four-pronged forks, and every other convenient article. A standing dish is soup, composed of buttermilk boiled and thickened with flour or rye bread. Potatoes, salt pork, salt fish, various vegetables, and eggs are the articles of daily consumption, with occasionally fresh meat and fresh fish, and always abundance of butter or rendered lard. All these provisions are made palatable by tolerable cooking. The potatoes are always peeled, and generally stewed in milk. A kind of kidney beans, sliced and stewed in milk, is a constant dish. No respectable farmer

* Mr. Nicholls' Three Reports on Poor Laws for Ireland, pp. 153, 4.

† They vary a good deal, however. In some parts of Belgium a day labourer earns as much as fifteen or sixteen-pence a day. See Mr. Symons' very interesting Report to Hand-loom Weavers' Commissioners.

is without a well-cultivated garden, full of the best culinary vegetables, and apples, all of which appear at his own table." *

The employment of hired labourers in husbandry is not, however, very common in Belgium, most of the farms being so small that the farmer needs no other aid than that of his own family. There are some few farms of more than 100 acres, but most are under fifty, and the most usual size is between five and ten acres. These small holdings lie so thickly together in the north and west of the kingdom, as to give the country the appearance of one continued village, and a most flourishing village it seems to be. Every " cottage is built substantially, with an upper floor for sleeping, and is kept in good repair : it has always a small cellarage for the dairy, a store-room for the grain, an oven, an outhouse for potatoes, a roomy cattle-stall, a piggery, and a loft for the poultry. The premises are kept extremely neat, and an air of comfort pervades the whole establishment." † These appearances are not deceitful. All the wealth upon these small farms belongs absolutely to the farmers, who are almost always their own landlords, and having no rent to pay, can apply all their produce to their own use. The proprietor of fifteen acres " brings up his family in decent independence, and in the course of his life accumulates sufficient means to put them in possession of a little farm of their own." If he

* Ratcliff's Agricultural Survey of Belgium, apud Macculloch's Geographical Dictionary, art. " Belgium."

† Nicholls' Three Reports, p. 165.

have only five or six acres, he can still contrive to keep a couple of cows, besides calves, pigs, and goats, and some poultry. He has plenty of rye bread and milk, and dines off mashed potatoes and onions, flavoured occasionally with slices of bacon. His dwelling is decently furnished, "the bedding amply sufficient," and no member of his family is ever seen ragged or slovenly, but all are decently clothed, though perhaps with the coarsest materials.* In short, the condition of the petty proprietors who constitute the bulk of the Belgian peasantry, leaves little to be desired. Their happiness is not of recent origin, but dates from the dawn of civilisation in many of the surrounding countries, and is the result of very singular causes. Eighteen hundred years ago Europe did not contain a more dreary region than these same Netherlands. The rich pastures of Holland, the garden-like surface of Zealand and Flanders, which cannot now be matched for fertility on this side the Alps, were then literally a series of sandy plains and salt marshes. The only provinces that offered any attractions to colonists were those to the eastward, which are now the least valuable,— Namur, Limburg, Liege, and Luxemburg. These, amidst the mountains, moors, and swamps of which they are chiefly composed, are interspersed with extensive forests and meadows, affording pasturage sufficient for numerous herds of cattle. As in these natural features they resembled the neighbouring parts of

* Nicholls, ut supra. See also Chambers' Tour in Holland and Belgium.

Germany, so also was their political condition for a
while the same: their first inhabitants were herdsmen, who were succeeded by an abject race of serfs.
In the maritime provinces, on the contrary, it is
probable that serfdom was never very general, if
indeed it existed at all. These districts must have
remained for a very long time very scantily peopled,
— the tribes must have been small, and individuals
poor, and nearly on the same level with respect to
wealth, power, and rank. The distribution of the
land, therefore, whenever it took place, was probably
effected with considerable regard to equality, and a
share was most likely allotted in full property and
unconditionally to every family. On a soil so sterile, and subject, moreover, to be devastated by
inundations of the sea and rivers, people could not
exist without the utmost industry and foresight,
and these qualities were doubtless still further encouraged by the labourer's knowledge that he
worked for himself, and not for a master. Still,
unceasing toil could at best only enable the inhabitants to live. It may be true, that where nature
does most, man generally does least, but something
else is necessary besides poorness of soil to make a
nation or a country rich. The Dutch and Flemings
might have persevered in cultivating their fields,
and have dug and redug the ground with unwearied
assiduity, without ever sensibly improving its quality: at the end of hundreds of years the sand
would have been sand still. In rendering it what
it is, wealth as well as labour has been expended,
and wealth far greater than the Netherlands them-

selves could have produced, and which can only have come from abroad. Very powerful reasons must, no doubt, have been required to induce wealthy foreigners to migrate to so ill-favoured a region, and to expend their capital in fertilising such an ungrateful soil; but it is not impossible to conjecture adequate motives for their conduct. The civilisers of the Netherlands were not improbably citizens of Gaul and Spain, who, when those countries were overwhelmed by barbarian invaders, took refuge in their ships, and sailed in search of an asylum elsewhere. The very dreariness of the Dutch and Belgian coasts, which in other circumstances would have been so repulsive, may now have been most welcome, for it was only where the natives were too few to molest them, that the wanderers could hope for security. We know that considerations of this kind induced the fugitive citizens of Aquileia to choose the muddy islets at the mouth of the Brenta, whereon to lay the foundations of Venice. Like the Venetians, too, the colonists of the Low Countries must at first have devoted themselves entirely to foreign commerce, from sheer inability to practise any other business:— they could not gain a livelihood except by becoming the carriers of northern Europe. The example of Venice, again, shows how great wealth may be acquired in this way: wealth supplied the means of establishing manufactures, and manufactures and commerce procured from abroad the means of subsistence for a large population. Where large bodies of men are gathered together, the materials for fertilising land are procurable in abundance. The new settlers had brought with them a knowledge of agriculture, and found in the native inhabitants apt and diligent scholars, so that round all the towns in the western Netherlands belts of rich land began to appear, which, rapidly widening till they met, gave the whole country its present character. If the conjecture be well founded, that the peasantry of these provinces have always been free, no further explanation of their progress can be needed. Even if they were ever serfs, it is easily understood that the growing influence of the cities, by curtailing the power of the barons, must very soon have loosened their bonds, and have permitted them to rise early to a height of social comfort from which they have never since descended. The same influence extended, but more gradually and less effectually, into the inland provinces, and there also put an end to prædial slavery, and converted the serfs into yeomen, although in some districts the traces of ancient feudal privileges were not entirely effaced until the French Revolution, and the consequent annexation of Belgium to France. Centuries ago, however, the peasantry very generally possessed, in the ownership of portions of fertile land, abundant means of livelihood. Population has ever since retained pretty much the same proportion to subsistence, and the people of this generation are consequently as well off as their ancestors. Their inheritance seems likely also to be transmitted unbroken to a distant posterity; for it is acknowledged, even by those who look upon small farms as the great promoters of pauperism, that they produce very different effects among the Flemings. " The too rapid increase of population," is observed to be " checked by the universal desire to marry only when the subsistence for a family can be readily and honestly obtained by industry."* What is it that disposes the Netherlanders thus to control their inclinations ? What but that, having been always used to plentiful food, warm clothing, and commodious dwellings, they duly appreciate domestic comfort, and are not disposed wilfully to forfeit such advantages.

Two other countries, in which the peasantry are eminently happy, and have been so ever since they became civilised, are Switzerland and Norway. Both are countries of small proprietors. In Switzerland, except in the canton of Tessin, the Emmenthal, and a few other districts, it is rare to find a person possessing an estate of more than 150 or 200 acres, or worth more than 100*l.* a year ; and frequently the properties are too small to afford full employment to a family. Almost every family, however, has at least a patch of ground of its own, on which it resides, and from which it derives the greater part of its subsistence. The little domain is cultivated chiefly with the spade, and so carefully that every separate plant often seems to have had a share of attention devoted exclusively to itself.† Much of the produce serves as winter provender for the cows, of which most

* Chambers' Tour, p. 81.   See also Mr. Nicholls' Three Reports, &c., p. 167.
† Inglis's Switzerland, p. 25.   Laing's Notes of a Traveller.

Swiss peasants have at least one, besides a few goats or sheep, and which in the summer graze on the " Alp," or mountainous pasture belonging in common to the parish. The produce of a farm is commonly abundant enough to place the owner at his ease; and the traveller in Switzerland cannot fail to remark the healthy looks and comfort of the people, and the neatness of their dwellings and plots of ground. The Swiss peasantry are not, however, entirely dependent upon agriculture. When confined within doors by winter or bad weather, they employ themselves in some sort of manufacture; and their earnings at this work, though trifling in themselves, are important as an addition to their income from other sources. It has been calculated that a Swiss artisan-peasant, having a wife and three children to support, lives in a way which would require 30s. a week in England*; and Mr. Macculloch, who calls this a very exaggerated statement, and thinks that agricultural labourers in most parts of Great Britain have no cause to envy those of Switzerland, admits in substance that the latter are much better lodged and fed. They use, he says, the same articles of food as the English, and in addition much more porridge, milk, and cheese, and wine instead of beer; their houses, he adds, though mostly of wood, are capacious, and furnished with all the articles required for daily use. This is really an acknowledgment of the superiority claimed for the Swiss.

* Report of J. C. Symons, Esq., to Hand-loom Weavers' Commissioners, p. 109.

In Norway, estates are larger than in Switzerland; few, perhaps, are under forty acres, and they are very often above 300 acres, independently of an extensive tract of upland waste, called the "seater," belonging to every farm, which furnishes summer pasture for the cattle. To supply the latter with winter provender, two-thirds of the cleared land about a farm are generally left under natural grass, and only one-third is reserved for corn, potatoes, and other such crops; but there must, nevertheless, be plenty of work for hired labourers. Of these, however, there is no great number. In the year 1835 there were 72,624 proprietors in Norway, living on their own estates, and 30,568 tenants of farms. At the same time, the whole male population of the country was 585,381, of which 309,000 persons were connected with agriculture, either as proprietors, farmers, or servants, so that on an average there could not be more than two male labourers, including boys, to a farm. They are, as might be expected, exceedingly well paid. If unmarried, they are lodged in an outhouse adjoining the farmer's dwelling, which it resembles in appearance, neatness, and comfort; they are allowed four meals a-day, consisting of oat or bean-meal, rye-bread, potatoes, fresh river and salt fish, cheese, butter, and milk; and once or twice a week they have meat, sometimes fresh, but more frequently in the shape of salt beef, or black puddings. At one of their meals they have also beer, or a glass of potato-spirits. Their money wages, in addition to all this, are about $4\frac{1}{2}d$. a day.

A married labourer lives on the outskirts of the farm, in a cottage of his own, generally a " good log-house of four rooms, with glass windows," which is held on lease for the lives of his wife and himself, together with a piece of land large enough for the keep of two cows, or a corresponding number of sheep and goats, and for the sowing of six bushels of corn, and three quarters of potatoes. The usual rent of these tenements is from four to six dollars, and is commonly paid for by work on the main farm, each day's work being valued at a fixed rate of three-pence or thereabouts. After the labourer has paid his rent, he is allowed his food as well as the usual money payment for every additional day's work. It need scarcely be said, that a houseman, as a married labourer of this kind is called, is in a very comfortable situation: in fact he wants few, if any, of the comforts which his master possesses; his house, though smaller, is as well built; his food and dress are of the same materials. The peasant proprietors, like their servants, are satisfied with enjoyments of home growth, and are little desirous of foreign luxuries. They build their own houses, make their own chairs, tables, ploughs, carts, and harness, spin their own flax and wool, and weave their own linen and woollen cloth; almost every thing they use is the produce of their own farms, except glass, pottery, and ironware, sugar, coffee, spices, and tobacco. Nevertheless, it would be difficult to find anywhere a happier race; they enjoy plenty, without having to work so hard for it as the Swiss and Belgians of the same class; they care little for

outward show, and are consequently exempt from
the painful desire to outvie their neighbours, and
to rise above their station.   Almost the only thing
in their condition which is much to be regretted, is
the deficiency of mental culture, which prevents
their turning their leisure to the best account, and
heightening their material enjoyments with intellectual pleasures. *

It has been said that the happiness of the Swiss
and Norwegian peasantry dates from a very early
period : it seems indeed to have resulted from the
characters of their respective countries.   A glance
at the map of Switzerland will show, that in a
territory so curiously intersected by mountains,
lakes, and rivers, there can be few if any extensive tracts of good land, and that the first settlers
must consequently have been both too much
scattered and too poor to allow of their being
generally divided into the classes of masters and
slaves.   In Norway, it is quite certain that serfdom never existed.   The Scandinavian peninsula,
of which that country forms part, is only accessible by land at the northern extremity, where the
rigour of the climate is only endurable by reindeer and Laplanders.   Its Gothic colonists must
therefore have approached it by sea.   But a pastoral people could not effect an extensive migration in boats, without leaving most of their cattle
behind them, and if they waited till the winter,
when the Gulf of Bothnia is frozen over and may

* Laing's Norway, *passim.*

be crossed on foot, their cattle would have perished from exposure and want of food. Most probably, therefore, the emigrants were not numerous tribes ranged in regular subordination under their chiefs, but little bands of adventurers, all poor, and nearly equal in rank; and this equality would long remain undisturbed in their new territories. Great part of Norway is merely a narrow slip of land between a chain of mountains and the sea, and the whole is traversed laterally, not only by numerous offsets from the main ridge, but also by a succession of inlets of the sea, which run for many miles inland. The soil too, even of the valleys, is for the most part sandy and poor, so that altogether there was as little room as in Switzerland for the increase of flocks and herds, or for the growth of great differences of wealth among their owners. Moreover, the need of substantial habitations for themselves and for their cattle, which in so cold a climate must be housed in winter, must very soon have compelled the herdsmen in both countries to lay aside their wandering habits, and to provide themselves with permanent abodes. The appropriation and distribution of the soil must therefore have taken place while all the inhabitants were still free, and entitled to demand their shares, and every family probably obtained an allotment sufficient for its maintenance. Thus, almost immediately after the settlement of either country, the peasantry were placed in a position which only required the improvements gradually introduced by increasing civilisation to become that which they still occupy.

The inference intended to be drawn from this
brief sketch of the history of society in the several
countries mentioned, is, that the originally happy
condition of the peasantry has been the cause of
its own continuance: that the people are comfortable now because they have never been otherwise,
and because the wish to retain their advantages
has prevented them from increasing beyond the
number that could be adequately provided for.
Yet it must not be concealed, that in most, if
not all of these countries, a certain amount of
pauperism exists, which may seem at first sight
opposed to such a conclusion. In Berlin, a city
of 300,000 inhabitants, exclusive of expenses of
hospitals and of a house of correction for beggars,
and exclusive also of aid afforded to sick poor
at their own homes, about 20,000*l.* is annually
expended in the relief of outdoor poor, which,
at the rate of 2*s.* 6*d.* weekly per head, would
suffice for the constant maintenance of about
3,000 persons, or about one per cent. of the whole
population. * In the Netherlands, the number
of persons accepting charitable relief of one kind
or another, is 14 or 15 per cent. — a very
much larger proportion than in any other European country, not even excepting England. This
must not however be mistaken for a proof of
extraordinary distress ; it merely shows, that
wherever subsistence can be obtained gratuitously,
plenty of people will be found ready to accept it.

* Laing's Notes of a Traveller, p. 255.

Both Holland and Belgium are almost unrivalled for their numerous well-endowed charitable institutions, which, together with many proper objects of compassion, maintain in idleness a multitude of persons who might support themselves by their own exertions. Excluding the inmates of these institutions, the number of poor is so small, that the annual sum raised for their support by compulsory taxation does not exceed 150,000*l*. in Holland, or 30,000*l*. in Belgium.* In Switzerland the parishes generally possess funds destined for the relief of the poor, which it is sometimes necessary to augment by means of a poor's rate, but the latter is always of inconsiderable amount, and if we may judge from the practice in the canton of Zurich, where it is likely to be as high as any where, does not exact more than $2\frac{1}{2}d$. annually from each individual. † In Norway, the only burthen resembling a poor's rate to which even a considerable landholder is subject, seems to be the obligation to maintain for a few days in the course of the year perhaps one old man; but it is probable that poverty is somewhat less rare in the towns. ‡

It has been already shown that the destitution of the aged or infirm, or of idle vagabonds, is not a sign of over-population, and much of the small amount of pauperism just alluded to may be that of persons of these descriptions. It need not be

* Laing's Notes of a Traveller. Macculloch's Geog. Dict.
† Symons' Report on Hand-loom Weavers.
‡ Laing's Norway.

denied, however, that there may still remain some
able-bodied poor whose distress arises really from
their inability to procure work, and it may be
thought that this would not be the case in such
countries as Germany, the Netherlands, and Switzerland, if the possession of the comforts of life were
as effectual in restraining over-population as it has
been described. To this objection it may be replied, that many circumstances may occasion a
diminution of employment in particular districts,
when there is no general deficiency of it, and that
the prudential considerations which have been supposed capable of checking the progress of population do not act with unerring precision, but admit
of fluctuations, which sometimes raise the numbers
of a community a little above, and sometimes sink
them a little below, the proper limit. However
careful every person may be to postpone marriage
until he is able to maintain a family, still, as all
marriages are not equally fruitful, population will
not always bear the same proportion to the means
of subsistence, and a greater number of persons than
can be adequately provided for will sometimes be
brought into the world. In rural districts, where
the bulk of the people are well off, this evil seldom
becomes very great, or lasts very long. A few
agricultural labourers in excess of the exact number required, can generally make themselves useful
enough to be able to earn at least their own livelihood, until by the death of some of their companions they succeed to more regular and better-
paid employment. Till then they are not likely

to think of marrying. The nature of agriculture enables them to estimate pretty accurately the exact quantity of work to be done in their neighbourhood, and to see distinctly whether the share which each will be able to obtain will suffice for the support of a family ; and a couple, who are living in comfort singly, will scarcely, however deeply enamoured, plunge into matrimony with a perfect certainty that it must render them miserable. It would be in vain for a man to attempt to supplant another in a better situation than his own by offering to take his place with lower wages. Such an offer might be greedily accepted by a farmer, whose landlord extorted from him every penny beyond the mere expenses of cultivation; but thriving peasant proprietors, having all their own wants abundantly supplied, would be ashamed to lower the condition of their servants for the sake of a paltry saving. Thus, in districts purely agricultural, where the inhabitants in general are well off, the surplus labourers must wait quietly until the class to which they belong is again restored by natural causes to its just dimensions, and thus every appearance of excessive population gradually vanishes. If, however, a considerable town be near, most of the surplus labourers will resort to it in the hope of obtaining employment in some of the numerous businesses carried on there. Where so many occupations are concentrated in one spot, it is impossible to ascertain exactly the total quantity of work afforded by them, and the amount, being indefinite, is apt to be over-rated, and often fails to satisfy all the applicants. It consequently happens, that a large town is scarcely ever entirely free from unemployed labourers, and if destitution prevail at all in the surrounding country, the town is invariably the focus in which it chiefly collects itself, and becomes most glaringly visible. There is reason to believe that permanent destitution among the able-bodied inhabitants of towns is seldom produced by any other cause than emigration from the country, and that the urban population is never rendered excessive by natural increase alone. Whether it be that prudential restraints are sufficient in themselves, or that the facility with which licentiousness may be indulged acts as an additional dissuasive from marriage, certain it is, that in towns holding out no attractions to immigrants, population generally remains stationary. In large and rapidly growing towns, where marriages are most encouraged, the mortality of children is so great, that the proportion of births to deaths would not always suffice to prevent depopulation, and never contributes more than a very small fraction of the addition annually made to the number of inhabitants.

There are two European countries in which the condition of the people, although at present on the whole satisfactory, was, until lately, decidedly the reverse. These are Poland and France. In the former, serfdom was mitigated in 1791, and totally abolished in 1807, when the peasants were converted into proprietors of the lands occupied by them, on condition of working a specified number of days in each week for their former lords, and paying them in addition certain fixed quantities of poultry, eggs, yarn, &c. The extent of land which thus came into the hands of the peasantry was very considerable, and the portion belonging to a family is generally from thirty to forty acres, for which about two days' work in the week, with a pair of oxen, seems to be the usual rent.* The owners of farms of this size have evidently the means of making themselves very comfortable, and considerable improvement has in fact taken place of late years in their condition. They are reported to be very filthy in their persons and dwellings, but the latter, even in the early part of the present century, were substantially built of timber, and large enough to contain at least two or three rooms, in every one of which a bed was generally found. Their diet formerly consisted entirely of vegetable substances, such as pease, black bread, and soup or gruel, washed down with quantities of cheap spirits; but in addition to these articles, milk, butter, cheese, and occasionally a little meat, are now probably supplied by the cows and oxen which every peasant keeps, to cultivate his own and his master's land. If the Polish peasantry have hitherto derived less benefit than might have been expected from their abundant resources, the reason must be sought for in the indolent and improvident habits engendered by ages of oppression, which are not easily to be got rid of. While Poland remained independent, all power and influence were monopolised by the nobles; the king

* Jacob's Report on the Agriculture of Northern Europe, 1826, p. 26.

was their creature, owing his office to their election, and quite unable to cope with them; and the distractions of the country prevented the growth of a considerable middle class. The authority of the nobles over their serfs consequently continued without diminution. They could not only exact from them an unlimited amount of work, and seize upon whatever wealth they had accumulated: they could also sell them like cattle, and even kill them with impunity. The introduction of foreign commerce, which elsewhere facilitated the enfranchisement of the peasantry, here only rendered their servitude more intolerable. By offering to the nobles extended markets for their produce, and new commodities in exchange for their previously useless wealth, it gave them a motive for rapacity, and for extorting the utmost they could obtain from their wretched tenantry. The latter accordingly, except on the estates of a few proprietors less unfeeling than the rest, were reduced to a state which all contemporary travellers agree in describing as most deplorable.

In France, previously to the Revolution, the state of the peasantry was equally melancholy. The nobility had indeed been early shorn of political power, and the serfs, at least nominally, emancipated; but what the nobles lost was gained almost entirely by the Crown, which, confident in its own strength, and needing not the support of the inferior classes, oppressed the peasantry quite as cruelly as their lords could have done. The French serfs, after their enfranchisement, either never possessed proprietary rights in the soil, or very soon lost them, and had then no other means of gaining a livelihood but by cultivating lands hired from the rich.  As however, they were, for the most part, destitute of capital, it was necessary that the landlords should provide them with farming-stock, cattle, seed, tools, &c., in return for which, and for the use of the land, they were bound to give a certain proportion, generally a half, of the yearly produce.  There does not seem to be any thing in these conditions which would necessarily prevent farmers from prospering, but in France, under the old government, a metayer, as a person in this situation is called, was exposed to so many taxes and exactions of various kinds, not only exceedingly grievous in themselves, but liable to be increased arbitrarily in proportion to his apparent ability to bear them, that he lost even the desire to acquire wealth which was sure to be taken from him.  He was satisfied if he obtained the means of subsistence, and never aimed at any thing further.  The consequence was, that the whole body of husbandmen were reduced to the most extreme poverty. Marshal Vauban, in 1698, calculated that, of the whole French population, one-tenth were in a state of mendicancy, and five-ninths of the remainder very little above it; and Arthur Young, ninety years after, did not discover improvement enough to require this assertion to be much modified.  It is scarcely possible to open any English book of travels in France, written during the last century, without finding the author exulting in a comparison between the ragged, half-starved French peasantry and the stout, sturdy, well-clad, and well-fed yeomanry of his native land.

A mighty change for the better in the condition of the lower orders of the French people was wrought by the revolution of 1789. Not only did all arbitrary exactions and all feudal privileges cease, but the division of extensive tracts of common land, and the confiscation and sale, at a very low price, of the vast estates of the nobility and clergy, enabled almost every cultivator to become a proprietor. At this moment one seventh of the whole nation are landholders, a much larger proportion probably than in any other part of the world. Most of the properties are of course very small; but, cultivated as they are with the minute and assiduous attention which are never bestowed except by small occupiers, they are sufficient to furnish their owners in general with a comfortable maintenance, or at least to contribute very materially towards it. That the French people in general are at present very well off, is remarked by every one who passes through the country; and it is of importance to observe, that their happiness is partly the effect of very recent improvements. In order to perceive that great progress has been made, it is not necessary to go back to the last century : so lately as twenty or thirty years ago, the Duc de la Rochefoucault, M. Lafitte, and others, could descant on the misery endured by multitudes of their countrymen, whom they described as clothed in rags, and subsisting entirely on coarse roots.* Whether faithful or not at the time it was drawn, this picture is certainly exceedingly inaccurate now. The French peasantry enjoy great abundance and variety of vegetable food, of which, with the aid of plentiful supplies of milk, eggs, &c. they compose savoury dishes, such as it never occurred to an English ploughman to imagine; and the increased and increasing cheapness of all articles of clothing also enables them to dress much better than formerly. Their habitations likewise are very good, and are well provided with all needful furniture, particularly bedding, and with utensils of earthenware, pewter, copper, and iron. It is only in some manufacturing districts, particularly in and about the towns of Lyons, Rouen, Lille, Valenciennes, and Cambrai, that destitution is at all prevalent; and there it has been produced by causes not unlike those from which it has sprung in similar situations in Great Britain, viz. the decay of branches of industry, which, after collecting large masses of people on one spot, are now unable to afford them adequate employment. In Lyons, whose silk manufactures were long the most flourishing in the world, the weavers have now to withstand the keen, and, in many respects, unequal competition of English and Swiss rivals. In the northern towns, where the cotton manufacture is chiefly carried on, great numbers of handloom weavers are to be found, whose once ample wages are now reduced to an amount barely

* Smith's Wealth of Nations, Macculloch's edit. vol. iv. pp. 467—71.

sufficient for their subsistence. Many of these operatives dwell not in the towns, but in the districts immediately adjoining; and their forerunners of a preceding generation probably possessed at one time, like other peasants, a piece of ground large enough for the maintenance of a family. While their manufacturing business continued prosperous, they probably looked upon it as an ample resource, and neglected the cultivation of their land; so that, on a man's death, his children, intending to establish themselves as weavers, and requiring sites for separate dwellings, may have divided his little estate amongst them. This was probably the manner in which the land around some French manufacturing towns has become split into portions too small to produce any considerable quantity of food; so that the owners, now that their looms no longer enable them to earn a competent livelihood, are reduced to extreme wretchedness. The tendency of misery to perpetuate and extend itself is strikingly illustrated in these manufacturing districts. While, in other parts of France, the condition of the people is continually improving,— thereby showing that population, although increasing as the resources of the country become developed, increases more slowly than the means of subsistence,— here, on the contrary, where multitudes are suffering extreme privation, the means of subsistence are no sooner increased than a corresponding increase takes place in the number of persons to be subsisted; and every addition to the fund for the payment of labour, instead of benefiting the actual dependents on that fund, only calls more of them into an equally wretched existence. In the Departement du Nord, which contains most of the principal seats both of the French cotton manufacture and of French destitution, population increases at a rate considerably more than double the average rate of the whole kingdom, or about thirteen per cent. in ten years.* It is probable that the greater part of the increase is created by natural causes within the department, considering how little attraction is held out to emigrants from more favoured parts of the country. Other, though less obvious examples of the same tendency, were presented throughout the whole both of France and Poland, previously to the great social revolutions which have been mentioned as having taken place in both countries. As long as the exactions of the crown and the nobility left to the common people nothing but a bare subsistence, the numbers of the latter not only did not diminish as they would have done if every one had resolved to keep for his own use what little he possessed, but they even increased as fast as the extension of industry rendered it possible for a greater number to subsist. Arthur Young, writing in 1789, did not hesitate to assert that France was then decidedly over-peopled. He had observed everywhere " most unequivocal signs of distress," and had found " numbers dying of diseases arising from insuffi-

* Laing's Prize Essay on National Distress, part ii. chap. 2.

cient nourishment;" and he declared himself convinced that the kingdom would be " much more
powerful, and infinitely more flourishing, with five
or six millions less of inhabitants."*   It was not
till the people became possessed of the means of
making themselves comfortable that they began to
restrain their inclination to marriage; but, ever
since, sufficient restraint has been exercised to
prevent population from advancing even so fast
as it might have done, without causing any deterioration in the actual condition of the people.

The wretchedness of the peasantry is very great
in many parts of Italy, — in the Roman and Neapolitan states, and in the island of Sardinia.   In
the latter the agriculturists are for the most part
either small metayer farmers, or cottiers, paying for
their patches of land by work on the proprietor's
estate, and are kept in extreme poverty by the
shortsighted rapacity of the landlords, and by
absurd laws.   The estates in the papal dominions
are in general very large, and are divided amongst
a number of metayer tenants as much depressed as
those of Sardinia.   As for the continental portion
of the Neapolitan kingdom, Ireland itself is scarcely
more decidedly over-peopled.   The bulk of the
lower classes in the towns as well as in the country,
are clothed in skins of beasts with the hair on, or
in tattered cloaks two or three generations old; live
almost entirely in the open air, without even at
night, or in wet weather, better shelter than that

* Travels in France.

of a mere shed, and are almost as ill fed as clothed and housed, except during the short seasons in which the great demand for rural labour, combined with the extraordinary bounty of nature, enables them to feast for a while upon maccaroni, maize, legumes, fruit, and vegetables. In every respect they are said by one * who has had ample opportunity for comparison, " to be more wretched, and in food, lodging, property, sense of decency in their habits and ways of living, in a lower condition, than the Laplander on the Norwegian fielde. In an earthly paradise the people are not merely in rags and wretchedness; it is difficult even to conceive humanity in so low a condition. — The sense of decency is apparently little higher than among irrational creatures." It may perhaps be argued, that such social and moral degradation is not in this instance a decisive proof of over-population. If the Neapolitan peasant or lazzarone be destitute of what are elsewhere esteemed necessaries of life, he is also free from the wants which make them necessaries. In such a delicious climate it is no hardship to live almost entirely out of doors : fuel is only requisite for cooking, and very little even for that, where food is to be bought ready cooked in every street ; clothing is not necessary for warmth, and rags will serve well enough to hide one's nakedness. All that a man requires is food, and he must not be called poor merely on account of the fewness of his wants. It must, however, be

* Laing's Notes of a Traveller, pp. 387. 396.  See also Madame Wolfensburger's Letters from Naples, in Tait's Magazine.

recollected, that Neapolitans of the lower orders do suffer very frequently and severely from scarcity of food, the only want they are capable of feeling; and it may, moreover, be shown, that the warmth of the climate, though it enables them to dispense with most of the conveniences of life, would not of itself cause the latter to be rejected, nor prevent considerable exertion being made in order to obtain them. The people of Tuscany have almost as much reason as the Neapolitans to boast of the favours of nature: they are no doubt naturally quite as fond of basking in the sun, and would suffer as little by going about half naked, yet a more industrious race than the peasant-proprietors of the Val d'Arno can nowhere be found, and the district is not more remarkable for the excellence of its cultivation than for the thriving appearance of the inhabitants. Climate, then, cannot be the sole cause of the idleness of the Neapolitans, nor idleness the sole cause of their wretchedness; they would probably be as industrious as the Tuscans if industry among them had always been equally well rewarded. But having been for ages in a position in which it was impossible for them to procure more than a bare subsistence, they have ceased to aim at an impossibility, and have recklessly bred up to the utmost limit which the means of subsistence would permit. They are wretched now because wretchedness has, during many generations, been the portion of their forefathers.

The emancipation of the peasantry took place much earlier in the south and south-west of Europe, than in other parts of the same continent. In Italy, especially, promoted both by the interposition of the Church of Rome, and by the contests between the free cities and the rural barons, it was effected before the serfs had acquired any prescriptive rights over the soil, so that after their enfranchisement they were obliged, as in France, to cultivate the lands of others. Savoy indeed, like other poor mountainous regions, has probably been always inhabited by petty proprietors, and in Tuscany, the persecution which the nobility endured from the democratical governments of the towns, and the frequent confiscation of their estates, soon enabled the farmers to become landowners. But throughout the rest of Italy, the cultivators of the land were, and indeed are still, generally metayers. In Lombardy, and generally in the great northern plain from Susa to the Adriatic, the condition of this class of men has always been at least tolerable, for there the nobility, though not so much depressed as in Tuscany, have always been subject to some control, and landed property has long been a good deal subdivided. But, in the Roman and Neapolitan States, in the former of which, down to the present time, and in the latter, until very recently, the land was for the most part divided among a few noble families retaining every tyrannical feudal privilege not absolutely incompatible with the personal freedom of their tenantry, the latter were from the beginning ground down by the heavy burdens imposed upon them; little more than a bare subsistence was left to them, and their industry was extinguished by the certainty that it could only expose them to increased exactions. Becoming thus inured to misery, they likewise became careless of the future, and laying aside every sort of self-restraint, multiplied to the utmost extent that misery would permit.

It would be easy to accumulate examples of this kind; but it will probably be thought that sufficient space has already been devoted to subjects only collaterally connected with the special business of this work. Enough has been said to show that misery is the great promoter of over-population. Returning therefore from this digression, let us now, by means of the principles which it has been designed to elucidate, endeavour to point out the circumstances to which the present condition of our own countrymen is attributable.

# 161

# CHAPTER V.

CAUSES OF OVER-POPULATION IN ENGLAND.

Prosperous Condition of English Labourers in early Times. —
History of the English Peasantry. — Peculiarities of the
Saxon Conquest. — Structure of Society among the Anglo-
Saxons. — Establishment of Serfdom or Villenage. — Its
modified Character and rapid Extinction. — Growing Importance of Villains after the Norman Conquest. — High Wages
of agricultural Labourers in the 14th and 15th Centuries.
— Ineffectual Efforts of Parliament to reduce them. —
Causes of the high Price of Labour at this Period. — Deterioration of the Condition of the Peasantry after the Accession
of Henry VII. — Growth of Pauperism and Mendicity
during the 16th Century. — Explanation of the Change in the
Situation of the Peasantry. — Temporary Improvement of
their Condition in the latter Part of Elizabeth's Reign. — Too
rapid Progress of Population. — Renewed Advance of Pauperism in the 17th and 18th Centuries. — Simultaneous Rise
in the Remuneration of Labour. — Operation of the Poor-
Laws. — Formation of Parks. — Enclosure of Common Land.
Great Distress of the labouring Classes during the six concluding Years of the 18th Century. — Dearness of the Neces-
saries of Life during the first ten Years of the 19th Century. — Severe Privations of agricultural Labourers. —
Encouragement given to Marriage by the Poor-Laws. —
Increase of National Wealth. — Rapid Progress of Population.
— Improvement in the Condition of the Peasantry in the
ten Years ending with 1820. — Prodigality of Poor-Law
Administration. — Unprecedented Advance of Population. —
Its accelerated Progress in the Period ending with 1830. —
Unexampled Increase of National Wealth. — Reform of the

Poor-Law in 1834.—Beneficial Consequences of the Change.
— Recurrence of Distress among agricultural Labourers. —
Deterioration of their Condition since 1836. — Results of the
Census of 1841. — Causes of Over-population in particular
Districts.—Obstacles to an excessive Increase of Population
in Towns from natural Causes.—Distress of Town Labourers
occasioned by the Withdrawal of their Occupation. — Immi-
gration from rural Districts. — Recapitulation of foregoing
Statements.

WE shall not be able in England, as in one or
two of the countries already noticed, to trace over-
population back to a very early period. The indigence which is at once its sign and its most
powerful cause, did not in England, as in southern
Italy, exist at the first formation of the nation,
continuing ever since to propagate and extend
itself. On the contrary, when the Anglo-Saxons
first became a distinct people, the lowest class were
placed in circumstances in which they were abundantly supplied with every thing which was then
considered a necessary of life; and the condition
of their descendants, several centuries later, not
only had not deteriorated, but had improved with
the progress of freedom and civilisation, so that the
English labourer, duly estimating all his advantages, might look down with pity on his fellows
in almost every other land. This state of things
might, it may be thought, according to the theory
proposed in the last Chapter, to have ensured its
own continuance; and it did so in effect as long as the
prudent habits which it was calculated to promote,
were sufficient for the purpose. But at length
extraneous influences, which the labourers could

not control, precipitated them from their high social position; and other circumstances, at a later period, by offering them temporary protection from the consequences of improvidence, prevented them 'rom again recovering the station they had lost. Prudence was replaced, first by the recklessness arising from extreme poverty, and afterwards by the indifference arising from supposed impunity. Population, being thus freed from the checks which formerly kept it within proper bounds, advanced with too great rapidity; its progress has perpetuated the indigence by which it was in the first instance promoted, and has produced the distress which is now so prevalent among certain sections of the labouring class.

Some particulars shall now be stated in order to show the grounds for these assertions. The Saxon subjugation of South Britain was effected in a very different manner, and produced very different effects upon society, from the conquests of the barbarians who overran the continental dominions of Rome. The latter, proceeding from their native territories by land, migrated in entire tribes, in which the distinctions of chiefs and re-tainers, masters and servants, were well marked, and their overwhelming numbers quickly beat down all opposition. After a short contest, the Roman provincials submitted to the invaders, and permitted them to select lands sufficient for their support. Every freeman, it may be presumed, obtained a portion, but the division was far from being made equally. The chiefs not only appropriated large domains entirely to their own use, but continued to exact from such of their followers as were now converted into small landholders, the same acknowledgment of their supremacy as they had been accustomed to receive in the forests of Germany. Their more immediate dependents, the servants, or slaves, who had been entirely supported by them, remained in the same situation; or if lands were assigned for their maintenance, the only change that took place in their condition was a change from domestic to predial slavery. The latter continued to be the state of the native peasantry: they had been serfs under the Roman, and they remained serfs under the Gothic domination.

The insular position of Britain caused its invasion to be attended by circumstances of a very opposite character, for the ocean, which separates it from the Continent, forbade the simultaneous transfer to its shores of entire hostile communities. The first descents were made by mere handfuls of adventurers, Hengist and Horsa, for example, having been captains of a squadron of only three small barks. The insignificant numbers of the invaders encouraged the natives to resist; and so stout was their defence, that fifty years elapsed before the Saxons could make themselves masters of Kent and Sussex, and a hundred and fifty more before the Heptarchy was completely established. The war that raged without intermission throughout this period was as bloody as it was lasting, particularly in the maritime counties, the conquest of which seems not to have been completed until all the original inhabitants were exterminated or expelled. The consequence was, that in the Saxon kingdoms situated on the coasts, which of course were the first formed, the new proprietors of the soil found no ready-made serfs long accustomed to the yoke, and amongst their own countrymen, who had accompanied them from the Continent, there were probably few whom they could compel to supply this want. The first invaders were sea pirates, whose profession, it is obvious, can scarcely be carried on except by freemen, since all engaged in it are, in a great measure, self-dependent. When news of the rich prize discovered by these robbers in England reached the opposite shores of the German Ocean, preparations for invasion were made on a somewhat larger scale; but it is not likely that many men of property joined in an enterprise, which, whatever prospects it might hold out for the future, required that they should not only abandon their native land, but should likewise leave behind the bulk of their present wealth.

Such an expedition was more likely to attract needy adventurers, too poor either to have much to leave behind, or to be able to take with them the means of maintaining any companions. The invading bands that crossed over into England consisted then, it may be presumed, for the most part, of freemen, nearly equally poor, and nearly equal also in rank and power. The lands conquered by such men would be divided pretty

equally amongst them ; but, although every man
may have got a share, there are two reasons for
supposing that no man's share was very large.
First, as the Saxon conquests were made very
gradually, the quantity of land to be distributed
at any one time must have been proportionably
inconsiderable ; and, secondly, however great the
extent of land might have been, a man without
servants could have no reason for appropriating
a larger portion than he and his family could
manage between them. It may therefore be concluded, that the Saxons who crossed the sea,
and established themselves in England, became
small landowners, or what we might now call
peasant proprietors or yeomen, and that the bulk
of the population in all the settlements formed
along the coasts consisted originally of families of
ths description.

These remarks do not apply to the interior of
the country. When the Saxons had firmly established themselves in the maritime districts, they
were able to collect forces which the Britons found
it useless to oppose. It was no longer a few daring
adventurers, who had to fight hard for every acre,
but hosts of warriors, who, rushing into the heart of
the island, over-ran more territory in one campaign
than their fathers could have subdued in twenty.
The conquest, too, was effected with comparatively
little bloodshed ; the natives were neither expelled
nor exterminated, but quietly submitted to the
victors, who, dividing among themselves the lands
they had seized, became proprietors of large, well-

peopled estates. It is particularly recorded, that in the kingdom of Mercia, the last-formed member of the Heptarchy, comprehending what are now the midland counties, the vanquished intermingled wit' the Saxons. Such of them as had been landowner: were probably either entirely deprived of their property, or were only allowed to hold some portions of it on conditions implying degradation and inferiority, and the cultivators of the soil were, no doubt, retained in the state of bondage in which they were found. An aristocracy was thus established in the central parts of England, similar to what existed at the same time in most Continental countries, and contrasting strongly with the democratic form which society had assumed in the maritime kingdoms of the Heptarchy. But, even in the latter, the peasantry were ere long thrust down from the independent position at first occupied by them. The operation of natural causes alone would have sufficed to impair the equality of condition which once subsisted amongst them, to enrich some families, and to impoverish others; but these effects were powerfully promoted and accelerated by the anarchy, the intestine broils, and foreign invasions, which, with short and partial intermissions, harassed the country as long as the Saxon dynasties endured. In those times of rapine and confusion, many families were utterly extinguished, and many others were reduced to slavery, not merely predial, but domestic. Even when no foreign enemy was near, the poor man was in almost equal danger from the tyranny of his powerful neighbours, against which his only remedy was to subject himself entirely to some one of his oppressors, in order to obtain protection against the others. In this manner a species of serfdom was established, even in those parts of England in which it had been previously unknown.   It appears from Domesday Book, compiled a few years after the Norman conquest, that in all England, exclusive of Northumberland, Cumberland, Westmoreland, Durham, and part of Lancashire, there were at that time (independently of the great tenants in chief) only about 26,000 freeholders, or free occupiers of land, to 184,000 villains or predial serfs, and 26,500 domestic slaves; and whether these numbers refer to the whole population, or only to the dwellers on the domains of the Crown, they may perhaps be regarded as sufficiently indicative of the relative proportions of the various classes into which the nation was divided. Yet it must not be supposed, that the English villains had sunk to the level of the serfs of France or Germany.  Most of them were, as we have seen, the descendants of freemen; and although freemen, seeking the protection of a master, may have placed themselves and their property entirely at his disposal, the recollection of the proprietary rights they had formerly enjoyed may have prevented the latter from abusing his power, or exacting from them any thing but certain fixed services or other payments in token of his superiority.  This, which was at first voluntary moderation on his part, would, if long practised, become a positive restraint upon his power, and render it impossible for him, without incurring the reproach of tyranny, to claim any thing unsanctioned by custom. When the obligations of one set of villains, distinguished from others only by their pedigree, came to be thus limited, a similar limitation would probably be expected by all, howsoever descended, and the serfs of Mercia might be raised to an equality with their brethren nearer the sea. At any rate, and by whatever means the change may have been effected, it seems certain that, towards the close of the Saxon period, the peasantry throughout England had very generally ceased to be in any respect the property of their lords, or to have any thing servile about their condition, except the name. Even *theowes*, or domestic slaves, had acquired the right, recognised by law, of possessing wealth, and of demanding their liberty when rich enough to purchase it at the established price. Villains had advanced much farther. From predial serfs, if indeed they could ever have been properly so designated, they had been metamorphosed into perpetual tenants of land at a quit-rent. When they had paid the accustomed dues, no further claims, either for work or goods, could be legally made upon them by their lord, nor could they be ousted from their land. They were quite as much proprietors as the copyholders of the present day, and their tenure indeed already differed in only one essential particular from the copyhold tenure by which it was afterwards succeeded. Villains were attached to the soil, that is to say, they could neither alienate nor otherwise abandon their lands, nor in any way free

themselves from the obligation to fulfil the conditions by which they held them; but it is obvious
that this disability was more nominal than real,
and that in those days, when agriculture was almost the only occupation open to the common
people, a legal prohibition was scarcely necessary
to prevent a peasant from selling his patrimony,
still less from parting with it without an equivalent.

At the period at which the villains were most
depressed, they must still have been allowed to
retain a portion of the fruits of their industry,
sufficient at least for their subsistence: when their
rents became fixed, any increase that took place in
the whole produce of their land was an equal increase of the portion which they retained for themselves.    Their holdings, if we may judge from
existing copyholds, as well as from the analogy
of Continental countries, were often of considerable
extent, and capable of producing much more than
the owners could consume: nothing, therefore, but
markets for their surplus produce, were required
to enable them to grow rich, and to surround themselves with many new comforts.    Now, in the three
centuries which immediately succeeded the Norman
conquest, civilisation made very considerable progress in England; internal and external trade were
greatly extended, foreign commodities introduced
in abundance, and native manufactures established
and improved.    The importance of villain-propri-
etors of land increased in proportion.    The most
considerable of them almost ceased to belong to the
class of labourers.    What services they were bound

by the conditions of their tenure to render, were performed by deputy, and the cultivation of their own farms was also performed chiefly by hired labourers.

Of these latter, a large body, possessing personal freedom, but destitute of property in land, had sprung up. It is probable that they were originally emancipated slaves, or sons of small freeholders, or of villain occupiers of land; but villain tenants themselves, after performing their bounden services to their lords, were at liberty to serve others for wages, the lords having only a prior claim to such further services from their own bondsmen as they might be willing to pay for.* Having been accustomed to plentiful living at home, these men could not be induced to enter a stranger's service, except by the assurance of liberal treatment. Married men, engaged as labourers in husbandry, seem to have been provided with a cottage and a few acres of land to cultivate, for their own profit, in the intervals of their master's work. Some direct payment, either in provisions or money, was also made to them, though it may be difficult to estimate the amount of their receipts from this source. Servants who had no land, if boarded and lodged, as they almost invariably were, by their employers, were, in the latter part of the twelfth century, rated at about a penny a day.† Whether this sum included the cost

* This important point is established by the language of the Statute of Labourers, 23 Edw. III. cap. 1.

† Eden, Hist. of the Poor, vol. iii. Appendix, and vol. i. p. 115 note.

of their victuals, is somewhat doubtful; but in either case, as a penny would at that time have bought a couple of fowls, or the fifth part of a sheep, we may be pretty sure that they were well fed. Early in the fourteenth century, a day labourer received a penny a day, and his food; and the daily ration served out to him, at harvest time, seems to have been two herrings and a loaf of bread (of which fifteen were made from a bushel of wheat), besides milk or cheese, and beer. No exception can be taken to the *quantity* of this allowance, and there can be no doubt that the *quality* was frequently varied, seeing that in those days a joint of meat might commonly be bought for the price of two loaves.*

By the year 1349 the wages of agricultural labourers had become "excessive" in the opinion of the landholders who had to pay them, and whose representatives in parliament attempted to limit them, by means of the famous Statute of Labourers, passed in that year, which required all servants to accept the same wages as had been customary eight or nine years before. A similar statute †, passed in the following year, tells us more particularly what those wages had been, viz. a penny a-day in hay-making, but five-pence a-day for mowers, and two-pence or three-pence for reapers of corn. Such rates were intended to be applicable only to men not boarded by their masters, for the act forbade the giving any victuals " or other courtesy," in ad-

* Eden, vol. iii. Appendix.
† 25 Edw. III. stat. 1.

dition; but it must be recollected that labourers who had to find their own food were almost always in possession of a few acres of land; and the Act likewise informs us, that servants were in the habit of refusing to work for less than double or treble the prescribed sums. Thirteen years later, in 1363, another effort was made to put an end to high wages by rendering them useless to the receivers; and a law * was passed, enjoining carters, ploughmen, and all other farm-servants, not to eat or drink " excessively," or to wear any cloth except " blanket and russet wool of twelve-pence." Domestic servants, whether of gentlemen or of tradesmen or artificers, were at the same time declared to be entitled to only one meal a-day of flesh or fish, and were to content themselves at other meals with "milk, butter, cheese, and other such victuals."† These ordinances of course failed entirely of their intended effect, as attempts to control the natural laws which regulate the price of labour must always do; but the parliament, little discouraged, proceeded, in 1388, to lay down another tariff of wages‡, according to which a bailiff was to receive 13s. 3d., a master-hind, carter, or shepherd, 10s., and a common labourer in husbandry 6s. 8d. or 7s. annually. Of course board and lodging were to be allowed in addition, though the law does not mention them. In 1444 these rates were raised to 23s. 4d., 20s. and 15s. respectively, independently of food and of

* 37 Edw. III. cap. 14.
† 37 Edw. III. cap. 8.
‡ 12 Ric. II. cap. 4.

clothes of a specified value. Day-labourers were to have not more than three-pence a-day, without food, except in harvest, when they might be allowed five-pence or six-pence.* These limitations were, however, as vain as the preceding ones. Wages continued to rise in spite of opposition, and enabled the working classes to indulge in a degree of luxury which quite scandalised the parliament, and which it was attempted to check by sumptuary laws. Accordingly, by a statute enacted in 1463†, servants in husbandry were restricted to clothing of materials not worth more than two shillings a-yard, and were forbidden to wear hose of a higher price than fourteen-pence a-pair, or girdles garnished with silver. The price of their wives' coverchief or head-dress was not to exceed twelve-pence. In 1482 it was found necessary to loosen these restrictions, and labourers in husbandry‡ were permitted to wear hose as dear as eighteen-pence a-pair, while the sum which their wives might legally expend on a covering for the head was raised to twenty-pence. This legislation, considering the fall which has since taken place in the value of money, was really much as if a law should now be necessary to prevent ploughmen from strutting about in velvet coats and silk stockings with silver buckles in their shoes, and their wives from trimming their caps with Brussels lace. It exhibits the English peasantry in a condition which was probably never

---

* 23 Hen. VI. cap. 13.
† 3 Edw. IV. cap. 5.
‡ 22 Edw. IV. cap. 1.

attained by the same class in any other age or country, unless perhaps by the emancipated negroes of the British West Indies, and which they could scarcely be believed to have really occupied, upon slighter evidence than has been brought forward. Such evidence is not of a character to require confirmation, yet it may not be uninteresting to add to it the testimony of Sir John Fortescue, Lord Chief Justice to Henry VI., who thus exultingly contrasts the abundance enjoyed by the lowest class of his own countrymen with the misery of the French peasantry. Of the latter he says, " Their shamewes (smock frocks) are made of hemp much like to sackcloth; woollen cloth they wear none, except it be very coarse, and that only in their coats, under their said upper garments; neither use they any hose but from the knee upward: the residue of their legs go naked. The women go barefoot, saving on holydays. Neither men nor women eat any flesh, but only lard of bacon, with a small quantity whereof they fatten their potage and broths. As for roasted or sodden meat of flesh, they taste none, except it be of the inwards sometimes and heads of beasts that be killed for gentlemen and merchants." But the English " are rich, having abundance of gold and silver, and other things necessary for the maintenance of man's life. They drink no water, unless it be so that some for devotion, and upon a zeal of penance, do abstain from other drink; they eat plentifully of all kinds of flesh and fish. They wear fine woollen cloth in all their apparel; they have also abundance of bed coverings in their houses, and of all other woollen stuff. They have great store of all hustlements and implements of household. They are plentifully furnished with all instruments of husbandry, and all other things that are requisite to the accomplishment of a quiet and wealthy life, according to their estates and degrees."*

In the face of testimony like this, it has been gravely argued, that the English peasantry of the middle ages were less comfortably situated than their living descendants, because they used barley instead of wheaten bread, ate off wooden platters, never knew the luxury of a cotton shirt or of a cup of tea, and slept on straw pallets within walls of wattled plaster. All the details of this picture are not perhaps perfectly accurate; at least there are grounds for believing that in very early times wheaten bread was commonly used by people of the lowest class in many parts of England †; but

---

* Fortescue de Laud. Leg. Angliæ, pp. 82—85, and 86.

† The Statute of Labourers (25 Edw. III.) ordains that ploughmen, swineherds, and all other servants, shall in the country, "*where wheat was wont to be given*," take for their wages either money or wheat at the will of the giver. In the "Visions of Piers Ploughman," written in the same reign, it is said that after harvest,

> "Would no beggar eat bread that in it beans were,
> But of cockit and clemantyne, or else *clene whete*."

Long afterwards, when agricultural labourers were fallen from their former high estate, Massinger's Marrall, to express the extremity of Wellborn's poverty, says that he "durst wish but cheese-parings and brown bread on Sundays," as if both were equally eligible articles of diet, and equally unfit for any but beggars.

even if the representation be quite faithful, it only shows that certain modern refinements and conveniences were formerly unknown and uncoveted. But although ruder means were employed to supply the wants of nature, every want was abundantly satisfied, which is far indeed from being the case at present. Many advantages of an advanced civilisation which are now within every one's reach were once equally unthought of by rich and poor. Our Plantagenet kings, as well as their courtiers, were fain to drink beer at every meal, and to drink it too out of wooden bickers: — they were as ill provided with under linen as the meanest of their subjects; and so little did they regard what are now considered the most indispensable requisites of domestic comfort, that the bedchamber furniture of so magnificent a monarch as Henry the Eighth consisted only of a couple of joint cupboards, a joint stool, two hand irons, a fire fork, a pair of tongs, a fire-pan, and a steel mirror covered with yellow velvet.* At this day little of any grain beside oats is used in many respectable families in Scotland, and many a continental baron, whose domain stretches for miles around his princely château, seldom eats any but rye bread.† This is

* Pict. Hist. of Eng. vol. ii. p. 880. The Spaniards who came to England in Queen Mary's time wondered when they saw the large diet used by the inmates of the most homely-looking cottages. "The English," they said, "make their houses of sticks and dirt, but they fare as well as the king." See *Bernan's Hist. and Art of Warming and Ventilating Rooms, &c.*

† See the lively description of an Esthonian nobleman's household in Miss Rigby's charming Letters from the Baltic.

mere matter of taste, and no one would think of mentioning it as a mark of social inferiority; but it would be quite as reasonable to do so as for the Dorsetshire labourer to look back with pity on his well-clad, beef-fed ancestors, because some of his own rags are made of cotton, and because the baker, of whom he now and then buys a loaf, sells only wheaten bread.

The scarcity of labourers in England, in proportion to the demand for them, during the latter part of the fourteenth and the greater part of the fifteenth century, which was, of course, the immediate cause of their astonishing prosperity, was ascribed at the time, and has also been ascribed by succeeding writers, to the dreadful pestilence which visited England, as well as most other countries of Europe, in the year 1349, and, according to Dr. Mead, swept away more than one half of the inhabitants. Although this is plainly an extravagant exaggeration of its ravages, the epidemic was indisputably exceedingly destructive: perhaps, as Dr. Mead asserts, the most destructive recorded in modern times. Doubtless it occasioned a corresponding rise of wages; but, that the extraordinary rise which ultimately took place was mainly, or even in any great degree, owing to this cause, is disproved by the single fact, that wages did not reach their maximum until more than a hundred years later. The effects of an unusual mortality, in diminishing the supply of labourers, would be felt most sensibly immediately after the mortality had occurred, and before time had been allowed for the partial repair of its ravages; but although the "Statute of Labourers," passed in 1349, the very year of the great pestilence, shows that wages immediately rose somewhat above the level of preceding years, subsequent enactments equally show that the advance was at first moderate. In 1363 it was still thought possible to compel farm-servants to dress themselves in stuff like horse-cloths, and it was not till 1463 that their habit of arraying themselves in broad-cloth, as dear probably as 2s. a yard as it might now be at 20s., excited the loud indignation of their superiors. It is true, that subsequently to the great pestilence of 1349, down almost to the close of the fifteenth century, minor epidemics from time to time occurred, and the land was also frequently devastated by civil war, or drained of its men for foreign expeditions. But experience has shown that a country may annually lose a very considerable number of its inhabitants in these ways, without being thereby in any degree depopulated, the offspring of those who are enabled to marry by the removal of their neighbours sufficing to fill up the places of the latter. In order to have any permanent effect upon population, the ravages of war or pestilence must be so prodigious that they cannot possibly be repaired by natural increase within a moderate period; the diminished body of labourers may then obtain a durable as well as a considerable advance of wages, and becoming accustomed to new conveniences and comforts, may learn to look upon them as necessaries of life, and may abstain from marriages which would require them to be given up. If, however, the great plague of 1349 failed to produce this effect, still less could it result from the very inferior mortality of subsequent years. As far, indeed, as regards the civil wars which harassed England during the reigns of the Yorkist and Lancastrian kings, if, on the one hand, the slaughter that attended them contracted the supply of labour, yet, on the other, the suspension of industry which they occasioned may have equally diminished the demand for it, and wages or the price of labour may have been little or not at all affected.

There does not, then, seem to be sufficient ground for supposing that any positive decrease of population took place during the period under review, and the extraordinary improvement in the condition of the labouring class would, therefore, seem to have proceeded from an opposite cause — not from a diminished supply of labour, but from an increased demand for it, consequent upon the extension of commerce, manufactures, and agriculture. That all these occupations were actually extended very considerably in the latter part of the fourteenth century, and very remarkably in the fifteenth, is unquestionable; and it is not difficult to conjecture by what circumstances their progress was favoured. The increase of foreign trade is sufficiently explained by the flourishing condition, at that time, of some continental countries, particularly of Flanders and Italy, whose ships and merchants began to resort, in unprecedented numbers, to the British shores for certain commodities for which this island had long been celebrated. Foreign commerce is often the nurse of domestic industry; but notwithstanding its aid, the growth of English towns seems to have been long retarded by the difficulty of procuring workmen for the various businesses carried on in them. As long as the mass of the people remained attached to the soil, or were retained in the still more galling chains of personal slavery, one chief resource of citizens requiring servants was in runaway bondsmen, who, if they could conceal themselves within the walls of a town for a year and a day, became free by law. Predial slavery, however, which was perhaps at no time very rigid in England, was continually more and more relaxed after the Norman conquest, until at length villains occupying land were, by a process already alluded to, converted into copyholders, and they and their children became in all respects free. Even before this change took place, and while the tenant himself was still attached to the soil, his children, if more numerous than was requisite for the cultivation of the landlord's estate, may frequently have had little difficulty in obtaining their manumission from a master to whom they were rather an encumbrance than otherwise. Emancipation of slaves was, moreover, strongly recommended by the clergy, whose influence over dying sinners often caused hundreds to be set free at once. These various causes long produced their effects, almost imperceptibly; but there is historical testimony that their operation was exceedingly powerful in the early part of the fifteenth century, when the enfranchisement of the English peasantry, though not quite complete, advanced with rapid strides towards completion.   One of the chief objects in 1381 of Wat Tyler's hundred thousand followers was the extinction of slavery; whereas Sir Thomas Smith, who wrote about the year 1550, declares, that he had never met with any personal or domestic slaves; and that the villains, or predial slaves, still to be found, were so few as to be scarcely worth mentioning.*   No sooner did the bondsmen obtain their liberty, than numbers of them flocked to the towns and applied themselves to handicrafts, or some sort of manufacture or trade.   This fact is sufficiently attested by repeated statutes, passed by the influence of the landholders in the House of Commons, two of which in particular ordained — the first, that all persons who had been employed in husbandry till the age of twelve should thenceforth abide at the same labour, and be incapable of being put to any mystery or handicraft† ; and the second, that no person should put his son or daughter, of whatever age, apprentice to any business within any city or borough, unless he had land or rent of the yearly value of 20s. at least.‡ The migration towards the towns indicated by these acts of the legislature occasioned an accession to the urban population, which created an increased demand for all sorts of rural produce, for materials of manufactures as well as for provisions.   The demand for wool, in particular, increased amazingly. British wool had been for ages an article in great

* Eden, vol. i. p. 103.
† 12 Rich. II. cap. 5.          ‡ 7 Henry IV. cap. 17.

request, but principally for the purpose of exportation; but about 1537 a colony of Flemings, invited over by Edward the First, established a domestic manufacture, which sixty or seventy years afterwards was able to compete successfully with its foreign rivals, and afforded to the British farmer a nearer, and consequently better, market for his wool. Thus a powerful stimulus was given to every branch of rural industry; and while part of the agricultural labourers were betaking themselves to other employments, those who remained were sought for with redoubled eagerness, both on account of their diminished numbers, and of the great addition made to the quantity of work to be done. Add to this the necessity which, during the wars of the Roses, every great man felt of keeping in pay as large a number of retainers as possible; and perhaps no other circumstance need be mentioned, in order to account fully for the extraordinary rise of wages which took place, and continued without interruption during the greater part of the fifteenth century, notwithstanding all the efforts of the legislature to restrain it.

It is, however, very important to observe, in this place, that the increase of employment, however great it might eventually have become, might not have affected the rate of wages very sensibly, if it had grown up by slow degrees, for the progress of population might then have kept pace with it. The principal effect of a slightly increased demand for labour is generally merely to hasten the marriages of parties who would otherwise have deferred their union for want of sufficient means of support, and the scarcity of labourers is consequently very soon remedied. But if a considerable augmentation of employment take place suddenly, the benefit which it confers on the labouring class is not only much greater immediately, but is much more likely to be lasting. Additional conveniences are brought within reach of the whole body of labourers, and notwithstanding the temporary encouragement given to marriage, the next generation grows up in the enjoyment of advantages unknown to the preceding one, and regulates its notions of comfort by a higher standard. A high standard of comfort tends, as has been shown, to check the undue frequency of marriage, and to prevent the progress of population from reducing the people below whatever point on the social scale they may have attained. It certainly operated in this manner at the time now spoken of. The amelioration of the condition of the common people, in the beginning of the fifteenth century, accelerated the progress of population very little, if at all: the extension of the field of employment proceeded at a much more rapid rate; and the benefit of this extension was felt by the labourers, in the shape of an almost equally rapid rise of wages, which did not cease until it reached its acmé about the time of the accession of Henry VII.

It will naturally be asked how the high social position which the English labourer had now attained came to be abandoned; how the ease and comfort which he once enjoyed have since been exchanged for difficulties and privations. It has been argued, that the diffusion of the comforts of life among all ranks of a community (a decisive proof that the numbers of the people, as compared with the amount of employment for them, are not disproportionably great) is sufficient to prevent population from increasing more rapidly than the amount of employment. How then has it happened that the numbers of the people are now, and have been throughout the last three hundred and sixty years, in excess of their former proportion to the amount of employment? For the present degradation of the English labourer has not been effected within a recent period; the golden age of the working class was followed without any interval by the iron age which still subsists. We have seen that, in the middle of the fifteenth century, every man could obtain as much work as he pleased at extravagant wages. So late as 1496, and even as 1514, parliament thought it advisable to pass laws for the purpose of keeping down wages, though the rise which was then taking place was occasioned entirely by the depreciation of the precious metals consequent on the discovery of America, and was not only not real, but concealed a positive fall in the real price of labour. Very soon afterwards, however, legislation took a new turn; and parliament, instead of attempting to curtail the labourers' honest earnings, had to exercise its ingenuity in providing for the crowd of destitute for whom no work could be found. England had probably never been entirely free from sturdy beggars; for wherever a livelihood can be obtained without labour, there will generally be some persons who prefer an idle vagabond life to one of patient industry, however richly rewarded. In this way we may understand the preamble to the " Statute of Labourers," passed in Edward the Third's reign, which declared, in the same breath, that though " many, seeing the necessity of masters and great scarcity of servants, will not serve unless they may receive excessive wages," others are " rather willing to beg in idleness, than by labour to get their living." These, however, and their successors, for more than a century, were beggars from choice, but they were at length replaced by a race of beggars from necessity. Repeated statutes, commencing with one passed in 1494 *, attest the rapid spread of destitution. For a time, misled by the experience of the preceding age, parliament imagined idleness to be still the fruitful parent of this evil, and punishment its best cure; no other asylum, therefore, was offered to able-bodied vagrants than the stocks, and no milder treatment than whipping at the cart's tail. After being admonished in this way, they were to be sent to the place of their birth, there to set themselves to work " as true men ought to do." In 1535, however, it was discovered that the aforesaid " valiant vagabonds," after returning home, could find no work to do; and the parish authorities were in consequence enjoined to collect voluntary contributions for the purpose, not only of relieving the impotent and infirm, but of enabling the strong and lusty to gain a living with their own hands.† In

* 11 Henry VII. cap. 2.        † 27 Henry VII. cap. 25.

1547, the number of beggars still rapidly increasing, in spite of the " godly acts and statutes" already directed against them, another was passed, which, though repealed two years afterwards, deserves to be mentioned, not merely on account of its astonishing barbarity, but as showing how genuine the distresses of the lower classes must have been, which even these atrocious measures could not induce them to conceal. It was enacted, that every able-bodied person found loitering about should be branded with a hot iron, and adjudged to two years' slavery to the man by whom he had been apprehended, during which time he might be fed upon bread and water, and refuse meat, and forced to work by beating or otherwise; that if he ran away he should be branded a second time, and should be condemned to slavery for life, and that if he absconded again, he should suffer death as a felon.* Threatened with slavery, stripes, and death, men chose to run every danger in seeking to better their condition, rather than pine with hunger at home, and beggars and vagabonds continued daily to increase. In 1562, voluntary alms being found insufficient for the relief of the poor, the parish authorities were empowered to assess persons obstinately refusing to contribute.† Mendicancy and vagabondage continuing still unabated, in 1572 ‡ power was given to tax all the inhabitants of a place for the relief of its poor. Other acts followed; and in 1601 the necessity of providing

---

* 1 Edw. VI. cap. 3.
† 5 Eliz. cap. 3.       ‡ 14 Eliz. cap. 5.

employment for the able-bodied poor by means of parochial assessments was fully admitted, and a matured plan for that purpose was established.*

It cannot be denied that the scene described in this series of statutes was one of real destitution; that the prevalence of mendicancy arose from the inability of labourers to procure sufficient work; that the supply of labour was consequently larger than the demand, and that in a word, the country was already over-peopled. It will again be demanded how this state of things, contrasting so strongly with the character of the age immediately preceding, was brought about. If it was produced by a positive addition to the population, it is obvious that the possession of comfort is not sufficient to prevent the numbers of a community from becoming excessive, and the principles laid down in the last chapter must be abandoned as untenable. I trust, however, that the reader may be persuaded not to adopt this conclusion, and may be convinced that the over-population of England in the sixteenth century, or the disproportion between the numbers of the labouring class and the amount of employment, proceeded not from the augmentation of the former, but from the diminution of the latter.

Most writers on the subject have indeed imagined that the growth of mendicancy at the period in question is attributable to the dissolution of monasteries by Henry the Eighth; but in opposition to this opinion, it need only be said, that monasteries

* 43 Eliz. cap. 2.

were not abolished till 1535, many years after the continual increase of vagrancy had become a standing topic of parliamentary lamentation. Besides, admitting what is very much more than doubtful, that any large portion of the monastic revenues had been appropriated to the relief of the poor, it can scarcely be supposed that habitual relief had been afforded to any except the aged and infirm. But the vagrants with whom the country was now swarming, and upon whom the legislature emptied the largest vessels of its wrath, are described as " sturdy, lusty, mighty of body;" and as these had never been dependent on the monasteries for sub-sistence, it is evident that they could not have been impoverished by their dissolution. If that measure had any effect in increasing the number of sturdy beggars, it probably did so by turning adrift some thousands of monks who had been originally taken from the lowest classes of society, and who, when their accustomed means of support were withdrawn, were obliged to seek a livelihood from other sources. But, after all, an equal or a greater accession to the labouring class had frequently before been occasioned by the disbandment of an army, without being followed by any sensible inconvenience; and there can be no doubt that the monks would have found new occupations as quickly as soldiers had done on former occasions if novel obstacles had not been thrown in their way.

The truth is, that the field of employment had of late been very greatly contracted. Both previously, and for some time subsequently to the abolition of villenage, England contained a vast number of small landholders. Besides owners of freeholds of the yearly value of forty shillings or thereabouts, who, at a time when land was commonly let for no more than sixpence an acre, must have formed a class important for its property as well as its numbers, and, besides the tenants in villenage, or their successors, the copyholders, who must have been at least as numerous as the copyholders of the present day, there were likewise many tenant-farmers, paying a rent of not more than 4*l*. a year, but occupying, as appears from Bishop Latimer's account of his father, corn land enough to employ half-a-dozen men, and pasture enough to keep thirty cows and a hundred sheep. * Besides these, there were the married servants in husbandry who were employed upon the estates of large proprietors or farmers, and whose remuneration consisted in part of the loan of a cottage, and of a piece of ground which was seldom of less extent than three or four acres. Most of the landholders of all these different classes, except the one last mentioned, must have required the aid of hired labourers, particularly as much land was under tillage, and large quantities of corn were grown. There was consequently a great demand for agricultural labour; and as the supply was limited by the causes elsewhere alluded to, wages became very high. But the high rate of wages, combined

* Latimer's Sermons, p. 101. Cambridge, 1844.

with the increasing abundance and cheapness of corn consequent upon the improvement of agriculture, must have rendered tillage less profitable than formerly, more especially to large landholders, who did not consume at home the principal part of their crops, but raised large quantities for sale. At the same time, the extension of the woollen manufacture was raising the price of wool; and the little attendance which sheep require was an additional motive for causing sheep-farming to be preferred to tillage. Arable land therefore began to be converted into pasture; and the seemingly interminable corn-fields, which, like those of Germany at this day, probably extended for miles without having their even surface broken by fences or any other visible boundaries, disappeared. After being sown with grass, they were surrounded and divided by enclosures, to prevent the sheep from straying, and to do away with the necessity of having shepherds always on the watch. By these changes, the quantity of work to be done upon a farm was exceedingly diminished, and most of the servants, whom it had been usual to board and lodge in the manor and farm-houses, were dismissed. This was not all. The married farm-servants were ousted from their cottages, which were pulled down, and their gardens and fields were annexed to the adjoining meadows. The small farmers were treated in the same way, as their leases fell in, and were sent to join the daily increasing crowd of competitors for work that was daily decreasing in quantity. Even freeholders

were in some instances ejected from their lands. *
This social revolution had probably commenced
even before the prosperity of the peasantry had
reached its climax ; but in 1487 it attracted the
notice of Parliament, and an act was passed to
restrain its progress ; for already it was observed
that enclosures were becoming " more frequent,
whereby arable land, which could not be manured
without people and families, was turned into pasture, which was easily rid by a few herdsmen," and
that " tenances for years, lives, and at will, where-
upon most of the yeomanry lived, were turned
into demesnes." †    In 1533 ‡, an act was passed

* One of the ways in which this might be done is described
very graphically by Massinger's Sir Giles Overreach : —
> " I'll buy some cottage near his manor ;
> Which done, I'll make my men break ope his fences,
> Ride o'er his standing corn, and in the night
> Set fire to his barns, or break his cattle's legs ;
> These trespasses draw on suits, and suits expenses
> Which I can spare, but will soon beggar him.
> When I have harried him thus two or three years,
> Though he sue *in forma pauperis*, in spite
> Of all his thrift and care, he'll grow behind-hand.
> Then with the favour of my man of law,
> I will pretend some title : want will force him
> To put it to arbitrement; then, if he sell
> For half the value, he shall have ready money,
> And I possess his land.—(*New Way to pay old Debts.*)

Sir Thomas More also, in his Utopia, speaks indignantly of
" husbandmen *thrust out of their own,* or else by covin and
fraud, or by violent oppression, put beside it, or by wrongs and
injuries so wearied that they be compelled to sell all."
    † Lord Bacon's Hist. of King Henry VII., Works, vol. v. p. 61.
    ‡ 25 Henry VIII. cap. 13.

strongly condemning the practice of "accumulating" farms, which it was declared had reduced "a marvellous multitude" of the people to poverty and misery, and left them no alternative but to steal, or to die "pitifully" of cold and hunger. In this act it was stated, that single farms might be found with flocks of from ten to twenty thousand sheep upon them, and it was ordained that no man should keep more than two thousand sheep except upon his own land, or rent more than two farms. Two years later it was enacted, that the King should have a moiety of the profits of land converted (subsequently to a date specified) from tillage to pasture, until a suitable house was erected and the land was restored to tillage. In 1552 a law * was made, which required that on all estates as large a quantity of land as had been kept in tillage for four years together at any time since the accession of Henry VIII. should be so continued in tillage. But these and many subsequent enactments of the same kind had not the smallest effect in checking the consolidation of farms. We find Roger Ascham, in Queen Elizabeth's reign, lamenting the dispersion of families, the ruin of houses, the breaking up and destruction of "the noble yeomanry, the honour and strength of England." Harrison also speaks of towns pulled down for sheep walks, "and of the tenements that had fallen either down or into the lord's hands," or had been "brought and united together by other

* 5 & 6 Edw. VI. cap. 5.

men, so that in some one manor seventeen, eighteen, or twenty houses were shrunk." * "Where have been a great many householders and inhabitants," says Bishop Latimer, "there is now but a shepherd and his dog †;" and in a curious tract published in 1581 by one William Stafford, a husbandman is made to exclaim, "Marry, these enclosures do undo us all, for they make us to pay dearer for our land that we occupy, and causeth that we can have no land to put to tillage ; all is taken up for pasture, either for sheep or for grazing of cattle; insomuch that I have known of late a dozen ploughs within less compass than six miles about me laid down within this seven years, and where threescore persons or upwards had their livings, now one man with his cattle hath all. Those sheep is the cause of all our mischief, for they have driven husbandry out of the country, by which was increased before all kinds of victuals, and now altogether sheep, sheep, sheep." ‡ While numbers of persons were thus being continually driven from their homes and deprived of their means of livelihood, we need not be at a loss to account for the increase of vagrancy, without ascribing it to the increase of population.

It is perfectly true, that at this very time, while her noble yeomanry were being degraded into common day labourers and mendicants, England, owing to the extension of commerce and manufactures,

* Eden, Hist. of the Poor, vol. i. p. 118.

† Latimer's Sermons, p. 100.

‡ Pictorial History of England, vol. ii. p. 900.

was advancing with unexampled rapidity in wealth and power, and the increase of employment in the towns must have been more than equal to the decrease of employment in the country. It may therefore be thought, that unless a positive addition had been made to the numbers of the labouring class, all the labourers dismissed from agriculture might have obtained abundant occupation in the towns. But there cannot be a greater error than to suppose that the substitution of one employment for another is not detrimental to the workmen originally employed, if the amount of work to be done remain the same. Even when the new business is carried on in the same place as the old one, the work may be very unsuitable to men who have always been differently employed; and if the business be removed to a distance, innumerable difficulties will prevent the workmen in general from following it. The starving labourers of the sixteenth century might have earned a very comfortable maintenance if they had been weavers and artizans instead of ploughmen and carters, but as husbandry was the only business they understood, few of them may have thought it worth while to offer their services in any other capacity, and those who did may have been much obstructed in their search for work by the tyrannical laws which endeavoured to prevent husbandmen from leaving their place of birth. Agriculture, the only occupation really accessible to the great body of the peasantry, had, as we have seen, been greatly contracted, and this

cause was quite sufficient of itself to reduce them
to destitution.

Perhaps the condition of the peasantry was never
worse than during the greater part of the sixteenth
century; towards the end of that period it began
sensibly to improve. It has been attempted to
show, that misery up to a certain point promotes
the growth of population, but beyond that point it
has a much greater effect in increasing mortality,
and so counteracts its opposite tendency. The
misery of the homeless outcasts with whom England was swarming during the domination of the
House of Tudor, was much too severe to allow them
to increase and multiply. On the contrary, want
and disease no doubt greatly thinned their numbers,
and might possibly have swept them away almost
entirely, if circumstances had not at length occurred
to rescue those who remained from their precarious
position. While the rural districts were being
desolated in the manner above described, the towns
were advancing fast in wealth and population, and
the increasing wants of the citizens, by greatly en-
hancing the price of corn, again altered the direction of agricultural industry, and occasioned a
strong reaction in favour of tillage. This augmented
the demand for agricultural labourers, and seems
for a time to have afforded sufficient employment
for all who sought it. Such at least is the inference
which may be drawn from the remark of Sir Edward
Coke, that an act passed in 1597 for the punishment of rogues, vagabonds, and sturdy beggars,
caused that class to disappear entirely as long as

the law was strictly enforced *, which could not have been the case unless every one had been able to earn a livelihood by honest industry. But although agricultural labourers were now raised a good deal above the depth to which they had sunk, they were very far from having regained the prosperity which they had once enjoyed. The cottages which were every where springing up to replace those that had been pulled down in the preceding period, had not in general any land attached to them. In most parishes there were common lands, on which a poor householder might keep a cow — a most valuable privilege; but otherwise a labourer was often entirely dependent on his daily earnings, and these were very inferior in value to the income of a cottager a few generations earlier. Their nominal amount was indeed greater, for, owing to the depreciation of the precious metals consequent upon the discovery of America, the rate of money-wages had about doubled, but the price of provisions and other commodities had risen in a much larger proportion. The price of wheat, for example, rose in the course of a hundred years from about 7$s$. to about 30$s$. a quarter, and in the year 1610, $4\frac{3}{4}d$., or about a penny less than a whole sheep had once cost, was given for a pound of mutton. An outdoor labourer at the beginning of the 17th century, therefore, who had to buy his own food out of sixpence or eight-pence a day, was not nearly so well off as a man of the same class would have

* Eden, vol. i. p. 145.

been in the 14th with only $3\frac{1}{2}d$. a-day, even supposing that the latter had not possessed in addition
the produce of a cottage farm.   The wages of the
former seem to have borne about the same proportion to prices, and to have enabled him to share in
the necessaries and conveniences of life about as
largely, as seven or eight shillings a-week might do
now.

Such a modicum of comfort could not, as we
may infer from the habits of the Dorsetshire peasantry of this day, act as a very effectual restraint
upon population, and we need not be surprised,
therefore, that in a few years labourers increased
beyond the number that could procure employment.
The anonymous author of a pamphlet published in
1622, speaks of the daily increase of poor, and
describes the country as being " pitifully pestered"
with " lusty labourers" out of work, who, because
no man would be " troubled with their service"
were fain to " beg, filch, and steal for their maintenance."   Sir Matthew Hale*, writing about 1660,
confirms this statement, and the preamble of an
important statute passed in 1662, dwells upon the
" necessity, number, and continual increase of the
poor" throughout England and Wales.†   In the
last thirty years of the same century the annual
produce of the poor rates was variously estimated
at from 600,000*l.* to 840,000*l.*, which, at the rate of
relief then customary, must have sufficed for the
constant maintenance of at least a hundred thou-

* Eden, vol. i. p. 216.
† 13 Car. II. cap. 12.

sand persons, or one-sixtieth part of the whole population. Of the persons thus relieved, one-half, according to a report drawn up by Mr. Locke in 1697, were able-bodied, and might have maintained themselves if they had had work.* A temporary reduction in the annual expenditure on the poor is supposed to have been effected by an Act passed in the 9th year of Geo. I., and in the three years ending with 1750, the average amount is shown by parliamentary returns not to have exceeded 690,000l. But by 1776 the amount had risen to 1,521,000l., and in the three years ending with 1785, the annual average was 1,912,000l. Now in the 17th and 18th centuries every branch of national industry flourished at least as vigorously as before. Commerce and manufactures prospered exceedingly, and if agriculture did not quite keep pace with them, it was, nevertheless, very much promoted by their growth, and an additional stimulant was given to tillage by the introduction of turnip husbandry and artificial grasses. As therefore the demand for labour of all sorts must have increased considerably, instead of diminishing, the simultaneous increase of pauperism can only be attributed to a still greater increase in the number of labourers. It has already been hinted, that this advance of population received its first impulse from the depressed condition and consequent improvidence of the labouring class at the beginning of the 17th century, but its prolonged continuance was the

---

* Eden, vol. ii. p. 245.

result of circumstances of a somewhat different
nature.

It is very remarkable, that while pauperism was
advancing in the manner above described, the condition of the labourers who obtained employment
was not injured by the competition of the unemployed, but on the contrary was gradually improving. We have no information as to the state of
things in this respect throughout the country, but
some general deductions may be drawn from the
records of particular counties. The average wages
(including extra earnings in harvest) of an outdoor
agricultural labourer who had to find his own
food, had been in Rutland, in 1610, about 6½d.
a-day, or 3s. 3d. weekly. In Essex in 1661,
they were about 1s. 1d. a-day, or 6s. 6d. weekly;
in Suffolk in 1682, 11d. a-day, or 5s. 6d. weekly;
in Warwickshire in 1685, 8d. a-day, or 4s. weekly;
in Devonshire in the same year, 10d. a-day, or
5s. weekly; in Lancashire in 1725, 10d. a-day, or
5s. weekly for inferior labourers, and 1s. a-day, or
6s. a week for those of the best sort.* In 1768
Arthur Young, who had been making a tour through
the south of England, principally with the view of
noting the state of agriculture and the condition of
the people, reckoned the average rate of agricultural wages the whole year round to be, within twenty
miles from London, 10s. 9d. a-week; at a distance
of twenty to sixty miles from London, 7s. 8d.; at
from sixty to one hundred and ten miles, 6s. 4d.;

* Eden, vol. iii. App. 3.

at from a hundred and ten to a hundred and seventy miles, 6s. 3d. He observed the rates to be highest in the eastern, and lowest in the western counties: in some parts of Gloucestershire and Wiltshire they were not higher than 4s. 6d. in winter, and 6s. in summer. In 1770, Young published a Tour through the North of England, in which he describes the weekly rate of agricultural wages as ranging from 4s. 11d. to 9s. 9d., the average being 7s. 1d. This last sum was also the average within fifty miles of London: between fifty and a hundred miles the average rate was 6s. 9d.; between one and two hundred miles from London it rose to 7s. 2d.; between two and three hundred miles it was still 7s., but beyond that distance it fell to 5s. 8d. The enhancement of wages which thus appears to have been going on for more than a hundred years, was not merely nominal, nor a consequence of the depreciation of money: on the contrary, the prices of provisions and of others of the most important articles of consumption were frequently falling while wages were rising. The average price of wheat was 2l. 11s. 7¾d. per quarter in the ten years ending with 1655. In each of the next ten decennial periods it was as follows:—

| In the ten years ending with | | | £ | s. | d. |
|---|---|---|---|---|---|
| 1665 | - | - | - | 2 | 10 | 5¾ |
| 1675 | - | - | - | 2 | 0 | 11¾ |
| 1685 | - | - | - | 2 | 1 | 4¼ |
| 1695 | - | - | - | 1 | 19 | 6¾ |
| 1705 | - | - | - | 2 | 2 | 11 |
| 1715 | - | - | - | 2 | 4 | 2¼ |
| 1725 | - | - | - | 1 | 15 | 4¾ |

In the ten years ending with       £   s.   d.

| | | | £ | s. | d. |
|---|---|---|---|---|---|
| 1735 | - | - | - 1 | 15 | 2 |
| 1745 | - | - | - 1 | 12 | 1 |
| 1755 | - | - | - 1 | 1 | 3¾ |

Mutton was sold in London in 1610 for about 3¾*d*. per lb. From 1660 to 1690 its price is said to have been about 2*d*. per lb., and though it became dearer afterwards, it cost only 2½*d*. per lb. from 1706 to 1730, and only 3*d*. as late as 1760. The prices of beef per lb. are said to have been in 1610, 3¾*d*.; in 1710, 1¹⁄₁₀*d*.; from 1740 to 1760, 2½*d*. Of wool, the prices were per tod, for some years previously to 1622, 33*s*.; in 1641, 24*s*.; in 1648, 37*s*. 6*d*.; in 1649, 40*s*.; between 1650 and 1660, they ranged from 22*s*. 6*d*. to 60*s*.; in 1671, the price was 28*s*.; in 1680, 12*s*.; in 1681, 18*s*.; in 1707, 16*s*.; in 1717, 23*s*.; in 1738, 23*s*.; in 1760, 18*s*. 6*d*.* The industrious labourer must thus have had at his command a larger share of the good things of this world than before, and a corresponding change for the better took place in his mode of life. Wheaten bread, which there is reason to suppose had been commonly used by the lower class of people in many parts of England, in the golden days that preceded the accession of Henry VII., had afterwards ceased to form part of the food of the peasantry; and had been superseded by rye and barley, except in the northern counties, where oats, either alone or mixed with peas, had always been the usual bread-corn. In the concluding years of

---

* The prices of meat and wool are taken partly from Eden's Hist. of the Poor, and partly from the Pict. Hist. of England.

the seventeenth century, however, wheat began to come again into more general use. Early in the following century, it was certainly eaten by the poorest people in some of the southern counties; and in 1764, according to calculations made with great care about that time, very little besides wheaten bread was eaten in any part of England except the northern and some of the north midland counties. With respect to meat, it was supposed by the eminent political writer, Gregory King, in 1696, that there were no persons in England, except paupers, who might not eat it twice a week. As for beer, in order to prove it to have been the universal beverage, it need only be said that the annual average quantity which paid duty in the ten years ending with 1693, was sufficient to allow more than a barrel for every individual, man, woman, or child, in the kingdom. It appears unquestionable, from all these statements, that the real price of labour rose considerably at a time when the market was greatly overstocked. Such a phenomenon, of course, could not have occurred, if the price had been suffered freely to adjust itself, according to the proportion between the supply and the demand, but this was prevented by the influence of the Poor Laws, the operation of which must now be briefly explained.

The act which is popularly regarded as the foundation of the existing Poor Laws, is the 43d Eliz. cap. 2., which ordained that, in every parish, a fund should be raised by taxation of the inhabitants, not merely for the relief of the aged and infirm, but for setting to work. all persons having no means to maintain themselves, and using no ordinary or daily trade of life, to get their living by. The momentous consequences with which this ordinance was pregnant, were not at first discovered. For many years the law remained nearly a dead letter: in most parishes no assessments at all were made, and in few or none was the amount collected sufficient for its object; so that the poverty in which the lower classes were very generally sunk, was left almost unopposed to exert its natural influence, in increasing the numbers and necessity of the poor. The country again became as much infested with vagrants as ever, and the evil, aggravated no doubt by the disorders of the civil war, at length reached such a height that, in 1662, Parliament, undismayed by former failures, once more attempted to put a stop to it. With this view was passed the celebrated act of the 13 Car. II. cap. 12. which, deviating from former principles of legislation, refrained from threatening wandering beggars with whipping, branding, slavery, and death, but strove to rouse the activity of parish officers, by enabling any needy intruder into a strange parish, who should not be removed within forty days, to obtain a settlement there, and a consequent claim to relief in the event of his afterwards becoming destitute. This law was completely successful, and, so long as it remained in force, which, with some modifications, it did till the year 1795, the English labourer was almost literally imprisoned within the bounds of his parish. The success was, however, dearly purchased. When people were forbidden to seek a livelihood elsewhere, it was impossible to refuse to maintain them in their place of birth, and the benevolent intentions of the 43d Elizabeth could be no longer disregarded. Able-bodied paupers could not indeed be set to work, according to the directions of that statute. In every place there is only a certain amount of work to be done, and only a certain amount of capital to pay for it; and, if the number of workmen be more than proportionate to the work, employment can only be given to those who want it by taking it from those who have it. But there could not in general be any reason for replacing one set of workmen by another; and those who had been unemployed were therefore, for the most part, permitted to remain in idleness, and were subsisted gratuitously. But they were not merely furnished with a bare subsistence. The parish authorities, in some instances, moved by the pity which the sight of undeserved misfortune naturally excites, and willing enough to be charitable at other people's expense,—perceiving also numerous ways in which they themselves might profit from a large expenditure upon the poor,—did not confine themselves to relieving the necessities of the destitute, but supplied the paupers whom they maintained in idleness with comforts which many a hardworking man could not hope to obtain. We learn from writers of the second half of the seventeenth century, that, at a time when two-thirds of all the bread used in England was made of rye, barley, oats, or peas, parish paupers seldom condescended to eat any that was not made of the finest wheaten flour, and drank none but the strongest beer. Even in the years immediately succeeding 1723, when the formation of workhouses was authorised, although most of those establishments were at first economically managed, there were some whose inmates were served with meat dinners at least three or four times a week; the rest of their diet consisting of suet and hasty puddings, bread and cheese, broth, milk and peas porridge, potatoes, fresh vegetables, and beer. When idleness was so liberally rewarded, and when the poor might obtain a more comfortable subsistence from the parish than they could possibly earn by their own exertions, their desire for employment must have greatly abated. They had no inducement to compete with their neighbours, or to offer to work for lower wages than were commonly paid. If they could not obtain the usual wages, they had recourse at once to the parish; and all of the very numerous class that prefer ease to independence were glad of an excuse for so doing. Thus, although the market was greatly overstocked with labour, the price did not fall, because only part of the whole stock was really offered for sale; and the same cause afterwards permitted the price to rise with the increasing demand for labour, although the whole stock in the market was increasing at the same time in a still larger proportion. It cannot be denied that one immediate effect of the Poor Laws, as administered at this time, was to keep up the rate of wages, and to raise the whole body of labourers, whether employed or unemployed, from their former state of want and wretchedness; and it may seem that, by removing one principal source of recklessness and improvidence, they must have acted as a check upon population. They seem really to have had this effect for some time. At least, if the calculations of the late Mr. Rickman* may be trusted, the population of England and Wales, which, in the sixty years ending with 1630, had increased from 4,123,708 to 5,600,517, a difference of nearly a million and a half of souls, increased by less than half a million in the seventy years succeeding 1630, having reached to only 6,045,008 in 1700. For some years after the commencement of the eighteenth century it seems to have even declined, and was very little more than six millions and a half in 1750. But whatever tendency the Poor Laws may at first have had to retard population in this way, was ultimately more than counterbalanced by their influence in another. If they rendered the poor man unwilling to forfeit his newly acquired comfort by any act of imprudence, they also went far to convince him that there was no imprudence in marrying without the means of maintaining a family, since additional parish assistance would be readily afforded to enable him to bear any burden which he might bring upon himself. If, by raising the rate of wages, they elevated the position of the independent labourer,

* Population Returns, 1841. Preface, pp. 36, 37.

and made him careful to avoid any thing that might reduce him to a lower level; they, on the other hand, encouraged the dependent pauper to consult only his own inclinations, without regard to the consequences. After the middle of the eighteenth century, the thoughtless profusion which had formerly marked the administration of the Poor Laws, but which had been somewhat repressed by the 9th George I. cap. 7., became more extravagant than before; and thenceforward those laws weakened, instead of strengthening, the impediments to marriage, and stimulated population still more powerfully than the indigence they had temporarily relieved. In the forty years immediately succeeding 1750, an addition of more than two millions was made to the numbers of the people, which were then raised to 8,675,000. So vast an increase of population might seem sufficient of itself to account for the enormous increase of pauperism which took place at the same time, but some minor causes may be mentioned which helped to aggravate the evil. The facility with which parish relief could be obtained, no doubt rendered many idle who might otherwise have earned their own livelihood; and many, on the other hand, were deprived of their accustomed occupation by the partial abandonment of tillage, which, though in general very greatly extended, ceased almost entirely in particular places. Men who had amassed fortunes in trade or other pursuits, and desired to possess suitable country residences, if they could not persuade a decayed family to part with its hereditary seat, purchased some of the outlying lands of an estate, and cleared half a dozen farms and a score or two of cottages to make a park.  Goldsmith's "Deserted Village" is probably not too highly coloured a picture of the desolation produced by such a process; and its outlines, at least, were certainly copied from nature.  The poet must have seen

> "One only master grasp the whole domain,
> And half a tillage stint the smiling plain;"

or he would not have described so circumstantially how

> "The man of wealth and pride
> Takes up a space that many poor supplied;
> Space for his lake, his park's extended bounds,
> Space for his horses, equipage, and hounds;"

nor how

> "The seat where solitary sports are seen,
> Indignant spurns the cottage from the green."

He had also, perhaps, observed the villagers leaving their cherished abodes, and witnessed

> "The sorrows of that parting day,
> That call'd them from their native walks away,
> When the poor exiles, every pleasure past,
> Hung round the bowers, and fondly look'd their last;
> And took a long farewell, and wish'd in vain
> For seats like those beyond the western main."

Possibly he may have tracked them in their subsequent wanderings, and noticed, that when

> "To some common's fenceless limits stray'd,
> They drove their flocks to pick the scanty blade,
> Those fenceless fields the sons of wealth divide,
> And ev'n the bare worn common is denied."

Or "if to the city sped," he could not fail to meet with stragglers, who

> "By cold and hunger led,
> At proud men's doors would ask a little bread."

Among the lines here quoted is an allusion to a circumstance, much too important to be omitted from the list of causes which have contributed to the degradation of the English peasantry. I mean, the inclosure and partition of common land. A hundred and fifty years ago, there was scarcely a parish without a considerable extent of waste, on which every householder was at liberty to turn out a cow, or a pig or two, or a few sheep or fowls. The poor man, therefore, even after the loss of the fields anciently attached to his cottage, might nevertheless contrive to supply his family with plenty of milk, and eggs and bacon, at little or no expense to himself. He has since in most instances been deprived of this advantage also. His rights of common belonged to him only in his quality of householder; they were communicated and surrendered with the cottage which he inhabited, and the enjoyment of them consequently depended on the permission of the landowners of the parish, whose property the waste land within its precincts in reality was. Early in the last century, landed proprietors began to see with regret the neglect of these extensive portions of their estates, which might be made to add very considerably to their incomes, and applications were made to Parliament for power to divide and inclose them. Little opposition was made to propositions apparently so well calculated to promote the national welfare. More than two hundred inclosure bills were passed in the reign of George II., and between the date of the accession of George III. and the year 1832, not less than 3,635 became law. A vast extent of territory has been brought into cultivation, and great benefit it must be allowed has accrued, not only to the owners but to the bulk of the community; but these advantages have been obtained at the expense of one unfortunate class, and that the one least able to afford it. In the great majority of parishes, the agricultural labourer has been deprived of the right of pasture, and with it of one of his chief sources of wealth. He can scarcely ever keep a cow except in districts in which the " allotment system" has been lately revived, and has for the most part been reduced to dependence on the scanty and precarious wages of hired service. It is true that in inclosure bills compensation is usually awarded to every owner of common rights, but the compensation is obtained ultimately, if not immediately, by the proprietors, and not by the occupiers of cottages. The land annexed to a cottage is soon detached, and united to the adjoining farm, and even where cottagers are owners of their own dwellings, their allotments generally fall at last into the hands of some rich neighbour. In ninety-nine cases out of a hundred, the poor man has lost his rights of common without any permanent equivalent.

When Goldsmith wrote, and indeed throughout the first half of the reign of George III., the condition of the English peasantry must have presented a very melancholy aspect to all who could perceive how much the foundations of their independence were undermined. As far, however, as regarded the actual supply of their physical wants, there was as yet little reason to pity them. Prices of provisions, and particularly of corn, were indeed higher than they had been for many years, but the rise was not very material, and the earnings of an industrious labourer were in general sufficient to secure to his family an adequate supply of the necessaries of life, or if there were a deficiency, the parish was in general ready to supply it. But with the year 1795 commenced a new and distressful era. The price of corn rose at once from 52s. to 74s. per quarter, and the average price during the last six years of the century was 72s. 6d., being raised to that height principally by the prevalence of bad seasons, both in England and on the Continent. This cause, and others arising out of the war then raging, raised the price of other articles, as well as of corn. Butcher's meat, beer, butter, and cheese, became about twice as dear as before, and coals and candles about one-third dearer. Clothing and other manufactured articles, it is true, became cheaper, and house-rent, probably, remained unaltered; but on the whole, and considering how small a part these items form of a poor man's expenditure, it may be asserted that considerably more than one half was added between 1795 and

1800 to the cost of the necessaries of life. In the mean time, although the wages of some kinds of artisans were slightly augmented, those of agricultural labourers remained at their former rate; that is to say, at about 7s. a week, on an average. No calculation is needed to show, that on such an income, in such times, it was scarcely possible for a family to subsist, and the Poor Laws were found to be no longer adequate to afford the required assistance. This arose from no defect of zeal on the part of their administrators. Public opinion had undergone a wonderful change since the time when the poor were regarded as public nuisances, whom it was allowable to get rid of by every possible means, and it was now thought to be the duty of a community to maintain all its members in comfort. The justices of the peace, who by virtue of certain enactments, framed with a very different view, had taken upon themselves to order relief for whomsoever they pleased out of the parish funds, do not seem to have doubted their ability, with the means at their disposal, to discharge this duty for the community. Early in 1795, the magistrates of Berkshire attempted to "settle the incomes of the industrious poor," by issuing an edict which directed parish officers to make up the wages of a labourer to a sum varying with the price of bread, and the numbers of his family, and the example was followed in most of the southern counties. In the following year an act was passed, formally investing the magistrates with the powers which they had already begun to exercise, and enabling a single justice to order relief for any poor person at his or her home; and while discussing this bill, some of the most eminent members of the House of Commons took occasion to expound the principles by which, in their judgment, the grant of relief ought to be regulated. It was distinctly asserted by such men as Pitt, Fox, and Whitbread, that a labourer's remuneration should be proportioned, not to his services, but to his wants; that a single man ought not to be paid so much as a man with a family, and that if the earnings of the latter were not sufficient for his comfortable support, the deficiency ought to be made up out of the poor's rate. Maxims, promulgated by such high authority, and coinciding so exactly with the sentiments previously held by the majority of the administrators of the Poor Laws, were forthwith taken by the latter for their rule of conduct, but it does not appear that any important results followed immediately from their adoption. The amount annually expended on the poor became indeed about twice as great as previously to 1795, but the difference was not more than proportionate to the increased dearness of provisions, and could not provide for the maintenance of an additional number of persons. It was, in fact, impossible, when the whole stock of food in the country was reduced much below the usual quantity, to assign to every individual his usual allowance, or to increase one .person's share without diminishing that of another; and as it can hardly be supposed that people in easy circumstances curtailed their accustomed meals in order to give to the poor, the evils of the scarcity must have fallen almost exclusively upon the latter. It is not, indeed, so long ago but that many persons living can well recollect how severe the sufferings of the labouring class were at that time, and with what difficulty they contrived to struggle through them. Their indigence was, however, too recent as yet to produce those effects upon population, which have been elsewhere ascribed to it. Wretchedness must become habitual, in order to produce recklessness and indifference to the future. While the remembrance of happier times remains, happier times may be looked for, and a man may wish to wait till they arrive, before incurring fresh burdens. It seems, nevertheless, to have been, not a diminution in the number of marriages, but an increase of mortality consequent upon extreme poverty, that caused population to proceed at a somewhat slower rate between 1790 and 1801 than during the decennial period immediately preceding. The census taken in the last-mentioned year showed the number of inhabitants of England and Wales to be 9,168,000, or not quite half a million more than the number estimated in 1790. The increase in the ten years after 1780 is supposed to have been 722,000.

Between 1801 and 1810, prices rose still higher than before. The average price of corn was about 82s., and the cost of most other provisions increased in as great or a greater proportion. Some portion of the rise of prices was only apparent, being occasioned by the depreciation of the currency consequent upon the Bank Restriction Act of 1797, but, except in 1801 and 1802, when the price of gold rose about 8 per cent., the depreciation of money was as yet too trifling to have much effect. Some compensation for the increased expense of living was however at last afforded to several important sections of the labouring class by very considerable additions to their earnings. The continuance of the war, and England's pre-eminence at sea, gave to this country a superiority over her commercial rivals, which, by the genius and inventions of Arkwright, Cartwright, and Watt, was almost converted into a monopoly of foreign trade. Britain became the workshop of the world, and the greatly augmented demand for all kinds of skilled and manufacturing labour, caused the wages of artizans, and of most descriptions of operatives, to rise, until, by the year 1810, they were in general double what they had been twenty years before. This improvement was, however, almost confined to the towns, and was shared in only a very small measure by the inhabitants of the country. A vast extension of agriculture was indeed occasioned by the exorbitant price of corn, and much waste land was brought into cultivation, but it is doubtful whether much additional employment was given, in consequence, to agricultural labourers. The high profits of farming had caused that business to be undertaken by a new class of men ; and the small farmers of former days were in a great measure supplanted by large capitalists, renting each his one or two thousand acres.

By these, more expensive and more scientific

implements and processes were introduced, and the productiveness of the soil was probably increased, but at the same time a saving of labour was effected, which rendered the services of a smaller number of persons necessary. In spite then of the extension of tillage, the wages of agricultural labourers might very probably have remained stationary, if an upward direction had not been given to them by the operation of the Poor Laws. The principles which in the last years of the preceding century had been admitted into the theory as well as the practice of these laws, were still as fashionable as ever, and the wealth which commerce was rapidly pouring into the country, furnished much more abundant means of carrying them into effect. The amount expended annually on the poor, rose again about 50 per cent., or from about four to six millions sterling, and the provision thus made for a portion of the class of agricultural labourers, enabled the remainder to demand, and to obtain, an increase of wages. Their earnings were augmented by about one half, rising to, perhaps, 10s. a week on an average, though it is difficult to ascertain the average of rates which vary so greatly in different counties. But this augmentation of wages, disproportionate as it was to the advance of prices, was far from restoring agricultural labourers to the position they had occupied before the war broke out, or from relieving them from the necessity of still enduring very severe privations. Their discomfort was moreover aggravated, by a circum-

stance independent of the scantiness of their
incomes. Until recently, it had been common for
farm-servants, even when married and living in
their own cottages, to take their meals with their
master; and, what was of more consequence, in
every farm-house, many unmarried servants of
both sexes were lodged as well as boarded. The
latter, therefore, even if ill paid, might be tolerably
housed and fed, and many of them no doubt fared
much better than they could have done if they had
been left to provide for themselves with treble
their actual wages. All had at least an example
of good living before them, which, if they did not
otherwise benefit by it, could not fail to have a
salutary effect in raising their ideas of comfort,
and rendering them unwilling to place themselves
in a position in which those ideas could not possibly be realised.

It was only men of simple manners, however,
who could consent to associate so familiarly with
their servants. When gentlemen became farmers,
few besides domestic servants were admitted into
the house; the others received a pecuniary allowance in lieu of their old privileges of board and
lodging, and were left to obtain these as they could.
It will be easily understood, that this banishment
from the farm-house must have been keenly felt,
and that the rustic bachelor, whether he attempted
to keep house for himself, or lodged with a stranger's family, must have found a cheerless home
on his return from work in the fields. So disagreeable a situation, he may have thought, could

scarcely become worse, and bad as it was, he could scarcely hope that time would improve it; so that if he fancied a wife would enliven his solitude, he had little inducement to balk his inclinations, or to wait till a more suitable moment should arrive for gratifying them. One circumstance, it should be mentioned, which might have compelled him to delay his marriage, viz., the difficulty of procuring a separate habitation, now no longer existed. To pay the rent of a poor cottager had become a very common mode of affording him parochial relief, and parish overseers and vestry-men had discovered, that a very lucrative property might be created by building cottages for the poor.

This was not the only mode in which the en-couragement afforded to marriage by the Poor Laws had of late been materially increased. Although ever since the middle of the eighteenth century it had been more or less usual to extend gratuitous assistance from the parish funds to men with large families whose earnings were insufficient for their comfortable support, the practice was not legalised until 1796, and until that year no able-bodied per-son, not being an inmate of a workhouse, could *demand* relief, however little difficulty there might be in obtaining it; but in a very few years afterwards the plan recommended by the Berkshire magistrates and by Mr. Pitt, became very generally acted upon throughout the country. Heads of families were assumed to be entitled to certain incomes, varying with the number of mouths they had to feed; and if any one's wages were unequal to the amount

considered to be his due, the parish readily made
up the deficiency. Thenceforward a poor man
might lay aside all thought for to-morrow, and
solace himself with the belief, that whatever family
he might bring around him, he should be maintained in the position which he actually occupied;
nay, it might almost be said that a positive bounty
was placed on procreation, for as the more children
a man had, the more money he received, a large
family might be regarded as a source of wealth.
Even this was not all. If any resolute bachelor
were found capable of withstanding every temptation to marriage, and anxious to gain a livelihood
by other means than by begetting a pauper pro-
geny, it often happened that no choice was offered
to him. If married and single men were applying
for work at the same time, the farmers sagely
argued, that as the former would be the heaviest
burden on the poor-rates, it would be most politic
to enable them to earn something for themselves,
and the rejected bachelor found that he would not
be allowed to maintain himself unless he first got a
wife and children for the parish to maintain.

The carelessness arising in part from extreme indigence, and produced in part by the influence of
the Poor Laws, no doubt augmented exceedingly
the frequency of marriage among certain classes;
but it is not asserted that this is the sole or even
the principal cause of the vast progress which popu-
tion has made during the present century, as well
as during the latter part of the preceding one. The
imprudent marriages of the poor can only augment

the numbers of their own class, but between 1801 and 1811 the number of inhabitants of England and Wales rose from 8,872,980 to 10,150,615, a difference of 1,277,635, and it would be ridiculous to imagine that this immense addition was made to the number of persons destitute of adequate means of support. Although some important sections of the people became impoverished, the aggregate wealth of the nation was fast and steadily increasing *,

* The fact of the great and continued increase of the national wealth during this period cannot, I think, be reasonably questioned; yet it seems irreconcileable with the evidence of documents which are commonly appealed to as the best authorities. I allude to the Parliamentary Returns.

Increase of national wealth, it must be premised, implies increase of national income. A nation can scarcely, like an individual, grow rich by mere parsimony, for it must always expend the whole, or nearly the whole, of its average income. When an individual is said to save, it is not usually understood that he lays his savings by, and suffers them to remain idle; he commonly either employs, that is to say, expends them, in his own business, or lends them at interest to be employed or expended by others. At any rate, it is only money, plate, and jewels that are, strictly speaking, hoarded; for no man in his senses goes on filling warehouse after warehouse with bulky goods, to serve for his consumption in far distant years. Unless he has reason to think he can profitably dispose of the surplus, he produces little more than may suffice for present use. But money, plate, and jewels constitute only a very insignificant item in national property, which consists chiefly of bulky articles, — provisions, manufactures, buildings, ships, and raw materials, the annual production of all of which is proportioned as nearly as possible to the expected annual consumption. The only articles that can be called permanent acquisitions are those which, from their durable character, may remain long in use without being destroyed. But accessions of wealth of this kind, however conducive to the

and most of the miscellaneous classes that were
benefited by this increase of wealth, became enlarged in proportion as additional means of subsistence were supplied to them.   The increase of population was therefore in a great measure owing to the
increase of the means of subsistence, and if it had been
no more than proportionate to this latter increase,

convenience of the inhabitants, add nothing to a country's productive resources, or to the means of subsistence, except in so
far as they occasion an increase in the national income.

Now, a little reflection will show, that national income cannot
possibly be augmented except in two modes, viz., either by an
increase of the produce of the native soil, or by an increase of
foreign imports.  But although, during the first ten years of the
present century, British agriculture was undoubtedly very
greatly extended and very greatly improved, the good effects
of this progress were, in a great measure, counterbalanced by the
frequency of deficient harvests, so that probably no considerable
addition was made to the average annual amount of native
agricultural produce.   The principal increase must apparently,
therefore, have taken place in foreign imports ; but this conclusion is contradicted by the Returns of Trade, laid before
Parliament.   In these the *official* value of imports into Great
Britain, which, though affording no clue to their *real* value, is
considered a tolerable index to the relative quantities of the goods
imported, is stated to have been, —

| In 1801 | - | £30,435,268 | In 1806 | - | £25,554,478 |
|---|---|---|---|---|---|
| 1802 | - | 28,308,373 | 1807 | - | 25,326,845 |
| 1803 | - | 25,104,541 | 1808 | - | 25,660,953 |
| 1804 | - | 26,454,281 | 1809 | - | 30,170,292 |
| 1805 | - | 27,334,020 | 1810 | - | 37,663,284 |

It would thus appear that the quantity of goods imported in
1801 was greater than in any other year previous to 1810. But
if this was really the case, how could the national income be
continually increasing ?  This apparent inconsistency may, perhaps, be easily explained by persons better versed in statistics,
but I must confess myself fairly puzzled by it.

it would have been a national blessing rather than an evil; but that it greatly exceeded these just limits is manifest from the simultaneous extension of pauperism and indigence, and it cannot be doubted that the principal source of the excess was the frequency of marriage among the poor. Another cause, however, that sensibly contributed to the same result, must not be overlooked. There was already a by no means inconsiderable influx of Irish labourers, who could not, of course, obtain employment without depressing, or at least keeping down, the wages of labour, and compelling some of their English competitors to have recourse to the poor's-rates.

From the beginning of the year 1811 to the pacification of 1814, prices underwent no reduction, and were indeed apparently much increased, the average price of corn, for example, rising to 100s. The wages of labour, however, likewise rose to 12s. in 1811, and to 14s. in 1812, and remained at the same height during the two following years; and although the rise, like that of prices, was in part only nominal, and produced by the depreciation of the currency (which was 8 per cent. in 1811, and from 20 to 25 per cent. in 1812, 1813, and 1814), it was also in part a real and substantial benefit to the labourer. The value of the currency was not entirely restored until 1821, but subsequently to 1817 the depreciation was too trifling to have much influence upon prices, which were further depressed in consequence of the cessation of the political causes that had contributed to enhance them during the war. The average price of corn during the six years ending with 1820 consequently fell to 77*s.*, and the price of most other necessaries fell with it. On the other hand, the average of agricultural wages also fell to 12*s.* in 1815, and remained at about the same level until the end of 1820, but the fall being less than the fall of prices, not only did not cause a deterioration of the labourer's condition, but left it even somewhat improved. On the whole, therefore, it appears, that independently both of the fall of prices and of the effects of a depreciated currency, agricultural wages were considerably higher between 1811 and 1820, than in the ten years immediately preceding. That they should have become so at a time when every village was swarming with people out of employment, is an anomaly which cannot, perhaps, be explained except by reference to the cause which has already been mentioned as having formerly produced similar phenomena, viz. the influence of the Poor Laws. The profusion which had long characterised the administration of those laws, was not only unchecked, but, though assuredly needing no additional stimulus, was fondly encouraged by the legislature. In 1815, an Act, commonly styled East's Act, was passed, which, as if it were not enough that justices of the peace could order relief for whomsoever they pleased, as often as they pleased, empowered them further to order such relief to be continued for three months together; and not content with allowing the poor to be relieved at their own homes instead of in a work-

house, when the justices saw fit, now expressly declared that they should not be required to enter a
workhouse, but should receive relief at home as
matter of right. The historical importance of this
law, like that of most similar documents, lies less
in its own positive injunctions than in the light
which it throws on the opinions and principles generally current at the time it was framed; and with
such a proof before us of the prodigal liberality
with which the poor were treated, we may at first
be disposed to wonder that the amount expended
on them did not increase more rapidly than it actually
did. The amount of poor's rates, which was probably
about six millions sterling in 1810, was not more
than 7,330,254*l.* in 1820; but in consequence of
the fall of prices, the additional relief granted was
really much greater than these figures indicate.
Six millions sterling in 1810 would purchase only
1,132,075 quarters of wheat, whereas 2,155,957
quarters might have been purchased for 7,330,256*l.*
in 1820; and it may be presumed, that pauperism
had advanced in the interval in something like the
same proportion. If it be considered further, that
the independent labourer, notwithstanding the recent amelioration of his condition, was still very
scantily supplied with the necessaries of life, it will
be seen that the two causes which have been mentioned as the chief incentives to thoughtless marriages were still in existence. It may also be seen,
that they were acting with unusual force. The
census of 1821 showed the number of inhabitants
of England and Wales to be 11,978,875, or 1,828,260

more than in 1811.   So vast an accession of population in so short a space of time, and in a territory
of the same extent, was, perhaps, never made in any
other country; at least nothing equal to it ever
occurred either in the United States or in Ireland.
The greater part of it may, perhaps, be ascribed to
the progress of national wealth, and a further portion was, no doubt, the result of immigration from
Ireland; but after making every possible deduction
on these accounts, there is still an immense remainder, which may fairly be regarded as the effect
partly of poverty and partly of a mismanaged provision for the poor.

A somewhat similar explanation may be given of
the still greater progress of population in the next
decennial period, during which the indigence of a
considerable class remained unabated, and the abuses
of poor law administration uncorrected, while the
aggregate wealth of the country increased faster
than ever, and extraordinary facilities were afforded
to immigrants by the more general use of steam
navigation.   At the census of 1831, the number of
inhabitants in England and Wales was found to be
13,894,574, an increase of not less than 1,915,699
since 1821.   Subsequently to 1820, prices of provisions had continued to fall, the average price of
corn during the ten years ending with 1830 being
only 59s. the quarter, but agricultural wages had
likewise suffered a decline, the average, which had
been 12s. a week in 1820, having sunk to 10s. in
1821, and to 9s. in 1823, and not having risen above
11s. during the next seven years.   The principal

cause of this decline was the pecuniary distress of the farmers, occasioned by the decreased value of their produce, which compelled them to contract as much as possible the expenses of cultivation. The cheapness of provisions, however, which led the farmers to attempt a reduction of wages, also assisted them in effecting their object. A smaller sum being required for a pauper's maintenance, and less being consequently assigned for the purpose, the independent labourer could no longer command his former wages by threatening to throw himself upon the parish, for, rather than take this step, it was better for him to submit to a certain reduction.* Still, from a comparison of wages and prices, it does not appear that the labourer's condition was now further deteriorated : on the contrary, it was probably, if any thing, a little improved, though the alteration either way was too small to deserve notice. The impulse which population receives from poverty had consequently lost little, if any thing, of its force, and the encouragement afforded

---

* It cannot be denied that in this instance the rate of wages was in part determined by the price of provisions, but this can only happen where the circumstances which naturally regulate the price of labour are arbitrarily interfered with. When the money price of labour is suffered to adjust itself according to the proportion between the supply and the demand, it will remain unaffected by any variations in the prices of provisions or other commodities. But where, by means of a poor law, wages are raised above their natural level, and are forced up to a sum sufficient to purchase a certain quantity of necessaries, they may be expected to fall whenever a fall of prices reduces the sum required for that purpose.

by the poor laws was likewise still as strong as ever. It might therefore have been expected, that the amount expended in the relief of pauperism would have increased; but this was not the case. Whether calculated in pounds sterling, or in quarters of wheat, the amount so expended was greater in the first than in the last year of the series, or than in any of the intervening years, with one single exception. From this it would appear, that although pauperism undoubtedly increased considerably in several counties, the increase was more than counterbalanced by the decrease in others, and that population, notwithstanding its wonderful progress, did not become more redundant. Neither the aggregate number, nor the necessities of the poor, received any augmentation. This can only be accounted for by supposing that the wealth and resources of the country increased as fast as the population, and it is certain that they did increase with unexampled rapidity. The national income had never been so copiously supplied from each of the sources from which it has been shown to be derived. On the one hand, the productiveness of the soil had been so much augmented, that notwithstanding the vast addition made to the numbers of the people, the corn consumed by them in 1821, 1822, and 1823, though supplied in abundance, and at a moderate rate, was almost exclusively of home growth, — a phenomenon that had not occurred for more than thirty years. In 1824 and 1825 also, the imports of foreign corn were not very considerable. On the other hand, the official value of foreign imports of all kinds rose from 27,769,122*l.* in 1821, to 44,815,397*l.* in 1830, an advance to which, if it were not altogether unprecedented, at least no parallel can be found in the Parliamentary Returns of preceding years.

The causes, whatever they may have been, which between 1821 and 1830 prevented an increase of the expenditure upon the poor, continued to act in the four years next succeeding, in no one of which was the pecuniary amount so great as in 1820, nor the corresponding value in wheat so great as in 1822. Owing, however, to the low price of agricultural produce, the same amount of poor's rates as had once been easily borne, had now become an almost intolerable burthen on the land. On many estates, chiefly in the southern counties, the rates swallowed up nearly the whole rent, and it was evident that, if much more increased, they would cause the land to be abandoned, through the impossibility of cultivating it without loss. In some instances this result had already happened, and in particular one entire parish, that of Cholesbury, in Buckinghamshire, had been absolutely deserted by the proprietor. Meanwhile the demoralisation of the lazy, insolent paupers, who lived at ease at the expense of the industrious, was daily becoming more conspicuous, and frequent outrages, equally brutal and cowardly, committed upon those who attempted to bridle their license, showed to what lengths they were prepared to go on the slightest provocation, and how little they retained of those sterling qualities for which the English peasantry had once been renowned. In short, a crisis was at hand, which it was obvious would, unless averted, utterly overthrow the national greatness, leave the country a prey to anarchy and disorder, and reduce all classes of the people to misery. The approach of these calamities had long been perceived; but ordinary minds shrank from a struggle with evils of such magnitude, and successive statesmen held the helm of government without making one vigorous effort to steer the vessel of the state from the breakers upon which she was fast driving. Happily, the direction of affairs was at last entrusted to abler hands; and stronger heads were invited to consult on the measures which the dangers of the times required. After two years spent in anxious and careful deliberation, a plan for the removal of the existing evil was submitted to Parliament, and being carried through both Houses by great majorities, received the royal assent on the 14th August, 1834, and became the celebrated Poor Law Amendment Act. Without entering into a detailed account of this memorable statute, it will be sufficient to state, that its fundamental principle is the necessity of making the condition of the dependent pauper less agreeable than that of the independent labourer, and that a principal means by which this principle is proposed to be enforced, is the refusal of parochial relief to the able-bodied elsewhere than within the walls of a workhouse. No time was lost in carrying the new law into effect. In less than a year after its enactment it was in active operation in 112 unions, comprehending 2,066 parishes, and one tenth of the whole population of England and Wales. The change produced by its introduction was almost magical. The first unions were intentionally formed in the most intensely pauperised districts, in which there had previously seemed to be the most decided symptoms of over-population. Scarcely a parish could have been found amongst them, in which there were not some able-bodied labourers out of employment, and in many places a hundred and more were entirely supported, during one half of the year, at the expense of the parish. When, however, these men found that they would no longer be allowed to spend their days basking in the sun, or playing at pitch and toss, and their evenings in the alehouse, but must either submit to the confinement and discipline of a workhouse, or earn a livelihood by their own labour, it soon appeared that the latter alternative was attended with little real difficulty: very few who could work were really unable to procure employment, and compelled to apply for parochial relief. In the county of Sussex, for example, in which, in 1834, there had been 6160 able-bodied paupers, there were only 124 remaining in the summer of 1835: in four unions in Kent, the number was reduced from 954 to 5. All the rest found means of providing for themselves, and most of them without leaving their respective parishes. It appeared, after searching inquiries, that only about half a dozen men in each of the Kentish unions had quitted it in search of work elsewhere, and these were fellows whom no one would trust, and who were obliged to go to other places to renew their characters. One or two of them had been tempted, by the prospect of pay and glory, to enter the service of the Queen of Spain. Indeed, except from Suffolk and Buckinghamshire, from which about 200 families were persuaded to remove to the manufacturing districts, no considerable migration of agricultural labourers seems to have taken place from the southern counties.* Almost the whole of them remained in their native villages, but nevertheless found means of keeping themselves out of the workhouse. It is deserving of notice, that the absorption of so much additional labour was not accompanied by any reduction of wages. This might not be difficult to account for, in places in which it had been usual to eke out wages from the poor's rates, and to pay all men, whether industrious or idle, alike, — or at least without reference to any other distinction than their wants. There, the reclaimed paupers might be receiving the same sums as before, because, after they ceased to be chargeable to the parish, the funds for the remuneration of labour would be increased exactly as much as the poor's rates were diminished. But in many parishes it had been usual to make a difference, though generally only a small one, between paupers and independent labourers; and here it might have been expected, that the competition of the latter, when thrown upon their own resources, would lower the rate of wages. If, for example, where an industrious man could earn 12s. a week,

* Mr. Muggeridge's Report to Poor Law Commissioners on Home Migration.

the weekly allowances made to paupers were 10s. each, the farmers would save only 10s. in poor's rates for every one of the latter who ceased to be chargeable to the parish, and could not, it may be thought, pay him a larger sum in wages, without paying less to their other labourers. It appears, however, that when the remuneration of the quondam paupers was made to depend upon the value of their services, they exerted themselves accordingly, and their industry created new funds for its own recompense. The produce of labour became larger than before, and the farmers were enabled to appropriate a larger portion of this produce to the payment of wages, and were induced to do so by the wish to keep to themselves labour which had now become so profitable.

Although, however, the symptoms of over-population were so much lessened, it must not be imagined that they had been altogether deceptive. Work had been shown to exist for most of those who required it, but there were still a few persons who, being unable to procure employment, were obliged to take refuge in the workhouse. The earnings of the employed also, though sufficient for subsistence, were, in many parts of the country, inadequate to satisfy even the most moderate ideas of comfort. Besides, it must be observed, that the New Poor Law was introduced at a peculiarly favourable juncture. The unusually abundant harvests of 1835 and 1836 not only lowered the prices of provisions, but, added to the unnatural activity prevailing in the manufacturing districts, created an

almost unexampled amount of employment.   The
temporary prosperity proceeding from those sources
was followed by a cruel reaction.   The distress of
the manufacturing classes in the years 1840, 1841,
and 1842, which has been already described, caused
less attention to be paid to the condition of agricultural labourers, but the latter also had to endure
privations, which, if somewhat less severe at the
time, have been far more lasting.  Their employers,
the farmers, had been impoverished in 1835 and
1836 by the very abundance and cheapness of
provisions, which to other classes were unalloyed
blessings, and would thus have been disabled from
employing so much labour as before, even if less
had not sufficed to gather in the comparatively
scanty crops of subsequent years.   The labourers
were therefore injured in two ways, — by the decrease of their earnings, and by the enhanced price
of necessaries ; and although the farmers meanwhile
were enabled partially to repair their previous losses,
they were soon afterwards depressed lower than
ever in consequence of the alteration of the corn
laws in 1842.   The facilities afforded by that measure to the importation of foreign corn have permanently reduced the price of agricultural produce
so much, that farmers have, in many instances,
found it impossible to pay their former rents without reducing other items of expenditure.   Of these
the largest, and at the same time the one most
completely under the farmer's control, is labour.
Less labour has of late been employed in agriculture, and what has been employed has been paid for

at lower rates. Wages have fallen, and the number
of men out of employment has increased, and both
these phenomena were especially perceptible in the
spring and summer of last year (1844). To the
effects of the poverty of the farmers were then
added those of a long-continued drought, which
put an almost entire stop to many operations of
husbandry, so that in what is commonly one of the
busiest seasons, numbers of able-bodied men were
idling about, vainly offering to work for a shilling
a day, and in many instances manifested their dis-
appointment by setting fire to barns and hayricks.
Thus, since 1837, the condition of agricultural
labourers in many parts of England has been unquestionably deteriorated, and the recklessness
arising from this cause has probably made up in a
great measure for the cessation of the impulse formerly given to population by the mal-administra-
tion of the poor laws. In this way may fairly be
accounted for a considerable part of the progress
which population made between 1836 and 1841,
and a farther portion must be attributed to the
influx of Irish immigrants, the extent of which may
be estimated from the fact, that at the date of the
last census the number of persons of Irish birth
dwelling in Great Britain was no less than 419,256.
These two are perhaps the only causes of any excessive increase of population that may have taken
place in this decennial period — the only causes,
that is, why population increased faster than the
means of subsistence. That it did so to a certain
extent is placed beyond doubt, both by the severer

and more extended distress observable among certain classes, and by the absolute amount of the increase itself, which at the last census was found to have been not less than 2,009,642 in the preceding ten years. During the same period, however, the value of foreign goods imported had advanced from 48,161,661*l.* to 62,684,587*l.*, so that the greater part of this vast increase in the numbers of the people seems to have been the legitimate consequence of the increase of the national resources.

It is easier to point out the general causes which have rendered the whole population of the country redundant, than to distinguish the particular circumstances which have caused the redundancy to be more remarkable in some districts than in others. Those counties, however, in which the class of agricultural labourers is most depressed, have all one thing in common. Each of them was formerly the seat of a flourishing manufacture carried on by the cottagers at their own homes, which has now decayed, or been withdrawn to other situations. Thus, in Buckinghamshire and Bedfordshire, the wives and children of labouring men had formerly very profitable occupation in making lace and straw-plait. During the last war, a tolerable lace-maker, working eight hours a-day, could easily earn 10*s.* or 12*s.* a-week, and at straw-plaiting, there were examples of women earning as much as 22*s.* a-week. The profits of both employments have since been so much reduced by the use of machinery, and the competition of Leghorn hats and bonnets, that a pillow-lace-maker must now work twelve hours daily to earn 2s. 6d. a-week, and a straw-plaiter is not very much better paid. It is possible that these manufactures, growing up as they no doubt did very gradually, and presenting a new means of defraying part of a family's expenses, may have promoted population, by inducing labourers to marry sooner than they would have done if they had been entirely dependent on their own wages. If this were the case, the rate of agricultural wages must have fallen in consequence, and when, after the decay of the domestic manufactures, those wages became the main stay of a family, their deficiency would of course be more decided than elsewhere.

A similar explanation may be offered with respect to Dorsetshire, where the making of wire shirt-buttons (now in a great measure superseded by the use of mother-of-pearl) once employed great numbers of women and children. At several places in Wiltshire, Somersetshire, Gloucestershire, and others of the western counties, most of the cottagers fifty years ago were weavers, whose chief dependence was their looms, though they worked in the fields at harvest-time and other busy seasons. By so doing, they kept down the wages of agricultural labourers who had no other employment, and now that they have themselves become dependent upon agriculture in consequence of the removal of the woollen manufacture from the cottage to the factory, these reduced wages have become their own portion also.

In this attempt to explain the excessive increase

of population in England and Wales, the reader's attention has been directed almost exclusively to the condition of the peasantry, because it is suspected that the population of towns is rarely increased faster than the means of subsistence, except by immigration from rural districts. Further inquiries it must be confessed are wanting for the satisfactory determination of this question, but several considerations seem to warrant the opinion just expressed. Town residents have not the same inducements to marry as dwellers in the country. Independently of the greater facilities they possess for the criminal gratification of their passions, they have freer access to society and to various amusements, which take them a good deal away from home, and enable them better to dispense with domestic comfort. * If, however, in spite of every motive for remaining single they do marry, with insufficient means, the foul atmosphere of the crowded localities in which they are for the most part obliged to live, heightening the effect of insufficiency of food and clothing, occasions a mortality among their children, which generally prevents any considerable increase of population from

---

* It is no refutation of this argument that in Glasgow, Manchester, and other large manufacturing towns, the number of marriages, in proportion to the population, is extraordinarily great. Owing to the continual influx of operatives, the proportion of inhabitants of marriageable age is much larger in such towns than elsewhere; so that, notwithstanding the increased force of dissuasives from matrimony, it is not very wonderful that marriages are unusually frequent.

this source. Numerous towns both at home and abroad might be instanced, in which population has remained stationary, or nearly so, for several generations, although in all towns, probably, the number of strangers entering in search of employment is always greater than that of the natives leaving on the same errand. Bruges and Rome are good examples. The records of births and deaths in the former, from 1700 to 1814, show a natural increase of only 8214 in 114 years, that is, an annual average increase of 2 in 1000. * In the latter, though that city be the resort of multitudes of beggars, ever flocking in from the country round, the population was actually decreasing for some years previously to 1842. † The case of Amsterdam is very similar. In the twelve years ending with 1832, the average annual number of deaths was 7336 ; of births, only 7282. ‡ In places in which population is long stationary, the means of subsistence may also be presumed to fluctuate little in amount, but even where these are rapidly increasing, and are attracting thousands of settlers from without, the increase of population from natural causes is often exceedingly small. In two of the most thriving towns of Great Britain, Liverpool and Bristol, it is, as we have already seen, absolutely nothing, the annual deaths being more numerous than the

* Macculloch, Geog. Dict.

† Statistical Tables of Pop. of Rome, inserted in Athenæum, No. 886, 19th Oct. 1844.

‡ Chambers' Popular Statistics.

births; and the same result would no doubt be exhibited in many other places, if we had statements of births and deaths in towns strictly so called, apart from the healthy suburban districts invariably associated with them in the Reports of the Registrar-General. From one case, that of the metropolis, in which we are enabled to sever this connection, we may judge of the erroneous conclusions to which the statements respecting other great towns are likely to lead.

In what is called the metropolitan district, extending from Kensington to Greenwich, and from the foot of Highgate-hill to Camberwell, the births, in 1840-41, exceeded the deaths by 8814; but, if we confine ourselves to the quarters in which the poor most thickly congregate, we shall generally find that the deaths exceed the births. This is the case in the subdivisions denominated St. Martin's in the Fields, East and West London, Whitechapel, St. Saviour's and St. Olave's, and Greenwich. In St. George's Hanover-square, Westminster, St. Giles and St. George, Strand, Holborn, and the city of London, there is a slight excess of births, too slight, however, to make up for the deficiency in the first-named quarters. If, then, in eleven out of the thirty sections into which the metropolis is divided by the Registrar-General, natural causes are not of themselves sufficient to prevent a decrease in the number of inhabitants, how much less likely are they to occasion an increase in the still more crowded recesses of Manchester, Leeds, and Birmingham.

Although, however, it is not probable that the urban population has been rendered excessive by natural increase, another cause of over-population, viz., the withdrawal from certain classes of part of the funds formerly appropriated to their maintenance, has had some operation in most towns of Great Britain in which textile manufactures are carried on. Hand-loom weavers, who are generally to be found in greater or smaller numbers in such towns, were once among the best paid, whereas they have now become the very worst paid of English operatives. The change is commonly ascribed to the introduction of the power-loom, and there can be no doubt that it was partly brought about by that circumstance. The use of the improved machinery, though it occasioned a vast augmentation of national wealth, and a corresponding addition to the demand for labour, lowered the price of fabrics produced by the hand-loom, and must necessarily have likewise lessened the earnings of hand-loom weavers. Only a small part, however, of the distress of the latter can be accounted for in this way ; for, long before power-looms came into general use, the condition of the hand-loom weavers had become very little better than at present. So far back as 1808 they were described, by a very competent witness *, as scarcely able by unremitting labour to keep themselves alive ; and from that year down to 1818, when the

* Mr. W. Radcliffe, cited by Macculloch, Statist. of Brit. Empire, vol. ii. p. 84.

power-loom was still a rarity, they never rose
again to a state of any thing like comfort. Their
depression seems, indeed, to have been principally
the result of the reaction consequent upon the
extrordinary prosperity they enjoyed in the interval between 1788 and 1803. During that period
a weaver's income, derived from the united labour
of his family, ranged from 40s. to even 120s. a-
week ; but such earnings were too high to be lasting. Crowds of emigrants were attracted by them
into the manufacturing districts, beyond what the
demand for labour, considerable as it was, could
absorb ; and, as the business of the cotton-loom
is extremely easy, requiring little strength and
less skill, it was adopted by all who could find
nothing else to do, by boys and girls, as well by
adults. The rate of wages in this employment,
consequently, sank far below its level in every
other. Nevertheless, the long-established hand-
loom weavers continued from old habit to ply
their accustomed vocation, and although their
own receipts were fast diminishing, suffered the
well-paid situations in the factories to be occupied
for the most part by strangers. They have very
generally brought up their children to the same
decaying trade, and their numbers have been further reinforced by the needy candidates for employment, common in most large towns, but particularly numerous in the north of England, where
plenty of Irishmen are always ready to fill up
vacancies in the list of hand-loom weavers, as fast

as they occur. Thus is the race perpetuated, and its misery prolonged.

In some other towns, chiefly in the southern and midland counties, distress and over-population have been produced by the transfer of manufactures formerly carried on there to more advantageous situations. This is an event which no foresight could have prevented; but the over-population created in this manner would be of short duration, if the evil proceeded from this source alone. The persons deprived of their accustomed means of support would necessarily be exposed for a time to privations more or less severe, but, unless recruited from the country, they would all probably ere long discover new modes of getting a livelihood, and a single generation would most likely suffice to re-establish the former proportion between the supply and the demand for labour. Their temporary sufferings, however, may serve to show that, as has been before observed, a diversion of industry from its accustomed channels, even into others wider and more commodious, is seldom an unmixed good, but though, perhaps, a national blessing, is almost always a curse to some individuals.

The disturbing influence of the poor laws renders it more difficult in England than elsewhere, to trace the tendency of poverty to augment population; yet, even here, the proofs of the reality of such a tendency are sufficiently obvious. It will be recollected that the peasantry, having, at the time of the Saxon conquest, been placed in circumstances which secured to them a competent livelihood, continued in

the enjoyment of plenty until the reign of Henry VII.
Great numbers of them were then suddenly deprived
of their occupations, and were subjected to privations so severe as to counteract the recklessness
which ever accompanies extreme indigence, and to
occasion a decrease rather than an increase of population.   After the lapse of a century, the field of
employment was again enlarged, and all who chose
to labour were enabled to earn more than enough
to keep them alive, though too little to keep them
in comfort.   The fecundity of poverty was then
allowed to produce permanent effects, and soon
covered the land with a fresh swarm of beggars,
for whom adequate provision was at length made by
the public, soon after the restoration of Charles II.
The poor laws, which then first came into active
operation, for a while relieved destitution without
greatly, or at least generally, impairing the utility
of prudence, and as long as they continued to act
in this manner, the progress of population was
decidedly retarded.   But, about the middle of the
18th century, profusion became the distinguishing
characteristic of poor law administration, and offered direct encouragement to the marriages of the
poor; and this was, probably, the sole cause of the
excessive speed with which population proceeded
from that date to the commencement of the wars
of the French Revolution.   Then, however, agricultural labourers were again subjected to severe
privations, which, with only brief intermissions,
though with varying degrees of intensity, have continued to affect them ever since.   It is during this

last dreary period, that the largest accession has been made both to the numbers of the people and to the number of the poor; and although other causes have contributed towards the result, the coincidence may be fairly claimed as an illustration of the tendency of poverty to increase the redundancy of population.

# CHAPTER VI.

### CAUSES OF OVER-POPULATION IN SCOTLAND AND IRELAND.

Relations subsisting between Highland Chieftains and their
Clansmen in former Times. — Decline of the clannish Feeling
after the Rebellion of 1745. — Ejection of Highland Tenantry
and Formation of Sheep Farms. — Decay of Kelp Manufacture. — Effects of Misery on the Character and Habits of the
Poor. — Usual Explanation of the excessive Populousness of
Ireland — its Incompleteness. — Primeval Poverty of the
Irish Peasantry. — Pastoral Occupation of the primitive Irish,
and of their Descendants, until the latter Part of the 18th
Century. — Wretched State of the labouring Class down to
the same Epoch. — Slight Improvement of their Condition, in
consequence of the Extension of Tillage. — Effect of this
Improvement on Population. — Contrast between Ulster and
the rest of Ireland. — Tenant Right. — Proneness of the Irish
Poor to early Marriage.

In tracing the over-population of Scotland to its
source, it will not be necessary to review the earlier
portions of the social history of that country. A
reference to the events of recent years will suffice.
In the Lowlands the condition of the peasantry is
not only comfortable at present, but is said to have
improved very perceptibly within the last half
century; and in the Highlands, where the signs of
over-population are too prominent to be overlooked,
they have become conspicuous only within a still
shorter period.

As long as the Highland chieftains retained and
valued their patriarchal influence, and preferred
the charms of solitary sway to the pleasures of
intercourse with equals, their incomes were spent

entirely amongst their respective clans, and were devoted chiefly to the maintenance of the largest possible body of retainers. Such of their lands as were not managed by their own servants, were parcelled out among tenants, from whom the most valuable returns expected were fidelity and obedience. Most of the farmers, however, were freeholders, who paid no rent whatever, and were only liable to a contribution called *calpe*, in token of their personal subordination to the chief. Single men without property were maintained by the chief, or by some of their richer clansmen, whom they served in peace, and followed in war; but no one ever thought of marrying until, by inheriting a farm or procuring the lease of one, he had got a house of his own over his head. While these usages prevailed, population could not increase beyond the means of subsistence, and the poorest Highlanders, secure from actual want, and inured to hardships, lived happily and contentedly.

After the rebellion of 1745, however, the Highlanders were disarmed; the use of their distinctive garb was forbidden; the hereditary jurisdictions of their leaders were abolished, and by means of military roads and English garrisons, the authority of the general government was extended over every part of their wild country. Many of their chiefs fled, and those who remained soon became as undesirous as they were unable to resume their former social position. There was no longer any motive to maintain a crowd of dependents, who could offer no effectual opposition to the law; and the only advantage which a laird derived from the populousness of his estate, consisted in the ability to raise troops for the Crown, and so to obtain commissions for himself and his relatives. It was part of the wise policy of the great Lord Chatham, to allay the disaffection of the Highlanders, by raising regiments of them for his Canadian expedition; and it is said that, at one time, a fifth part of the men able to bear arms were in the army. When this resource failed, the Highland lairds, who had now imbibed a strong taste for the enjoyments of civilised life, had to seek other modes of improving their incomes, and for this purpose very extraordinary facilities had of late been afforded to them. By a series of changes the Highland tacksman, who was originally co-proprietor of his land, had become at first vassal, then hereditary tenant, and lastly tenant-at-will of the chief, and the latter had been declared by law absolute proprietor of the land occupied by his clan. The chiefs did not hesitate to avail themselves to the utmost of the advantages thus conceded to them, and, with the view of raising their rents, began to oust the tenants of the small grazing farms into which the Highland counties had been divided, in order to form extensive sheep-walks. To such an extent has this been done, that in many places where once were numerous black cattle farms, now not an inhabitant is to be seen for miles. This was a revolution very similar to the one which took place in England towards the close of the 15th century, and would have been followed immediately by the same melancholy consequences, but for certain circumstances which served for a time to furnish the dispossessed peasantry with new means of employment and subsistence. The construction of the Caledonian and Crinan Canals, of roads and bridges, and other public works, provided occupation for considerable numbers, and the pecuniary allowances made to volunteers during the last war, were also a very important assistance. But the most valuable resource was the manufacture of kelp, which attained to an astonishing degree of prosperity during the war, and drew off to the western coasts and islands the bulk of those inhabitants of the inland districts, who possessed no adequate means of livelihood at home. After the repeal of the duty on salt in 1822, however, the kelp manufacture rapidly declined, and it is now almost wholly extinct, and its decay has deprived multitudes of their principal means of subsistence. *

Meantime the consolidation of farms is still going on as actively as ever. It is only within the last five and thirty years that the straths and glens of Sutherland have been cleared of their inhabitants, and that the whole county has been converted into one immense sheepwalk, over which the traveller may proceed for forty miles together without seeing a tree or a stone wall, or anything but a heath dotted with sheep and lambs.† Even the few cot-

* Skene's Highlanders of Scotland, vol. i. ch. 6. and 7. Evidence taken by Highland Emigration Committee. Report of Scottish Poor Law Commissioners.

† Reports of "Commissioner" of Times Newspaper, June, 1845.

tiers who remain are considered too numerous. If an old couple dying leave a son behind, the latter is permitted to marry, and to occupy the vacant dwelling; otherwise the cottage is pulled down, and its land added to some adjacent tenement. The example of Sutherland is imitated in the neighbouring counties. During the last four years some hundreds of families have been "weeded" out of Ross-shire, and nearly four hundred more have received notice to quit next year. Similar notice has been given to thirty-four families in Cromarty, and only the other day eighteen families who were living in peace and comfort in Glencalvie, in Ross-shire, were expelled from the farms occupied for ages by themselves and their forefathers, to make room for sheep. Little heeds the ruthless oppressor what becomes of such outcasts: "the nearest loch is deep enough for them all." Lucky are they if they are permitted to settle down on some desolate moor, and obtain a temporary refuge there, until by cultivation they have given to the soil value enough to make it worth the landlord's while to drive them off again.

These wholesale "clearances," as they are called, are quite sufficient to account for the destitution of the districts in which they have been effected; but misery in the Highlands exhibits its usual tendency to perpetuate and extend itself. There, as elsewhere, it is remarked that early marriages are most frequent among the poorest of the people; and wherever an excessive increase of population takes place, it can generally be traced to the labouring class, whose members marry without a shilling, and without any other place to live in than their parents' houses.*

Writers on Ireland are almost unanimous in imputing the excessive populousness of that country mainly to two causes — the minute subdivision of land, and the adoption by the peasantry of the potato as their principal article of food. Until late in the last century nearly the whole territory was given up to pasturage, most of the occupiers of land being opulent graziers, who employed comparatively few labourers in the management of their extensive farms; but in the years 1783 and 1784 the Irish Parliament granted high bounties on the exportation of grain, and prohibited its importation from abroad; and the rise of price which took place in consequence, was further promoted by the demand for foreign corn in Great Britain after the commencement of the war with France, and by the abolition, in 1806, of all restrictions on the corn trade between this country and Ireland. Extraordinary inducements were thus given to landholders to exchange pasturage for tillage; but the tracts held by single graziers were in general much too extensive to be cultivated by their actual tenants, and they were therefore divided into farms of more convenient size, and let to such persons as were willing to undertake them. There was not, however, capital enough in the island for this sudden

* Report of Scottish Poor Law Commissioners, App. ii., especially pp. 9. and 163.

revolution in husbandry, and most of the new race
of farmers were so poor that they could not pay
their labourers in any other way than by assigning
to them pieces of ground to build cabins upon, and
to cultivate for their own subsistence.  Together
with the farmers, therefore, a considerable body of
cottiers was created, and the number of the latter
was further augmented through the desire of the
landlords to increase their political influence.  The
elective franchise belonged in Ireland, as in England, to forty-shilling freeholders, that is to say, to
the possessors of a life interest in land of the clear
annual value of forty shillings ; but previously to
1792 it was enjoyed only by Protestants, and was
consequently withheld from the great body of the
peasantry.  In that year, however, the privilege
was conceded to Catholics also, and landlords then
began to manufacture voters by thousands, by
granting them leases for life of small patches of
land.  In this manner the bulk of the people were
converted into occupiers of land, and furnished
with the means of rearing a family, of which they
did not delay to avail themselves, and an increase
of population took place in consequence.  Gavel-
kind, or the custom of dividing a father's landed
property, whether freehold or leasehold, equally
among his children, has always prevailed in Ireland.
When one of the newly-made farmers died, therefore, all his sons were able to establish themselves
on farms of smaller extent, and a cottier's sons
also generally inherited small pieces of ground.
Having thus some assured means of livelihood, they

married as hastily as their fathers had done. Their
example was in turn followed by their children, and
by a repetition of the process, most of the descendants of the original farmers have, in the course of
two or three generations, sunk to the level of cottiers, and most of the original cottage holdings
have been divided among as many families as can
contrive to obtain from the soil potatoes enough to
keep them alive.

This explanation, however, though perfectly correct as far as it goes, leaves the main difficulties
of the subject untouched. There are plenty of
countries, besides Ireland, in which the peasantry
are occupiers of land, and in which equal shares of
a man's property are inherited by all his sons; yet
we do not find that in such countries the land
is continually subjected to more and more minute
subdivision, and that the people in each succeeding
generation are content to fare worse than their
immediate predecessors, or marry as soon as they
can command a bare subsistence. The son of a
Flemish or German boor does not set up for an
independent householder as soon he becomes entitled to a piece of land. He first considers whether the land is large enough to maintain him in
the style he has been accustomed to. If not,
he either lets or sells it to a stranger, or more
commonly holds it in partnership with his brothers,
until, by the death of the other co-heirs, the whole
patrimony is left to a single proprietor. Mr. Laing
found properties in Norway which had remained
undiminished in possession of the same families

since the days of Harold Harfager, and Mr. Nicholl, whose prejudices are certainly not in favour of small farmers, confesses that among those of Belgium he could discover no tendency to the subdivision of their holdings.  The modern bonder and boors occupy farms as large, and enjoy as much abundance, and more comfort, than their ancestors of a century back.  In both these countries, as well as in France and Germany, population is so far from outrunning the means of subsistence, that it does not even keep pace with them.  In France more particularly, the condition of the people has been steadily improving during the last thirty years, or during the whole period in which they have enjoyed tranquil possession of their recently acquired land.

Again, where people subsist entirely on potatoes, the most productive of vegetables, a much greater number can be maintained upon the same extent of ground ; but the potato is as well known in most other parts of Europe as in Ireland, and some peculiar circumstances must have induced the Irish alone of European nations to submit to a potato diet.  The simple reason of their having done so is, that they could never afford any thing better, and in this — their primeval poverty, lies the true secret of their present condition.

From the earliest times, the Irish peasantry have been miserably poor, and have been as imprudent, and as prone, among other follies, to early marriages, as they are at this moment.  If their conversion into occupiers of land had sensibly improved their social position, the benefit would probably have been permanent. Their poverty and their improvidence would have been cured by the same means, and over-population, instead of being promoted, would have been checked in its progress. Unfortunately, the terms of their tenure of land prevented it from materially increasing their resources, and instead of giving them the means of living in greater comfort, only enabled them to bring up more children in the same misery as they were themselves accustomed to. Their children, when grown up, did not feel the want of comforts they had never known, and only sought for the means of supporting life; and, provided they could obtain land enough to grow a few potatoes, they fancied themselves quite competent to provide for a wife and children. The prodigious strides which population has made of late years have rendered the destitution of the people more obvious than before, but it is doubtful whether they have rendered it much more severe. Ireland was certainly never so populous as at present: it never before contained so large a population; but it has long, perhaps, been nearly as much over-peopled, that is to say, the number of inhabitants has long been nearly as much disproportioned to the means of subsistence. The mass of the people has always been subjected to such extreme privations, that although the number of sufferers is now far greater than ever, it is doubtful whether their sufferings have been much aggravated. A very hasty retrospect will suffice to discover the grounds for this opinion.

From the earliest times Ireland has been noted for the excellence of its pastures. Its level surface, overspread with the most luxuriant herbage, presented a wide field, over which the cattle of the first settlers might freely range, and multiply at an exceedingly rapid rate. Their owners became proportionably wealthy; but the possession of great wealth by individuals implies a corresponding disparity of ranks in the community. The authority of the leader of a tribe might depend on his personal character, or on accidental circumstances; but, whatever might be the political position of the chief with respect to his fellow herdsmen, the latter, no doubt, exercised almost unlimited power over their servants and dependents. It is indeed a recorded fact, that these retainers did, after a while, degenerate into absolute bondsmen, who were attached to the manor on which they dwelt, and, under the name of " betages," were as completely at the disposal of their lords as the serfs of continental Europe. The pastoral occupation of the primitive Irish was not laid aside as soon as they had divided their new country amongst them, and had stationed themselves on particular spots, but continued to be practised by their descendants for many generations. The principal obstacle to change was probably at first the nature of the climate, which, Mela says, was as unsuitable for grain as it was favourable to the growth of grass[*]; and this

* Pomp. Mela, de Situ Orbis, lib. iii. cap. 6.

was perhaps the sole reason why, so late as the twelfth century, the people could still be represented as despising husbandry, and as not having laid aside their ancient pastoral mode of life.*

When greater intercourse sprang up between them and more civilised nations, they would have been taught the advantage of cultivating the soil; but, unfortunately, in the long period of anarchy and confusion which succeeded to the conquest by Henry the Second, the incessant warfare between the English colonists and the natives acted as an effectual bar to agriculture, for both parties thought it wiser to keep their property in the shape of flocks and herds, which could be driven into a place of shelter, than in corn stacks or standing crops, which must have been left to the mercy of a successful invader. Cattle thus continued to be almost the sole produce of the country, so much so indeed that they were often used as the medium of exchange; and even in the beginning of the sixteenth century, the Book of Ballymote is said to have been purchased for one hundred and forty milch cows.†
More than a hundred years later we find the poet Spenser lamenting that " all men fell to pasturage, and none to husbandry;" and recommending that an ordinance should be made to compel every one who kept twenty kine, to keep one plough going likewise.‡ It is not likely that agriculture made

* " Gens agriculturæ labores aspernans, a primo pastoralis vivendi modo non recedens." — Giraldus Cambrensis, apud Moore, Hist of Ireland, vol. i. p. 317.

† Moore, vol. i. p. 191.

‡ Spenser, View of Ireland. Dublin, 1763, p. 230.

much progress after this, during the reigns of Elizabeth and of the first two Stuarts, and during the Protectorate—a period marked by the rebellion of the Earls of Tyrone and Tyrconnel, the massacre of the Protestants promoted by Roger Moore, the equally bloody invasion of Cromwell, and the confiscation of five-sixths of the island; and if it did, it must again have been thrown back as much as ever after the Revolution of 1688, when a twelfth of the land again changed masters, and a series of penal acts was directed against the Roman Catholics. These atrocious laws, among other monstrous provisions, forbade papists to purchase lands or to hold them by lease for more than thirty-one years, or to derive from leasehold property a profit greater than one-third of the rent. The great majority of the people, being Roman Catholics, were thus in effect restrained from the practice of agriculture, and the proprietors of estates had really no option but to divide them among the few capitalists who could legally compete for them, and who of course could not properly superintend the management of the immense tracts which fell to their shares, except by keeping them almost entirely under grass. So general and so recent was the neglect of tillage, that, in the year 1727, a law was made to compel every occupier of 100 acres of land to cultivate at least *five* acres.

From the earliest times, then, until about sixty years ago, Ireland was almost entirely a grazing country. Now, although every class, in a pastoral community, is commonly sufficiently supplied with

the necessaries of life, this is not likely to be the case, except when the people have little commercial intercourse with more civilised neighbours.  A rich herdsman has then, literally, no means of getting rid of his superfluous wealth, except by maintaining a large retinue of servants, and he is naturally liberal enough of the milk, cheese, wool, hides, &c., which must be wasted if he does not give them away.   But Ireland, from a very remote period, has carried on a considerable export trade ; and the lords of the soil have always possessed, in foreign countries, a market for their surplus produce.  They have therefore had good reasons for practising economy, and for restricting the remuneration of their servants to what was absolutely necessary for their subsistence.  When the servants became serfs, they were not, according to the custom in more agricultural countries, provided with portions of of land to cultivate for their own support; for the estates of their lords, however extensive, could scarcely be too large for pasturage.  They lived upon such fare as their masters chose to provide, went half-naked, and slept under trees, or the scarcely better shelter of a few branches cemented together with mud.  When they became enfranchised, they gained nothing but personal freedom.  Their condition, in most other respects, remained unchanged.  Froissart describes them as living in forests, in huts made of boughs, like wild beasts.*
There was so little demand for labour, that most

* Johnes' Froissart, edition of 1839, vol. ii. p. 578.

were still glad to serve for a bare subsistence, and the few who were permitted to be tenants of land obtained little more from their farms. Irish landlords, says Spenser, "do not use to set out their lands in farm, or for terms of years, but only from year to year, and some during pleasure; neither, indeed, will the Irish husbandman otherwise take his land than so long as he lists himself. The reason hereof is, that the landlords used most shamefully to rack their tenants, — laying upon them coigns and livery at pleasure, and exacting of them, besides his covenants, what he pleaseth." Spenser goes on to speak of the farm-houses, which he calls "rather swine-styes than houses;" and of the farmers' "beastly manner of life, and savage condition, lying and living together with his beast in one house, in one room, in one bed, that is, clean straw, or rather a foul dunghill."* Matters were not at all mended in 1672, when Sir William Petty made his survey, and estimated that, out of 200,000 houses then existing in Ireland, 160,000 were "wretched nasty cabins, without chimney, window, or doorshut, even worse than those of the savage Americans."

From these premises it may be concluded, that the present misery of the Irish peasantry is of no recent origin, but has been from time immemorial an heirloom in the race. The number of labourers has always been greatly disproportioned to the demand of labour, and the remuneration of labour

* Spenser, View of Ireland, pp. 125—7.

has consequently never been much more than sufficient to procure the merest sustenance. This was
as much the case when Ireland was one vast grazing farm, and contained few inhabitants besides
cattle and their attendants, as now that the face of
the country is cut up into potato gardens, and
dotted with cabins, each containing a separate
family. The inhabitants have always been as
numerous as the country in its actual circumstances
could support, and population has only advanced
in proportion as the limits set to it have been
widened. How much soever population may have
varied in amount at different periods, it has always
been nearly equally in excess of the means of subsistence for the labouring class, and the multiplication of the latter, much as it has increased the
mass of misery, has not perhaps sensibly aggravated the sufferings of individuals. The chief difference is, that whereas people were once starving on
a short allowance of meat, they are now starving on
an equally short allowance of potatoes. Abundance
either of one or the other they scarcely ever enjoyed.

Any thing like comfort certainly was never even
temporarily known to the Irish peasantry. A trifling and transient improvement in their condition
took place towards the close of the last century,
when the general adoption of tillage increased the
demand for farm servants ; but the increase was too
gradual to produce any material effect on the remuneration of labour. The Bounty Acts of 1783
and 1784 did not cause a large breadth of land to

be suddenly brought under the plough.  The increase in the exportation of grain, which may be
regarded as an exact measure of the increase of
cultivation consequent upon those acts, shows that
the latter was inconsiderable.  The quantity of
wheat and other sorts of corn exported from Ireland was 211,979 barrels in 1783, and 648,884
barrels in 1789, showing a difference in six years
of 436,905 barrels, or about 266,000 quarters; and
this quantity, divided by six, gives about 44,000
quarters as the annual ratio of increased exportation.  But to produce 44,000 quarters of corn, not
more than 11,000 acres are required, and five hundred men are many more than are commonly employed to cultivate 11,000 acres in the ordinary manner.
In each of the six years, therefore, ending with
1789, additional employment was created for no
more than five hundred labourers, at the very outside.  But such an increase of employment, in the
midst of a population of nearly four millions, could
not materially raise the price of labour.  The
wages of a labourer, or the piece of ground which
he obtained in lieu of money payment, did not
therefore raise his ideas of comfort, by enabling him
to procure new enjoyments and to satisfy new
wants, but merely gave him an ampler meal of
potatoes, and the means of feeding a greater
number of children on the same simple fare.  The
addition to the resources of the peasantry was just
sufficient to give a fresh impulse to population,
which advanced so rapidly, that although the extension of tillage continued to increase the demand

for labour, the supply of labourers fully kept up with it, and prevented it from working any beneficial change in the condition of the people. It is true that population could scarcely have advanced so rapidly as it did, if the facilities for acquiring land, and the general use of the cheapest diet, had not made the chief requisite of existence easily procurable; but these circumstances could only place the bare means of subsistence within reach of a larger number of persons, and could not compel any to be content with it. The peasantry of Norway, Belgium, Switzerland, and France, may, if they please, divide their farms into patches just large enough to supply a family with potatoes, but no one will be satisfied with such a provision, because all have been accustomed to comforts which it cannot afford them. It is only those who have never tasted the conveniences of life, that are ready to propagate their species, without any better prospect than that of ability to keep themselves alive. It is because the son of an Irish cottier has always considered a fill of potatoes to be the height of physical comfort, that he esteems a few square yards of ground a very competent marriage portion. The true cause of the over-population of Ireland must be looked for in the ancient and inveterate poverty of her people. But for this, the occupation of land would have produced effects the very opposite of those which have actually proceeded from it, and would have established the prosperity of the peasantry on a firm basis, instead of increasing the number of participators in their misery.

It is a conclusive proof that the occupation of land by the Irish peasantry does not of itself contribute to their misery, that it is precisely where the distribution of land amongst them is most general that population is least redundant, and the condition of the people most tolerable. In Ulster, the number of farms not exceeding five acres in extent, and the proportion of inhabitants occupying land, are greater than in any one of the other three provinces, yet it is in Ulster only that the English tourist is occasionally reminded of his own country by the neatness of the whitewashed cottages, and by the appearance of their comparatively well-fed and well-clad inmates. It is true that Ulster is the most densely-peopled portion of the whole island, but population has not outrun subsistence in the same manner as in the other provinces, and the inhabitants, though much more numerous, have long managed to preserve the same proportion between their numbers and their means of livelihood. The reason of this is, that they were always able to command something approaching to a comfortable subsistence. The terms of their tenure of land do not leave them just so much only of the produce as may suffice to keep them from starving. They are not mere tenants in the ordinary sense of the word, but possess a proprietary right over the soil, which limits the landlord's power, and in most instances virtually prevents him from raising his rent, or ejecting the actual occupant. This " tenant-right" as it is called, which is peculiar to the North of Ireland, has probably grown out of the privileges granted to the English and Scottish emigrants, by whom Ulster was colonised in James the First's time, to induce them to settle in so barbarous a region. Although founded solely on prescription, its operation is almost as effectual as if it were recognised by law, and its value to its possessor is self-evident. It stimulates him to exertion, by securing to him the entire produce of his additional labour, and enables him to procure sundry substantial advantages, the desire to retain which is only another name for prudence. A cottier's sons have the same power in Ulster as in Munster or Connaught of dividing their father's holding, but they see clearly that they cannot maintain separate families on their respective shares without sacrificing the few comforts they have been accustomed to. They seek, therefore, for some additional means of livelihood, and do not in general marry until they find it. The cottage farms are consequently transmitted from one generation to another without diminution of size, and population only keeps pace with the increase of means for its support. The only county in Ulster to which this description does not apply is Donegal, in which, as the indigenous Celtic inhabitants were never disturbed, the tenant-right has not been introduced, except partially, and in an imperfect shape. The peasantry of that county, ever since they became occupiers of land, have been kept as poor as their brethren in the most wretched districts of Connaught, and their numbers have increased as fast, and the partition of their holdings has been carried on to the same extent.

While it is thus clear, even from observation of the state of Ireland, that facilities for obtaining the tenancy of land give no excessive impulse to population, except among a people rendered desperate by misery, it is equally evident that familiarity with wretchedness, independently of other circumstances, is the most powerful of incentives to early marriages. The Commissioners of Inquiry into the Condition of the Irish Poor in 1836, found it universally admitted that the most destitute were also the most ready to marry, and that provided they could scrape together halfpence enough for the priest's fee, they would not always wait even till they could get a roof over their heads, and potatoes and whisky for the wedding feast. The witnesses only differed as to the reasons for such impatience. Whatever might be the motives, however, of the candidates for matrimony,—whether they were anxious to have children to take care of them in their old age, or thought that they could not fare worse coupled than they did singly, or whether they did not think of the future at all, is not of much consequence. Their conduct is equally corroborative of the opinion in support of which it is cited, and, like the other statements in this and the two preceding Chapters, points to the conclusion that the original cause of over-population is almost invariably misery.

# CHAPTER VII.

### REMEDIES FOR OVER-POPULATION IN ENGLAND AND WALES.

Restrictions on the Marriages of the Poor. — Soundness of the Theory of Malthus. — Its Incompleteness. — Consideration of various Schemes for the Cure of Poverty. — Vindication of the New Poor Law. — Emigration. — Improvement of Agriculture. — Free Trade. — Ability of foreign Countries to supply Great Britain with Provisions. — Imperative Obligation on foreign Merchants to accept British Goods in exchange. — Groundlessness of the Opinion that Cheapness of Food would occasion a Fall of Wages. — Examination of Objections to Free Trade in Provisions. — Loss of Revenue — Dependence on foreign Countries. — Reduction of Rents. — Possible Extent of such Reduction. — Circumstances by which it would be compensated. — Inadmissibility of the Objection that Free Trade might lower Rents. —Effect of Free Trade on the Demand for agricultural Labour — Subdivision of Farms. — Manner in which that Subdivision would affect Land Owners and agricultural Labourers. — Superior Productiveness of small Farms. — High Rents obtainable for them — Great Amount of human Labour required for their Cultivation. — Cottage Allotments.—Their Advantages. —Examination of their supposed Tendency to create an excessive agricultural Population.— Peculiar Circumstances which have led to the minute Partition of Land in Ireland. — Dissimilar Condition of England. —Actual Results of the Occupation of Land by the Peasantry in some Parts of England. — Its Influence in preventing and curing Pauperism, and in checking improvident Marriages. — Tendency of Cottage Allotments to promote the social and moral Improvement of the Occupants.

To cure over-population, is to restore the proper proportion between the number of labourers and the fund for the remuneration of labour. Either the first must be diminished, or the second must be augmented. But it is not sufficient to cure,—we must also guard against a return of the disease. Population must if possible be prevented from increasing beyond the means of subsistence. This can only be done by restraining people from marrying until they can bear the expenses of a family. Whatever other remedies may be prescribed, therefore, restrictions upon the marriages of the poor are an indispensable part of the regimen to be observed.

It requires some courage, in these days, to exhibit such principles, the very essence of Malthusianism, in all their naked simplicity. They are, indeed, as clear, and one would have thought as undeniable, as the sun at mid-day; but they have been so sternly denounced, and so mercilessly ridiculed, that few are now found bold enough to avow them. It is not merely benevolent declaimers or fanatical zealots who inveigh against the "detestable hard-heartedness of the system" that would keep people single until they can afford to indulge in the "luxury of marriage" *, who call it "an impeachment of God's providence" † to suppose that population can outrun subsistence, and in this fifty-ninth century esteem it a sin to disobey the ante-

* These expressions are Southey's, and occur in an article in the Quarterly Review, vol. viii. p. 326.

† See the late Mr. Sadler's "Law of Population," or rather an article in No. 102. of the Edinburgh Review, in which the most brilliant writer of the age has condescended to demolish Mr. Sadler's absurdities.

diluvian injunction, "to be fruitful and multiply, and replenish the earth." *   Even hard-headed and hard-hearted political economists shrink from one whom they were once proud to hail as a colleague. Mr. M'Culloch, the Coryphæus of the band, stigmatises the theory of Malthus "as a striking instance of the abuse of general principles † ; " and Mr. Laing contends, that to give the name of moral restraint to prudential abstinence from marriage is to " confound prudence and morality," and to " overturn the land-marks of human virtue." ‡ I will not be drawn into a regular defence of Mr. Malthus against his opponents, though the temptation is great to show that the poor have no more right than the rich to indulge in luxuries which they cannot afford, and that it is decidedly immoral to bring children into the world to starve.§   I will confine myself to one or two observations. Malthus asserts

---

* Mr. Alison has taken this for the text of his Discourse on the " Principles of Population."

† Principles of Political Economy.   Preface.

‡ Residence in Norway, p. 481.   Notes of a Traveller, p. 338.

§ Mr. Laing is not to be put down by authority, or I would quote Milton and Dean Swift against him.   The former makes Eve exclaim : —

" Miserable it is
To be to others cause of misery,
Our own begotten, and of our loins to bring
Into this cursed world a woful race."—*Par. Lost,* book x.

And the latter informs us that " the Lilliputians think nothing can be more unjust than for people, in subservience to their own appetites, to bring children into the world, and leave the burden of supporting them on the public."—*Voyage to Lilliput,* chap. vi.

that people ought not to marry until they are able to maintain the children they are likely to have. This is the great maxim which he labours to establish, the end to which all his reasonings point, the sole practical deduction to be drawn from his doctrines. Do his opponents maintain the contrary? Do Messrs. M'Culloch, Alison, and Laing, — does any one, in short, except doting mammas, impatient to behold their children's children, or young ladies still dreaming of love in a cottage, think that people ought to marry before they can afford to do so? If they do not think this, they are as much Malthusians as the founder of the sect, for Malthus himself has said no more. It is, indeed, his great defect that he has confined himself to this, — that he has said so little, not that he has said so much. Over the space of two goodly volumes he has heaped up proofs of what no reasonable man disputes, — the necessity, viz., in certain circumstances, for abstinence from marriage; but he has omitted to show how men can be induced to practise such abstinence. He apparently relied entirely on education. He seems to have thought that people might be persuaded to control their matrimonial inclinations by having the evil consequences of indulgence in them clearly explained. He overlooked or undervalued the tendency which the possession of property has to engender prudence, and seems, indeed, to have thought that that quality is rarely to be found among members of the labouring class, except under the pressure of misery. If he has not explicitly pronounced these sentiments, at least he has not

clearly expressed the contrary; and it is this deficiency on his part which it is the object of the present essay to supply. An attempt has already been
made to show that misery renders men reckless in
marriage, as in every thing else; and that, in order
to make them provident, it is first necessary to
make them comfortable, and to make the continuance of their comfort contingent on their own behaviour. It has been asserted that indigence, the
never-absent symptom of over-population, is likewise its principal upholder and promoter. If these
opinions be correct, a permanent cure of over-population may be effected by any means that will raise
the labouring classes from the poverty in which
they are sunk, and provide them with adequate
means of supporting themselves. How so desirable
a change can be wrought in the condition of the
British peasantry is now to be considered, and I
enter upon this part of my subject with the more
alacrity, because none can fail to be interested in
the immediate object of pursuit, however doubtful
they may be of the ulterior results expected from it.

Before, however, offering any suggestions as to
the proper course to be followed, it will be convenient to examine some measures which are
popularly regarded as likely to conduce to the
desired end, and it is particularly important to
demonstrate the hopelessness of any considerable
benefit from a relaxation of the present Poor Law.
Few persons are now disposed to deny, that a poor
law of some sort is essential to the well-being of
every community. Cases of destitution, arising

from physical infirmity, are everywhere liable to occur; and there ought certainly to be a public provision, to which the sufferers may have access, in default of private charity. A variety of causes, too, may deprive the able-bodied of their accustomed occupation; and humanity and policy equally demand that similar provision should be made for them also. But, although a poor law be highly useful, and indeed indispensable, there is no human institution which requires to be more strictly watched, to prevent it from doing more harm than good. If relief be bestowed too freely, even on the infirm, it is apt to create improvidence. If it be granted to the able-bodied, unless either very sparingly, or coupled with very stringent conditions, it fosters idleness and discourages independent industry. Even if this evil be avoided, the knowledge that there is a resource, other than his own proper business, from which he may derive a maintenance, deprives the labourer of the principal motive for postponing marriage until his earnings are sufficient for the expenses of such a change in his condition. Unless, therefore, some special precaution be taken, the supply of labourers, though already surpassing the demand, will be augmented by fresh swarms, and poverty will be extended by the very means adopted to relieve it. This can only be prevented by making the situation of the dependent pauper less desirable than that of the independent labourer.

It may savour of Quixotism to volunteer an apology for the New Poor Law, at a time when its very authors are for the most part awed into silence, and when some of them take credit for the wide deviation which has been lately made from its most important principles. Nevertheless, I shall not hesitate to express my conviction, that the administration of the law, where most rigid, is in all its principal features marked by at least as much gentleness and liberality as are consistent with proper regard to the dangers to be apprehended.*

The most unpopular part of the present system is that which, in certain circumstances, requires paupers to enter a workhouse. Yet inmates of workhouses are lodged, clothed, and fed so much better than independent labourers, that the latter would probably demand admittance in a body into the so-called bastiles, but for the discipline observed there. Still, it is asked, why should paupers be subjected to any peculiar restraints? Poverty is not a crime; why then should they be punished for it? If they really stand in need of relief, why is not relief afforded to them in their own dwellings? The chief reasons for requiring entry into a workhouse are—that this, besides being a ready and effectual mode of testing want, offers the cheapest means of relieving it, and admits of a

* In matters of detail there is certainly room for improvement. The large size of many unions, for example, however advantageous in some respects, often compels a poor person to make a journey of several miles in order to substantiate a claim to relief; and this, it is obvious, might in cases of emergency be attended with serious consequences. It would apparently be easy to devise some means of remedying this evil.

greater portion of relief being afforded with safety. When paupers are allowed to remain at home, it is often difficult to ascertain whether their distress is real or feigned; the cost of maintaining them is greater than it would be in a large establishment, where the most methodical arrangements could be practised; and, as no restraints can be imposed on their personal liberty, the only means of making them dissatisfied with their dependent condition is to abridge the assistance afforded to them. Poverty, it is true, is not a crime, but neither is the workhouse a place of punishment. On the contrary, it is really as comfortable an asylum as could be provided for the destitute, without encouraging pauperism\*; and the conditions attached

---

\* The late proceedings at Andover may perhaps be thought to require some modification of these sentences. Notwithstanding every testimony, it is difficult to believe that Englishmen, with tongues in their heads and with the national propensity to grumble, did really submit to a diet so meagre that they were glad to supply its deficiencies by gnawing putrid scraps of flesh from the bones they were set to crush, without at least complaining to the guardians of the scantiness of the food allotted to them. The reports on the subject cannot be otherwise than greatly exaggerated and overcoloured. Still, if they have the smallest foundation in truth, it can no longer be disputed that the workhouse allowance, however suitable for persons leading a comparatively sedentary life, is not sufficient for those who are set to hard labour. At the same time, we must be careful to distinguish between the intrinsic harshness of a system, and grievances arising out of a breach of its regulations. The late master of the Andover workhouse was unquestionably utterly unfit for his office; but his misconduct—his alleged peculations, licentiousness, and drunkenness, are no sign of any defect in the New Poor Law. In the administration of human affairs, confi-

to a participation in its advantages are necessary
to guard against this latter danger, and could not
be moderated without being rendered altogether
worthless. For, in what does the discipline of a
workhouse consist? The most tender-hearted philanthropist cannot disapprove of the inmates being

dence must needs be reposed in fallible agents, and while human
nature remains what it is, the trust will be often abused. But
although Macdougall's offences prove nothing against the Poor
Law, they prove a great deal against the Poor Law Commissioners, who have evinced an unequivocal desire to screen their
suspected servant from detection and punishment. Their par-
tiality is not perhaps difficult to account for. For years past
they have been so unceasingly subjected to the unscrupulous
assaults of political rancour, they have been so badgered with false
and frivolous accusations, and have seen the acts and motives of
themselves and their subordinates so industriously misrepresented, that they have not unnaturally become prejudiced against
all complaints, and disposed to regard every new charge as a fresh
invention of malice. But this, though possibly an explanation,
is no excuse for their conduct. In spite of every provocation,
they are bound fairly and patiently to investigate every complaint, without reference to the motives of those who make it,
and they must not shut their eyes to the delinquency of their
inferiors, merely because their attention is drawn to it by an
adversary. The watchful animosity with which they are regarded, instead of making them callous to public opinion, ought
in common policy to make them more studious not to give any
real ground for reproach; and they cannot better serve the
purpose of their enemies than by suffering themselves to be
irritated into declaring themselves the advocates of all under
their authority who are accused of oppressing the poor. In
that case, the prediction of a friendly journal may not improbably be speedily verified, and the Commissioners may be the
destruction of the law they are appointed to administer, and
which they are so anxious to uphold.

required to observe regular hours, to practise habits of cleanliness, and to perform stated tasks when able to work. There are, in fact, only two regulations to which any specious objection can be made. Paupers, with the exception of the aged (to whom considerable indulgence is allowed), are in general confined strictly to the workhouse premises so long as they choose to reside there, and are also restrained from associating with relatives or companions of the other sex. These rules have incurred the most vehement censure. Why, it is asked, should not free egress be permitted at stated hours, so far as the preservation of order in the establishment would permit? Simply because workhouses are designed solely for the relief of genuine want, and are not intended to be boarding-houses for labourers in general, as Mr. Wakley perhaps would have them, and as they would certainly become if such liberty were granted. As habitations, they are far preferable to cottages of the very best description. What cottager then would refuse to avail himself of their advantages, if he could do so unconditionally? Work in the workhouse is not worse than work elsewhere, and is often better remunerated; at least, agricultural labourers live much better in the workhouse than they do in their own homes. Unless there were some irksomeness to counterbalance its recommendations, a residence in the workhouse would be much more anxiously desiderated than it is now eschewed; workmen would be continually leaving their employers, and the parish would be the only popular master. It is, however, the separation of the sexes, and particularly of husband and wife, that has incurred the largest share of odium. The practice, although usual in hospitals and similar charitable institutions, has been styled inhuman and unnatural, and it has also been called an impious defiance of the Divine injunction, " What God hath joined, let no man put asunder." Of course, those who so strangely misapply our Saviour's reprobation of divorce, are not indebted for the quotation to their own biblical researches; but, even if the words really had the meaning attributed to them, they would be equally inapplicable. Whether it be or be not allowable, in any circumstances, forcibly to separate man and wife, no one will dispute that they have a right to part of their own accord, if any considerations of convenience render a temporary sacrifice of each other's society desirable. But the separation which takes place in the workhouse is a spontaneous arrangement of this sort. No compulsion is used: the parties are quite at liberty to live together at home, if they can afford to do so; but, if they cannot support themselves, and apply to the parish for subsistence, the parish has a right to dictate its own terms; and no conditions can be more reasonable than, that being themselves a burden to the public, they shall not employ their leisure in accumulating an additional burden.

If however the workhouse discipline be free from objection, how comes it that the poor are in general so averse to submit to it, and that in some instances they have preferred to endure the extremes of privation ?   The question may best be answered by those who have taken so much pains to inflame the minds of the poor, and to fill them with exaggerated notions of their rights.   Cases undoubtedly there are, in which a family, by taking up its abode in a workhouse, would disable itself from regaining an independent position, and in which the refusal of out-door relief would leave only a grievous alternative.   But such cases, though not uncommon, are still only exceptions.   In general, the poor ought surely to be thankful for an asylum in which the infirm may obtain a permanent retreat, and the able-bodied may take refuge from temporary distress, and in which the wants of all are supplied with a liberality to which they are unaccustomed elsewhere.   Left to themselves, they would surely never have spurned these advantages, or have dreamt of dictating in what mode charitable assistance should be afforded to them.   When however their superiors in station and knowledge are continually assuring them, not only that maintenance at the public expense is nothing more than their due, but that, in the arrangements for their support, regard to their comfort should be the foremost consideration ; that the workhouse is only a prison designed for the punishment of poverty, and that to yield to its restraints is unmanly and degrading; — when notions like these are industriously propagated amongst them, what wonder if they exclaim against a supposed invasion of their just privileges, and that some are willing to starve rather than submit to what they are taught to regard as insolent tyranny? Absurd as the prejudice is, it has become so strong, that it has been thought advisable to humour it. The workhouse test is not now applied to one in six of the whole number of applicants for parish relief, and the remainder receive assistance at their own homes. The relaxation is, however, the reverse of beneficial to the poor themselves. For reasons already explained, so large a supply of necessaries cannot safely be granted to out-door as to in-door paupers. When the restraints of a workhouse are wanting, the only means of keeping the pauper in a worse position than the independent labourer, is by reducing his allowance. This is of necessity the expedient actually adopted, and, as an inevitable consequence, the wants of the out-door poor are relieved more imperfectly, though perhaps at a greater relative expense, than those of inmates of workhouses. Fresh pretexts for indignation are thus furnished to the opponents of the New Poor Law, without however more real ground for invective than before. The principle upon which the regulations respecting out-door poor are based, is certainly sound, and could not be abandoned without causing the demoralisation of the industrious classes. Even if it were too closely adhered to, — if excessive frugality were exhibited in the treatment of the out-door poor, the privations occasioned by it might, except in the case of men with families, be said to be voluntarily borne. The more abundant diet and greater accommodation of the workhouse are offered to all who need them, and if any prefer

to receive smaller allowances at their own homes,
they can only blame their own choice. General
rules for the relief of the poor, like general rules
for any purpose whatsoever, affect different individuals unequally; and among those exposed to their
unvarying operation, are of course some whose
previous conduct, character, or other circumstances
entitle them to more than ordinary consideration.
But these are not deprived by the Poor Law of the
benefit of the sympathy which their situation is
calculated to excite. No larger allowance from the
parish funds is made to them than to others; but if
any such additional allowance were made, it could
only be obtained by means of increased contributions on the part of the rate-payers. The latter
are not compelled to wait until the collector calls
upon them. If they witness distress, which the
poor's-rates do not seem to relieve adequately, they
are at liberty to assess themselves voluntarily, and
to contribute what is wanting. A poor law is not
designed to supersede private charity. Its legitimate object is to prevent destitution, and it cannot
attempt much more, without undermining those
virtues which are the most effectual safeguards
against destitution. If, in particular cases, the
provision which it makes is less liberal than would
be consistent with wise economy, it is for private
benevolence to supply its deficiencies; and the true
friends of the poor would be much better employed
in stimulating by example as well as precept the
dormant charity of their neighbours, than by writing
letters for the newspapers in abuse of a law, which

at worst can only be accused of not compelling people to be as charitable as they ought to be of their own accord.

Far from extending the grant of out-door relief, true policy would perhaps suggest a much stricter enforcement of the rule which the authors of the Poor Law had in view; and, in the great majority of cases, would permit relief to be given only in the workhouse. From the operation of this rule, entire families, capable in ordinary times of supporting themselves, but whose means of livelihood were temporarily curtailed or withdrawn, might very properly be exempted. A little assistance afforded to these at their own homes, might enable them to struggle through their temporary difficulties, and to regain in a short time their independence; whereas, if they were compelled to enter the workhouse, they might be permanently detained there by the impossibility of again procuring and furnishing habitations elsewhere. Such families or households, however, appear to be the only exceptions which it would be really advisable to make. Of all persons otherwise circumstanced, whether old or young, married or single, infirm or vigorous, the workhouse should be the only certain dependence in distress, — the only place in which they could *claim* relief as their due. The discipline of the workhouse, so far as regarded the old or the very young, might probably be somewhat relaxed without any bad consequences ; not so much so, however, as to make the workhouse a desirable abode, and so to dissuade the labourer from making another provi-

sion for himself in old age, or for his children in
the event of his own premature death. But to
able-bodied inmates, while every requisite was supplied for their maintenance in health and strength,
the workhouse should undoubtedly be made sufficiently irksome to make them impatient to get out
of it. If among those to whom on their applying
for parish relief the workhouse would be offered,
were any deserving a more kindly treatment, it
would be the office of those who commiserated them,
to raise, by subscription or otherwise, the means of
supporting them at their own homes. Well-directed
private charity, thus employed, as its uncertain aid
could not be depended on, could do no harm, and
might offer to labourers an additional incentive to
good behaviour; whereas a legal and compulsory
provision for the out-door poor, unless very frugally
distributed, could not fail to engender improvidence.
Freedom from this tendency is the chief advantage
which the workhouse system possesses over every
other mode of relief. The expediency of keeping
the allowance of the out-door poor below the earnings of their independent brethren, may prevent
the wants of the former from being adequately
relieved, and may cause them to be retained in a
state bordering more or less closely on indigence.
Thus, one of the chief advantages of a poor law, that
of keeping up a high standard of comfort among
the lower orders of people, will be sacrificed, and
a course which must necessarily lower their ideas
of what is requisite will be intentionally adopted,
in order to avoid giving direct encouragement to

improvidence. In the workhouse, both these dangers may be avoided, and the poor may be well lodged, clothed, and fed, without by their example depriving poverty of its wholesome terrors. This is the principal recommendation of the workhouse; but another ground of preference is the comparative cheapness with which its inmates may be maintained. Two or three hundred persons, living together, may be supplied abundantly with every requisite for a sum which, if they were separated, would scarcely keep them alive. With the most skilful management, the expenditure on account of the poor must be very large, but certainly no means should be neglected of keeping it as low as may be consistent with the perfect attainment of its legitimate objects.

The present, however, is no time to sing the praises of the workhouse, at least with any expectation that its resources will be placed under increased requisition. The current of popular feeling runs too strongly the other way, to allow of the limits within which out-door relief is granted being drawn closer. To prevent their being still more widened is all that can be hoped for. Many powerful voices already swell the cry of " a fair day's wages for a fair day's work," and declare that, if a man cannot procure work for himself, the public are bound to find him employment, and to recompense his services as if they were really required. It is vain to urge the obvious objection to this proposition, that the deficiency of employment proceeds from the excess of labourers, in other words, from over-population; and that to offer a man the means of bringing up a family when his services are not needed, is the surest way to increase over-population. The dictates of a short-sighted benevolence are alone listened to. If a man be willing to work, it is not his fault that he cannot find employment. Certainly not; but although not his fault, it *is* his misfortune; and upon whom but himself should his misfortunes fall? Assistance to support the load, is all that he can expect from his neighbours, — he cannot reasonably ask them to take it wholly upon themselves; especially if by so doing they must cause it eventually to fall with redoubled weight upon his children. But the real question is not whether it be desirable to assign the same incomes to paupers and to independent labourers. The thing, whether desirable or not, is utterly impracticable, or only practicable by reducing both classes to an equality of indigence. When persons able to work are unable to procure employment, it is because there is not sufficient employment for them, — because the fund for the remuneration of labour is not sufficient for the comfortable maintenance of the whole body of labourers. It is impossible, therefore, to give occupation to the unemployed, without taking it from those in employment. It has been shown that the average annual revenue of a nation (with the exception of any specie or other valuables that may be hoarded), is wholly expended within the year.* The whole income of every individual is likewise expended within

* See ante, p. 221. note.

the same period, either by the owner himself, or by those to whom he lends his money at interest. In whatever manner expended, it serves for the support of industry, — it sets a number of persons to work, and enables them to gain a livelihood. Now, if from any one's income an unusually large deduction be made in the shape of poor's rates, exactly so much less remains to be spent with tradespeople, and the latter have so much less to pay their workmen. Every addition to the amount of poor's rates causes a corresponding deduction of the amount payable in wages, and the poor can only be relieved at the expense of independent labourers. This is, indeed, no reason why destitution should not be relieved, for it is better that one set of persons should be deprived of some comforts, than that another set should be left to starve. But it is an excellent reason why relief should not much exceed what is strictly necessary. If it be attempted, by means of charitable donations, to place paupers on a level with independent labourers in respect to income, some of the latter must necessarily be reduced below that level; or the level common to all must itself be lowered. This consideration ought to induce the opponents of the New Poor Law to pause. How much soever they may desire to elevate the pauper, they cannot surely wish to degrade the independent labourer, or to make the two exchange conditions. Yet this is obviously the end towards which all their efforts are tending.

It will be very easy to turn the preceding remarks against the writer, and to accuse him of callousness and indifference to the sufferings of the unfortunate. Although, however, what has been said may be misrepresented, it cannot, I am persuaded, be misunderstood by any who will take the trouble to examine for themselves. One who devotes a volume to an enquiry into the best means of promoting the welfare of the poor, may fairly claim credit for taking some interest in the subject, however widely his views respecting it may differ from those of his critics. He may entertain all the opinions expressed above with regard to poor laws, and yet be a very sincere and very ardent friend of the poor. Measures for increasing the dependence of the poor upon charity can only benefit one portion of the labouring class in the same proportion as they injure another, and, if carried far, must inevitably involve all in ruin. The true way to improve the condition of the able-bodied is, in all cases short of want of the necessaries of life, to throw them entirely on their own resources, but at the same time to augment those resources to the utmost, — to make their own industry their sole dependence, but to enlarge the field within which that industry may be exerted. To make them public pensioners, is at best only to alter the distribution of the fund for the payment of wages; but, to produce any unalloyed advantage, the equilibrium between that fund and the number of persons dependent upon it must be restored — the one must be augmented, or the other must be diminished.

In order to diminish the number of labourers in

a country, if such desperate measures be rejected as
the child-eating scheme of Dean Swift and the
"painless extinction" of infants, spoken of in "grim
earnest" by Mr. Carlyle, emigration is the only
expedient that can be recommended. In order,
however, to produce any durable results, emigration
must be carried on on a gigantic scale. Experience
has proved incontestably, that a country can afford
to lose annually a very considerable number of inhabitants without becoming less populous in consequence. Up to a certain point, the withdrawal
of part of a community only places a greater number of persons in a position to marry immediately,
and the gap is filled up, almost as soon as it is made,
by an increase in the number of births. It is only
when the number of persons removed is so great,
and the incomes of those remaining are so much
augmented in consequence, as to create among the
latter a higher standard of comfort, and to raise
their notions of what is requisite for ease and respectability, that marriages decrease in number, and
the progress of population is checked. These results might be expected in England, if the bulk of
the surplus population could be persuaded and enabled to emigrate at once, but of course such a
scheme is purely chimerical. The mere expense of
transporting the emigrants to their destinations
would not indeed offer a serious objection. The
average charge for a passage to the most distant of
our colonies is little more than the annual cost of a
pauper's maintenance, so that, supposing ships
enough to be procurable, the country might be

for ever freed from the burthen of maintaining all those who are not comfortable at home, for little more than the amount which they now cost every year. But the insurmountable difficulty is, that of providing at once for a million or so of fresh settlers, in any part of the world. Waste land of good quality is abundant enough, both in America and Australia; but land cannot be cultivated without capital, and in none of the countries available for colonisation is there capital more than sufficient to employ the limited supplies of labour which they already receive. At present, only about 100,000 emigrants annually leave the British Islands; yet in Canada, New Brunswick, and New South Wales, the labour market is often over-stocked, and out of 60,000 persons who emigrated to the United States in the year 1842, nearly 10,000 were compelled to return home by inability to procure employment.* It is obvious then, that for the present the resource offered by emigration is of no great national value. What it may become hereafter remains to be seen. Improved plans for the disposal of the waste lands in our colonies have lately been proposed †, which if adopted may greatly encourage the investment of capital in the soil, and furnish funds at the same time for the conveyance of emigrants to the enlarged field, which will then be opened to their

---

\* Parliam. Returns; and Hansard's Debates, 3rd April, 1843.

† The reader need scarcely be referred to the able speeches of Mr. Charles Buller on Systematic Colonisation, delivered in the House of Commons in the session of 1843.

labour. A really serviceable outlet will then be afforded to our redundant and cooped-up population; but years must elapse before this can happen, and in the interval emigration must continue to flow in its present restricted channels. Of the average annual number of emigrants who now leave the United Kingdom, probably one half, or about 50,000, may be natives of England and Wales; but the subtraction of so insignificant a proportion of the whole people cannot in the smallest degree ameliorate the condition of the millions left behind. All who now emigrate do so entirely of their own accord, and almost entirely at their own expense, and it would be a mistaken policy to assist them on their way, in the hope of diminishing population. Emigration cannot have the slightest effect of this sort, as long as its total amount remains as small as at present, and while it takes place from all parts of the country indiscriminately. It might be different if the emigrants proceeded from a few districts of limited extent. One over-peopled tract after another might then be cleared of its superfluous inhabitants, and plenty and social comfort might replace want and misery within slowly but surely extending limits. The produce of the poors' rates could hardly, perhaps, in some rural parishes, be applied more beneficially for the interests of all parties concerned than in furnishing all the able-bodied inhabitants who had no regular employment, with the means of transporting themselves to a foreign home, where industry would be sure of earning a competent livelihood. No very heavy contributions would be required from the rate-payers for this purpose, and the amount would, moreover, be applied to the reduction of future taxation, for pauperism would be almost extinguished, and the remaining labourers raised at once to independence. Such an expedient as this, however, ought not to be resorted to except in cases of extreme necessity. Banishment, even when voluntary and self-imposed, is still a painful resource. It is hard to bid a lasting farewell to kindred and friends, and to resign for ever the indescribable charm, the endearing associations that cling to every object in our place of birth, even though poverty has been our lot, and though brighter prospects entice us away. In some crowded parts of the Scottish Highlands and in Ireland, where the inhabitants have multiplied to a number for which it is almost hopeless to seek for adequate means of subsistence on the spot, emigration may seem to be the easiest way of escaping from misery; but before passing sentence of exile on the English peasantry, it behoves us to inquire what it is in the power either of the legislature or of individuals to do for them at home.

The numbers of the peasantry remaining the same, the only means by which their condition can be improved, is an increase of the aggregate fund assigned for their support. Such an increase may take place in two ways: an increased demand for labour may cause a larger amount of money to be distributed among the labourers, and occasion a rise of wages; or, money-wages remaining unaltered, the cost of food and other necessaries may fall in consequence of increased production at home, or of increased importation from abroad. Postponing the question of the possibility of affording additional employment to agricultural labourers, let us first consider how far their present earnings may be rendered more valuable by a reduction in the price of the necessaries of life.

Whatever makes an article more abundant, without at the same time increasing the demand for it, makes it also cheaper than before. If, then, by improved methods of cultivation, larger crops could be drawn from the soil, the price of agricultural produce would be reduced, and labourers and others would be enabled to live more comfortably, without any addition to their pecuniary receipts. Now, since the peace of 1815, British agriculture has made very great progress, so much so, that notwithstanding the simultaneous increase of population, the corn raised at home has, in some very fruitful years, been equal, or nearly so, to the total national consumption, and has been sold at not more than one half the average price of the earlier part of the century. Improvement has been particularly remarkable during the last few years, since the public has become familiar with the experiments and speculations of Professors Liebig and Johnstone, Mr. Smith of Deanston, and others, and since the alteration of the corn laws has forced farmers into double diligence, in order to protect themselves against foreign competition. The art, however, is far from being equally advanced in every part of these islands; and it has been supposed that, if the processes and implements of husbandry used in the best-farmed counties were generally adopted throughout the kingdom, the annual produce of the soil would be doubled. If this estimate make any approach to accuracy, (and no one will think it exaggerated who has witnessed the neglect of drainage, the waste and misapplication both of manure and of animal labour, in all but the most improved districts,) it is obvious that the native supply of food might be raised at once to a level with the demand. But for this purpose farmers must have more capital, and more encouragement to invest it in their business, as well as more skill and knowledge. Their resources must not be exhausted by rents so high as barely to leave them the means of continuing cultivation in the present antiquated manner, and they must be freed from the danger of ejectment, as a consequence of improving their lands. They must have long leases at moderate rents. The actual exorbitance of rents may be plausibly inferred from the abatements which are regularly made by many landlords, when payment bcomes due. Such landlords are called liberal, and their generosity is highly extolled in the local newspapers; but the quality for which they take credit would be better shown in fixing rents, in the first instance, at reasonable rates, from which no deduction would be requisite. Abatements are only made when farmers have not the means of paying in full. It seems, indeed, that in average seasons the nominal rent is not expected to be completely realised, but it is fixed so high, in order that when a year of unusual agricultural prosperity occurs, the principal advantage from it may go to the landlord. It is probable that such rapacity defeats itself, and that a farmer who finds, the more he exerts himself, and the more he produces, the more rent he has to pay, sinks into apathy, and does not trouble himself to raise more than the smallest sum which he thinks likely to satisfy the claims upon him. Still it is possible that the present high rents might be punctually paid without distressing the farmers, if the latter were encouraged to exert themselves by the possession of leases. But in most parts of England leases are almost unknown, and the practice of granting them is supposed to be on the decline.* Farmers, for the most part, are removable at the landlord's pleasure. Where this is the case, a tenant is seldom silly enough, by expensive improvements, to run the risk of having his rent raised, or of being ousted to make way for a higher bidder. It is no doubt true that improvers are rarely ejected, and that instances are numerous of a farm remaining in possession of the same family for many generations without the security of a lease; but the explanation of this is to be sought, not in the moderation of the landlord, but in the caution of the tenant, who, adding nothing to the value of his land, offers no temptation to others to bid more for it than he pays. A prudent man, however convinced of his landlord's good faith, will scarcely lay out capital upon his pro-

* M'Culloch, Statistics of British Empire, vol. i. p. 455.

perty without a written engagement that he will be allowed to reap the full benefit of it. How much soever opinions may differ as to the necessity of reducing rents, there can be no doubt that, until leases become general, agricultural improvement must be greatly retarded. What at present chiefly prevents farmers from obtaining the security they so much need is the Chandos clause of the Reform Bill (introduced, be it observed, by their especial friend and champion), which, by giving the elective franchise to fifty-pound tenants-at-will, a class completely in the power of their landlords, causes them to be preferred to leaseholders who can venture to vote as they choose. A greater service could scarcely be rendered to agriculture than by the withdrawal of this baleful privilege from men who dare not use it conscientiously, which only serves to rob them of their independence, and which entices country gentlemen to cultivate their political influence at the expense of their estates. Whenever the tenure of land shall be freed from its capital defects, when farmers are no longer drained of the funds necessary for scientific cultivation, and can prudently embark all their spare capital in their business, the season will have arrived for increasing their knowledge of their art, and of the best modes of turning their resources to account. Agricultural associations may then wisely take a lesson from the Anti-Corn-Law League — publish tracts and popular treatises on husbandry, and despatch emissaries all over the country to lecture both in public and private to agricultural auditors, explaining the practical deductions which have been obtained by researches into the properties of soils and manures, and into the chemical composition of plants and animals. A spirit of inquiry and reflection may thus be awakened in a class in which it is particularly wanting, and farmers at the periodical meetings of their clubs may have observations and opinions really worth communicating to each other. Many other expedients will readily suggest themselves as likely to be of service in combating the prejudices of the present race of farmers, but it is from the enlightenment of the rising generation that the most decisive results may be expected. Agricultural schools should be established, in which, with everything essential in the ordinary course of study, should be combined special instruction, practical as well as theoretical, in all branches of knowledge connected with husbandry. Colleges should also be founded for the benefit of those who desired a more intimate acquaintance with agricultural science, and the annexation of professorships of agriculture to the national universities would also do good, by at least making the study fashionable among young men of the higher grades of society. Indications are already visible of a disposition among influential persons to afford these facilities for training skilful agriculturists. The great benefit derived from the school existing at Templemoyle in Ireland, has caused the formation of similar institutions in this part of the kingdom to be at least talked about, and as the thing might be almost as easily done as

said, it is to be hoped that actions will soon follow
words.  For the establishment of an agricultural
school, little more seems to be required than that
the leading landholders of a district should seek
out some person qualified to undertake its management, and should promise him their countenance
and support.  If any pecuniary assistance were
required, it would probably be only a moderate
sum for the purchase or lease of a piece of ground
and the construction of the necessary buildings,
and might be a loan to be repaid at an early period.
The school would require no endowment.  If well
conducted, it would be abundantly supported by
members of the class for whom it was designed,
and who would undoubtedly prefer it to the wretched
places of education at present open to them. . It is
the more probable that the establishment of schools
of this kind will not be much longer delayed, as
agricultural seminaries of a higher character are
already springing up.  The completion of the college at Cirencester will probably be followed by
the erection of preparatory schools, in which future
collegians may imbibe the elements of instruction,
and from the college will, in turn, issue tutors qualified to take the management of the schools.  The
example thus set in the western counties will, it
may be presumed, be followed in the rest of England, until at length no part of the country is unprovided with adequate means of agricultural education.  When this desideratum is supplied, and
when the other circumstances which join with un-
skilfulness in cramping the farmer's energies are

removed, we may expect to see the capabilities of the soil fully developed; but a consummation dependent on such conditions can only be the work of time. In proportion as more accurate views are taken by landholders of the obstacles which have hitherto impeded the progress of agriculture, more capital will be invested in that department of industry, more judgment will be shown in the application of it, and a corresponding increase will take place in the annual amount of produce. This increase, however, must certainly be gradual, and will probably be slow. But a slowly progressive augmentation of the national stock of provisions will not necessarily render them cheaper, for the increase in the number of consumers, and in the consequent demand, may keep pace with it. In order to insure a fall of prices, the increase of supply must be rapid enough to arrest the growth of population, by improving the condition of the lower orders of people, and raising their ideas of comfort. Without denying the possibility of such a revolution being effected by greater activity on the part of the actual occupiers of land in Great Britain, it will not be superfluous to look elsewhere for the means of procuring a considerable immediate enlargement of our present supply of food.

Foreign commerce presents a very valuable resource. In almost every other part of the civilised world provisions are much cheaper than in England, and in most countries of easy access, the difference of price is much more than equal to the cost of conveyance to our shores. They are, however, shut out from what would otherwise be their best market, by the excessive duties levied on their importation into this kingdom. But for these restrictions, the price of food here would not in general exceed its price in any other country by more than the expense of transport from the latter. Elaborate calculations have been made, with the view of ascertaining the probable reduction of price which would be effected by the free importation of foreign provisions, and very different results have been obtained at different times, corresponding with the varying opinions and wishes of the calculators. The mistakes of conjectural estimates may, however, be avoided, if any country can be found situated in other respects like Great Britain, but receiving a large portion of its food from abroad, by means of a trade unshackled by fiscal burthens. This is the case with the islands in the British Channel. Guernsey and Jersey do not produce a fourth part of the corn consumed by their inhabitants, and are principally supplied with it from France, Denmark, and Prussia. France also furnishes them with fruit and poultry, and Holland with cheese. The freight of the two most important of these articles from the exporting countries, is certainly not lower, and is probably higher, than it would be to Great Britain. It is therefore our customs' duties alone that make corn, foreign cheese, and in general all sorts of provisions that will bear keeping, dearer in this country than in Guernsey and Jersey, where their price is commonly about one-sixth part lower than with us.

Consequently, most kinds of food might at once be made about one-sixth cheaper by the removal of the imposts now levied on importation from abroad.

It has indeed been asserted, and some persons possibly believe, that foreign countries would be unable to satisfy the additional demands that would be made upon them if the British provision market were thrown open to all the world. With respect to corn, more especially, statements have been put forth professing to specify the quantities that might be obtained from various sources, and suggesting the conclusion, that the total amount of importation would have only an inconsiderable effect on prices here, and would still leave them a good deal above their present level on the Continent. There seems to be no real ground for this opinion. For many years past Great Britain has had no regular trade in corn with foreign countries. Immense quantities have from time to time been imported, but there have also been several years in which the importation has been too small to deserve notice. The demand, though often exceedingly large, has been too inconstant and irregular to be safely depended on, and foreign growers, therefore, have no doubt been deterred from providing for it. Nevertheless, whenever a demand for foreign corn has arisen, no difficulty has been experienced in obtaining whatever quantity was required. The importation has several times exceeded three millions of quarters in a year, and in one year (1839), it amounted to more than 4,600,000 quarters. This, it must be borne in mind, was effected without any previous notice, and can only show at most what quantity of corn foreign countries are able to spare from their present average annual stocks. How much more they might be able to furnish, if they were encouraged to extend cultivation by the certainty of being able to dispose of the increased produce, it is impossible to say, but supposing, for the sake of argument, that all the corn-growing countries of Europe and America could raise only five millions of quarters in addition to their present average crops, even such an insignificant importation would much more than suffice to reduce prices in this country to their level in the Channel Islands. The average quantity of corn annually brought to market in the United Kingdom is supposed to be about thirty millions of quarters*, which would be increased one sixth by the importation of five millions of foreign grain; but it has been often observed, and it is well known, that the price of an article, particularly of one so indispensable as corn, does not vary merely inversely as the quantity, but in a very much larger proportion, and that an addition of one-sixth to the stock in the market would cause the price to fall very much more than one-sixth. The thirty millions of quarters just mentioned include grain of all sorts, barley, rye, oats, &c., as well as wheat. The quantity of wheat annually brought to market is probably not more than eight millions of quarters. To reduce the price of wheat from 48s. a quarter, which may

* M'Culloch, Commercial Dict., edit. 1844, p. 407.

now be regarded as the average rate in England, to
40s., an addition of one million of quarters to the
average quantity annually brought to market would
very nearly suffice, and it would be ridiculous to
question the power of procuring so moderate a supply from abroad. It may then be presumed that
free trade in provisions would provide us with corn,
and consequently with both bread and beer, at the
same prices for which they are now usually sold in
Guernsey or Jersey. Butter and cheese would become equally cheap, for Holland, the great dairy
farm of Europe, lies over against our shores, and
would find it more profitable to supply our wants
then to send her produce to more distant markets.
The imports of fresh meat and poultry would most
likely be inconsiderable, but the price of the former
would be indirectly depressed by foreign supplies
of salt beef, bacon, and hams. Potatoes and some
other sorts of vegetables might also be introduced
in any quantities from abroad, unless they could be
produced as cheaply at home. These are the most
important articles whose price would be materially
reduced by the repeal of duties on foreign provisions ; for rice, sago, and similar tropical produce
are already nearly as cheap as they can be made ;
tea and coffee are luxuries, and sugar, though habit
has caused it to be regarded as almost a necessary
of life, is not, strictly speaking, food, and is a very
proper subject for moderate taxation. Among the
articles first mentioned, however, are included
almost all those which enter largely into the diet of
the poor, and of these a stock sufficient for our

consumption would be immediately furnished at greatly reduced prices, if foreign commerce were relieved from her present restrictions.

It has been questioned, however, whether the enlarged supply obtained from abroad would be continuous. At first, no doubt, the high price of provisions in this country would ensure a considerable importation ; but it has been supposed that foreign producers might be deterred from accepting British goods in exchange by the high import duties to which the latter are liable on the Continent and in America, and that they might insist on being paid in money. In that case the country would quickly be drained of the precious metals, and the new-born trade would necessarily be brought to a close. It is important that these apprehensions should be shown to be unfounded.

Notwithstanding the measures adopted by foreign nations for the protection of their own manufactures, there is not a civilised country in the world that does not annually import a certain quantity of British goods ; from which it is to be inferred that foreign workmen do not manufacture sufficient for the other classes of their countrymen, and that the latter are obliged to have recourse to British assistance to supply the deficiency. British goods are therefore no where wholly excluded by the operation of hostile tariffs. The non-manufacturing classes of every nation, after purchasing what their own countrymen are capable of furnishing, purchase in addition as large a supply of British productions as they are able to pay for, and would purchase still

more if their means would permit. Now, if a new
or enlarged market for their produce were offered
to foreign agriculturists in England, their means of
purchasing would be augmented. The cultivation
of their waste land would yield an additional supply
of provisions, which at present could not be profitably disposed of, but which might then be sent
to Great Britain and exchanged for various kinds
of commodities; and these commodities might be
carried home without more obstruction from high
customs' duties than the British goods actually imported at present. It does not appear, then, that
any difficulty would be experienced in effecting an
exchange of British manufactures with foreign provisions; but even if the foreign merchant should,
for some inexplicable cause, persist in demanding
payment in coin, his unaccountable obstinacy would
not put a stop to trade, but would merely cause it
to take a more circuitous route. A very slight
exportation from this country would raise the value
of the precious metals to such a height, and would
consequently so greatly depress prices, that the
money sent out would be immediately returned to
be expended in a market where it could be laid out
to so much advantage. The goods purchased with
it would then be exported to the countries which
had supplied the provisions, and would thus in effect
be bartered for them, the employment of money
having served merely to prolong the transaction.
In this manner the trade might continue. Provisions might be sent to England from abroad, and
money might be sent back for them, — the money,

however, would immediately return to buy manufactures, and these manufactures would be finally
exported. So clumsy a process would indeed soon
be abandoned, or rather would never be adopted, and
a direct system of barter would be employed in preference; but in one way or the other foreigners would
assuredly be induced to accept our manufactures in
exchange for their provisions, and consequently, if
the importation of the latter were freely permitted,
it would not be discontinued from any inability on
our part to pay for our supplies.

But foreign tariffs might be raised, additional
duties might be imposed on British goods, or the
trade in them might be altogether forbidden. This
certainly might happen, but there is no probability
that it would. The admission of an additional
quantity of British fabrics into a foreign market at
the present duties would not interfere in the least
with the foreign manufacturer. He might still
retain all his old customers, and continue to sell as
many of his products as before. The British goods
would be paid for solely in food which he did not
require, and which indeed would not have been
raised except to pay for those goods, and would be
superfluous for any other purpose. The extended
trade with Britain would thus divert no capital
from established channels, but would as it were
create new funds for its own support, — would
cause provisions to be raised which could not be
disposed of except in purchasing the British products offered in exchange for them. A stoppage
of the British trade would leave these provisions

on the producer's hands. He could not sell them
to his manufacturing countrymen, for the latter,
having already a sufficiency of food, would not
require them. The producer, therefore, although
prevented from buying British goods, would not be
able to buy more of home manufacture. If the
blind selfishness of the foreign manufacturer demanded additional protection from British competition, his cry would be opposed by another equally
loud from the foreign agriculturist; and it is scarcely
credible that any government would be silly enough
wantonly to deprive one class of its subjects of a
source of wealth which could not be diverted to
the benefit of any other class.

It will then, perhaps, be conceded, that Free Trade
would greatly augment the supply, and proportionately reduce the price of food in this country:
still it is contended that a reduction of the price of
food cannot be advantageous to labourers, for that
it occasions a corresponding fall in their pecuniary
receipts. Though an oft-refuted, it is still a common opinion, that wages are regulated by the price
of food; so that, however abundant and cheap the
latter may become, the earnings of the labourer, decreasing in proportion, cannot procure for him a
larger portion of it. If this be true, the amelioration of the condition of hired labourers may be
abandoned as hopeless. Their principal complaint
is want of food, and if wages only rise when food
grows dearer, and if food never grows cheap without making wages fall, human ingenuity is at a
loss to conceive how their power of purchasing pro-

visions can be augmented. On the other hand,
their situation will be as secure from deterioration
as it is incapable of improvement. Whether provisions be dear or cheap, their ability to purchase
them will remain the same. Even a famine cannot
injure them; the evils of scarcity must fall exclusively on the rich. A theory involving such propositions as these cannot be sound. Every one
knows that the command which labourers possess
over food does vary very materially, both in different countries, and in the same country at different
times; that farm servants in Norway and Belgium, for example, are six times as well fed as in
Munster or Connaught, and that the meagre figures
who till the ground in Dorsetshire and Somersetshire are lineal descendants of an ancient race of
sturdy beef-eaters. It is also notorious, that wages
are often high where food is cheap, and low where
it is dear; that they are nowhere lower than in
Ireland, where provisions are dearer than in any
other part of Europe except Great Britain, and no
where higher than in the United States, where the
cost of subsistence is proverbially moderate. Still,
although the notion that wages and prices rise and
fall together, is in general utterly false, it must be
admitted, that there were till lately circumstances
which afforded some countenance to it in this country. Previously to the amendment of the Poor
Law, the rate of agricultural wages in most parts
of England depended on the decision of parish
vestries and county magistrates. By these, certain
sums, proportioned to their wants, were assigned as

suitable incomes for labourers, and if any one failed by his own labour to procure the amount specified for him, the deficiency was made up out of the poor's rates. The sum requisite for the supply of a person's wants necessarily varied with the price of food, and as the independent labourer would naturally refuse to accept less than he might receive as a pauper, and as he could not obtain much more while there were labourers out of employment maintained by the parish funds, his wages were commonly regulated by the pauper's allowance, and varied like it with the price of provisions. This has since ceased to be the case. The allowance now made to an out-door pauper, little, if at all, exceeds what is necessary for subsistence. Less than this an independent labourer need not, and does not accept, but the Poor Law interferes with the rate of wages only so far as to prevent its sinking below this extreme level. In all its fluctuations above this mark, the price of labour is at present governed, in England as elsewhere, by the circumstance which determines the price of all other commodities, viz. the proportion between the supply of, and the demand for, the article. When workmen are numerous and work is scarce, the former, in order to procure employment, will attempt to undersell each other, and wages will fall. If, on the contrary, the demand for labour be great and labourers few, the masters will bid against each other, striving to attract workmen into their service by raising wages, which will rise higher or lower in proportion to the amount of capital possessed by the masters. Thus

it appears, that the rate of money wages depends
entirely on the proportion between the supply of
labour and the amount of money applicable to its
remuneration, and has no connection with the price
of provisions; wages may be high when food is a
drug in the market, or they may be low when there
is a famine in the land. Their real value does, indeed, depend greatly on the price of food, for they
will buy more or less of it according as it is cheap
or dear, and if wages were paid in food instead of
in money, their nominal as well as their real value
would vary with the abundance of food. But it is
obvious, that the larger the stocks of food possessed
by the employers of labour, the more food would
they be willing to offer in order to procure servants, so that, directly or indirectly, an augmentation of the supply of food must always proportionately increase the labourer's ability to procure it.

Arguments like these, however, have already
been often employed in vain, and it cannot be expected that they will be more successful now than
when urged by abler writers. I shall therefore
attempt a new mode of demonstrating that wages
are not depressed by the cheapness of provisions.
When any considerable addition is made to the
stock of food in a country, the increased abundance
and cheapness do not induce people in easy circumstances to consume more than before; for
scarcity, though it may prevent many from indulging their palates, is seldom sufficiently intense
to compel any but the poor to stint their appetites.
The rich, therefore, in times of plenty, merely pay

less for their provisions ; but, as they do not use more than usual, an unusually large residue remains for the poor, to whom, as to the only willing purchasers, it must be sold, if sold at all. But if wages have fallen in proportion to the increased cheapness of food, the poor cannot have the means of buying more than previously, and will be unable to pay for the additional quantity offered to them. Yet this additional quantity is not wasted, but is eventually sold ; and, since none but the poor required it, it can only have been sold to the poor. The latter, therefore, must have had the means of paying for it, and their wages cannot have been reduced by the cheapness of food, seeing that they have continued sufficient to purchase the whole of the additional supply which occasioned that cheapness.

Although, however, the low price of food cannot of itself lower wages, it may be suspected that the adoption of the particular means here recommended of making food cheap, viz. the free importation of foreign provisions, might have that effect, by narrowing the field of agricultural employment in this country. This question shall be presently considered, but it will be convenient first to examine some other supposed impediments to a measure, which, provided it did not lessen the demand for labour, would apparently enable the labourer to purchase one-sixth part more food than at present.

The first and most obvious objection to the repeal of any import duties, is the loss of the revenue arising from them. But the duties on corn, the principal article of food imported, cannot be depended on as a source of revenue. In some years they are very productive, but in others they yield little or nothing. Their proceeds can at best be regarded only as an unexpected windfall for the Chancellor of the Exchequer; but as their amount is considerable only in bad seasons, when people, having to pay more for bread, cannot afford to spend so much on other taxed articles, it probably never does more than make up for a decrease of income from some other source, which with corn at free-trade prices would not have occurred. As for the duties on provisions of every other kind — on butter, cheese, salt meat, bacon, hams, eggs, rice, &c., their annual produce is very little more than 300,000*l.*, the loss of which sum might be compensated at least eight times over, merely by an equalisation of the duties on British colonial and foreign sugar.

Another objection to free trade in provisions, is that it would render us dependent, for part of our subsistence, on foreign countries, which might then at any time reduce us to great distress, by cutting off the supplies. This is perfectly true; but we are already exposed to a greater danger of the same kind. If many of our purveyors of food were foreigners, and should all with one accord resolve to shut up shop, they would certainly place us on short commons; but our own countrymen, the farmers and others, who now almost monopolise our custom, might starve us outright by combining among themselves, and refusing to sell

to us any more. Every one who does not
himself raise or make every thing he uses,
must be partially dependent upon others for
the necessaries of life, but the dependence gives
him no concern, because he knows it to be mutual.
My baker has it in his power to disappoint me of
to-morrow's breakfast, yet I reckon with unabated
confidence on the customary hot rolls, because if I
want his bread he wants my money, and can as ill
afford to spare the one as I can the other. It is
solely from such mercenary motives, and by no
means from any compatriotic prejudices in our
favour, that our own farmers keep our markets
constantly supplied; and foreigners, being not less
greedy of gain, would be equally ready to furnish
us with their surplus produce as long as we could
offer them what they desired in exchange. But the
crops would sometimes fail in foreign countries; all
the provisions might be required at home, and there
might be none to spare for us; and this would be
particularly likely to happen with respect to corn.
But all corn countries are not in the same climate
nor does any country consist of only one soil. The
same weather which makes the harvest defective in
one place makes it unusually abundant in another
and such local variations, compensating each other,
not improbably render the aggregate produce of
extensive regions much the same from year to year.
When the market was ill supplied at Dantzic, it
would probably be crammed at Odessa, or in Sicily
or Egypt; or if the scarcity were general on this
side of the Atlantic, the chances would be greater

of extraordinary plenty in the United States. But perhaps war might break out between ourselves and the supplying countries. We should scarcely however quarrel with all of them at once; or, if we did, it would be a sign of a pugnacious disposition on our part, which low diet would be very useful in correcting, and so the evil would cure itself. In truth, however, there would be little danger of a breach between countries so intimately connected by a mutually beneficial commerce. Nothing tends so greatly to prevent men from quarrelling as mutual dependence; and the remark applies quite as well to communities as to individuals. One nation would be as reluctant to make war with another in whose territories she enjoyed an extensive market for her goods, as a tradesman would be to quarrel with his customers. She would naturally be equally anxious not to give offence. Russia, although invulnerable by external violence, bridles her ambition at the bidding of other Powers, in order that they may continue to deal with her for hides and tallow. Without their help in getting rid of her superabundance, she would be choked in her own fat, and would perish from the dropping off of her constituent members. The youthful passions of America, in like manner, are constrained by nothing stronger than bonds of cotton. None but ourselves can take off her immense stock of this article, and she cannot therefore venture seriously to disoblige us. Her intemperance commonly vents itself in harmless vapouring, and notwithstanding her implacable ill-will towards us, she has long refrained from any action that would have compelled us to retaliate. France alone, amongst civilised nations, is tormented by an unqualified desire for war, and is withheld from it only by the poverty of her resources and the good sense of her ruler. This results from her commercial isolation. Having little trade with any of her neighbours, she has no tradesmanlike reasons for keeping the peace; and, envious of the prosperity which her narrow policy prevents her from equalling, she snatches eagerly at every pretext for dispute. The larger the dealings between different nations, the more certain are they to remain on good terms. The dependence of this country upon foreigners for part of her subsistence, instead of being a cause for uneasiness, would become more secure in proportion as it extended. As long as our imports of food are of trifling amount, or take place only at uncertain intervals, it may be easy for a capricious government to interrupt our intercourse with its subjects; but if a considerable portion of our population were dependent for subsistence on foreign supplies, the agricultural classes in almost every neighbouring country would be interested in opposing a stoppage of the trade. One principal design of Providence in assigning different products to different regions, was doubtless to prevent their inhabitants from being entirely self-dependent, and to force them into commercial and amicable intercourse. Every country in the world possesses peculiar advantages for the production of certain articles of human consumption, and so obvious is the advantage

of seeking every commodity where it can be procured most cheaply and of the best quality, that if
free trade were once universally established, the
common interest of mankind would secure it from
the risk of disturbance.   War would then become
an impossibility.   Political economy thus points out
the way to a state of tranquillity, for which philan-
thropists and philosophers of all ages have vainly
sighed.   The genuine Universal Peace Society is the
Anti-Corn Law League, and Adam Smith its most
appropriate patron saint.   The sword will not be
turned into a ploughshare, nor the spear into a
pruning-hook, until old iron is needed for tools
of husbandry, and till men are too busily engaged
in raising corn and wine to sell to their neighbours,
to have time to spare for cutting their throats.

These, however, are trifles.   The grand obstacle
to the repeal of duties on foreign provisions, is the
fear which is entertained of its injuring British
agriculturists, by reducing the price of their produce.   In the discussion of this part of the subject,
it must be premised that "agriculturists" is rather
too comprehensive a term for those classes of our
countrymen which can really be interested in
excluding foreign provisions.   Landlords and holders
of land on lease alone can possibly be benefited by
a continuance of high prices.   To the great majority
of farmers, who are merely tenants at will, and are
at liberty to break off their connection with their
landlords at the close of every year, it is a matter
of indifference what the average price of food may
be, or rather they are as much interested as any

other consumers in being able to buy it cheap.
Except during the short period for which their
landlord's demands upon them are fixed, their profit
does not depend upon the price of produce. If
prices are high, rents will be high also; and if they
are expected to fall, rents will likewise fall. In
arranging the terms on which land shall be let,
both owner and farmer calculate how much the
value of the produce is likely to exceed the expenses
of cultivation, together with the usual profit on
those expenses. The difference is, strictly speaking,
" rent," the whole of which it is the landlord's
object to obtain, while the farmer is equally anxious
not to engage to pay more. If the ordinary price
of agricultural produce be so low that the value of
the crop will probably only exceed the cost of cultivation by sixpence or a shilling an acre, sixpence
or a shilling an acre is all the rent that the farmer
will consent to pay; whereas, if prices be high, he
may be ready to pay two or three pounds per acre.
All that he demands is a means of profitably
employing his capital, and this, if he calculate correctly, he may have equally in either of the above
cases. Agricultural labourers, likewise, if the
employment for them remain the same, will receive
the same money wages, and with the same money,
will of course be better off when food is cheap than
when it is dear.

Of the whole body of agriculturists, therefore,
taking the term in its most extended sense, the only
portion that can be directly benefited by high
prices, consists of landlords and leaseholders. The

interest which these possess in them seems at first sight obvious enough. Rent has been explained to be that portion of the produce of land which remains after the expenses of cultivation, including the farmer's profit, have been paid. Consequently, when prices are high, the surplus remaining for rent is proportionably large, and when prices fall, unless the expenses of cultivation are reduced, not merely in the same proportion, but absolutely to the same extent, the landlord's claim must be reduced also, or must be paid in part out of the farmer's capital. It is difficult to avoid the conclusion that these results would follow the establishment of free trade in food. Grounds have already been assigned for the belief, that by that measure the price of British agricultural produce would be reduced one sixth. By such increased cheapness of many commodities, the cost of subsequent production would, no doubt, be affected, but it could not possibly be reduced in more than the same proportion; and it is obvious that a fall of one-sixth in the gross value of the crop would be far from compensated by a reduction of one-sixth in the cost of raising it. Moreover, the items of which the cost of cultivation is composed are not only not always the same, but vary both with the quality of the soil, and with the nature of the produce, and all the items are not equally susceptible of reduction. For this reason, the tendency of rents to fall would be counteracted in very different degrees in different cases by the diminution of the farmer's expenditure; but one or two examples may be useful in showing the probable average result. An acre of light land, of

medium quality, sown, according to the most approved rotation, with turnips, barley, clover, and
wheat, generally yields, in the course of four years,
mutton, wool, grain, clover, &c., to the value, at
present prices, of about 26*l.* altogether, or 6*l.* 10*s.*
annually. This last sum would, at present, be
distributed in something like the following manner: — The expenses of cultivation might absorb
about 5*l.* 4*s.* 9*d.* ; the farmer's profit, reduced as it
has been of late years, would scarcely exceed five
shillings*, and one pound would remain for rent.
The expenses of cultivation might be subdivided
as follows: —

|  | £ | s. | d. |
|---|---|---|---|
| Manure     -     -     -     -     -     - | 1 | 10 | 0 |
| Seed     -     -     -     -     -     - | 0 | 12 | 9 |
| Manual labour     -     -     -     - | 1 | 2 | 0 |
| Animal ditto, and wear and tear of cattle and agricultural implements     -     - | 1 | 13 | 0 |
| Poor's rates, church and highway rates, and tithes     -     -     -     -     -- | 0 | 7 | 0 |
|  | £5 | 4 | 9 |

Now a deduction of one-sixth from the gross
value of the produce would reduce the annual proceeds to 5*l.* 8*s.* 4*d.*, and would seem at first sight
to leave nothing whatever for rent. But on the
other hand, the fall of prices would occasion a considerable reduction in the farmer's expenditure.
Wages, indeed, a very important item, would not
fall unless the demand for labour were diminished,
which, I hope presently to be able to show, would

* It must be borne in mind, that to the farmer's profit arising
from the sale of his produce, should be added the value of the
possession of a rent-free dwelling house.

not be the case. But one-sixth less money would be required for seed, and for the purchase and keep of cattle, and as cattle could not be rendered cheaper without a proportionable increase in their number, the cost of manure would also be reduced one sixth. With the price of food, the cost of maintaining the poor, and the amount of poor's rates, would decrease, and tithes also would be eventually regulated by the price of corn. The sum total of all these savings would be not much less than 14s., reducing the expenses of cultivation to 4l. 10s. 9d., exclusive of 5s. for the farmer's profit. After deducting these two sums from 5l. 8s. 4d., the supposed value of the produce of an acre, there would remain 12s. 7d. instead of 1l. to be paid to the landlord; so that the reduction of rent would be rather less than three-eighths. In heavy clay soils of the same annual value, the produce of an acre in four years, in one of which the land was left fallow, might be $3\frac{1}{4}$ quarters of wheat, $4\frac{1}{2}$ quarters of beans, and 6 quarters of oats, besides straw, stubble, &c., and might be worth 25l. 10s. altogether. The average annual proceeds would therefore be 6l. 7s. 6d., which, by a deduction of one-sixth, would be reduced to 5l. 6s. 3d. The annual expenses of cultivation would average 5l. 2s., which, by a decrease of one-sixth in all the items, except that of manual labour, would be reduced to 4l. 9s. 6d. This sum taken from 5l. 6s. 3d. would leave 16s. 9d., of which five shillings would be taken as profit by the farmer, and 11s. 9d. would remain for the landlord. It is not necessary, however, to let land lie fallow so often as once in four years. In every alternate quadrennial period, one green crop and three of grain might be advantageously taken; and, by this means, half-a-crown at least might be added to the annual rent, raising it very nearly to fifteen shillings. These examples seem to warrant the inference, that the unrestricted importation of foreign provisions would, on an average of different soils, reduce rents nearly one-third; and, with every confidence in the inestimable advantages of free trade, I cannot persuade myself that, unless a great change took place in the practice of agriculture, rents would not fall to something like that extent. It is vain to urge that corn and dairy produce are the only articles of food that would be largely imported, and that the price of meat would be little affected by direct foreign competition. Supposing this to be true, if the cheapness of corn rendered its cultivation less profitable than the management of live stock, the former business would be contracted and the latter would be extended, until the relation between the prices of corn and cattle became the same as before. In this manner a fall in the price of corn must occasion an equal fall in the price of almost every sort of agricultural produce; and, if the one becomes one-sixth cheaper in consequence of foreign importation, the others almost without exception must do so likewise. It will be impossible to prevent a decrease in the value of the produce of the land by merely changing the sort of produce.

To one of the two classes of persons whom the

depreciation of agricultural produce would really
affect — to leaseholders, who would, nevertheless,
be bound to continue their accustomed payments
to their landlords, the diminution of their pecuniary
receipts would be a most serious evil, from which it
might, perhaps, be proper to protect them by a
legislative enactment, compelling a suitable reduction of rents to be made. Such a measure, however unprecedented, would be the less objectionable,
as the reduction which it would effect in the income
of landowners would not place the latter in a much
worse position than before. Money is only valuable
for what it will purchase; and if, in the altered
circumstances, in which rents were reduced one-
third, a corresponding reduction of taxation, and
in the price of commodities, should take place,
landlords would still possess the same power of
purchasing. Now, it may be taken for granted
(for upon this assumption the preceding calculations
respecting the probable fall of rents are based), that
the repeal of duties on the various foreign provisions
enumerated above would make them nearly as cheap
here as on the Continent, the expense of conveyance
to this country constituting the only difference of
price. Many other articles, only second in importance to these, would be cheapened in as great
or a still greater degree. When monopoly has been
driven from the citadel, she will not be suffered to
linger at the outposts. British landowners, when
deprived of their unjust privileges, will no longer
be disposed to make common cause with colonial
proprietors, but, being forced to sell cheap them-

selves, will be anxious to buy cheap from others, and will zealously join in an attack on their present allies. Coffee and sugar will then, assuredly, be admitted here on equal terms, from whencesoever they may come ; and the former will be sold nearly as cheap, and the latter much cheaper in our markets than in France or Germany. This will be effected, too, not only without any loss to the state, but with an increase of revenue, which will allow of the total repeal of the duties on tallow, soap, candles, bricks, and timber. We shall then have food, the requisites for light and cleanliness, and materials for building, almost as cheap as our neighbours. Moreover, with duty-free timber, ships may be built at less expense in England than in any other part of Europe; and by the cost of ships the price of all imported articles must neces- sarily be affected. The only important articles of desirable consumption (for tobacco and spirits should rather be classed among poisons) which will then be much dearer here than elsewhere, are wine and tea; and the difference in the price of these and of other things would be partly, if not entirely, compensated by the superior cheapness of clothing and of manu- factures in general. On the whole, it does not seem too much to expect that, by the abolition of provision-duties, and by the other financial reforms indicated above, the cost of living in Great Britain might be brought as low as in France, where it is notorious that an equal share of luxuries and com- fort, as well as of the necessaries of life, may be enjoyed, with two-thirds of the income which is

needed to procure them in England. It may be
thought strange that such a result should be supposed capable of attainment without a reduction of
the amount raised by taxation ; but it is a mistake
to imagine, that the necessity of levying so large a
sum for the service of the state, is the cause of the
extraordinary dearness of England. Our public
expenditure, enormous as it is, is certainly not so
great in proportion to our resources as that of the
French : it is certainly easier for us to pay fifty-five
millions than for them to pay forty-three millions
sterling annually. But the most grievous of our
taxes are imposed, not for the sake of revenue, but
for the protection of particular classes, and are designed to exclude foreign grain, sugar, coffee, and
timber. The abolition of the discriminating duties
on the second and third of these articles would
furnish the means of repealing between two and three
millions sterling of other taxes, without causing the
smallest diminution in the revenues of the state. We
should then pay a greater amount of taxes, but we
should not be more heavily taxed than the French.
We should pay more, simply because we were richer.
The taxes on commodities would not be higher, nor
in many cases so high, but they would produce
more, because more of the commodities would be
used.

The emancipation of trade, then, although it
might occasion a fall of rents, would raise the value
of money in the same proportion, and would enable
landlords, in spite of the decrease of their incomes,
to live in much the same style as at present.

"But," exclaim certain statesmen, with an art-
lessness truly engaging, "landed estates are in
general heavily mortgaged, or otherwise incum-
bered, and their owners, with reduced pecuniary
receipts, would be unable to make the annual
payments for which they are responsible." Certainly nothing can show more clearly how low the
advocates of the provision laws are sunk, than that
they should stoop to such an argument as this.
Because country gentlemen have got into debt, the
rest of the nation, forsooth, are to contribute to
their relief, and be punished for their extravagance !
To save them from the consequences of their imprudence, others are to be placed on a short allowance of food, and restricted to three-fourths of the
quantity which they both urgently require and can
afford to buy ! Upon what plea do landlords presume thus to place their own burthens on other
men's shoulders ? Why should not they, like every
one else, be left to get out of debt as they can, and
to satisfy their creditors, even by selling their property, if no other means present itself ? Is the fear
of their being driven to such an extremity a sufficient
reason why other people should be prevented from
buying food where they please, and compelled to
deal only at dear shops established for the landlords' benefit ? Is there indeed any conceivable
motive that would justify so audacious an abuse of
power ? In the preceding pages an attempt has
been made to show that the emancipation of trade
would not be injurious to landowners, at least to
such as were unincumbered by debt. Supposing,

however, this opinion to be erroneous — supposing that the fund from which rents are paid would be completely swept away by the repeal of the taxes on food,— even that would be no valid objection to the measure. What is sought is not a boon or an indulgence which may be honestly withheld — it is merely the redress of long-endured injustice. The people ask permission to buy provisions where they are to be found cheapest. Is this a request to be denied? Why, the very fact of its being made is in itself disgraceful to the legislature. Can the poor be much longer deprived of a right so incontestable for the aggrandisement of a particular class? If its concession be incompatible with the maintenance of existing rents, no further proof is requisite that those rates are iniquitous and ought not to be maintained. *Fiat justitia, ruat cœlum.* Let the people keep their own, though landlords be the sufferers.

Country gentlemen appear, from the language they are in the habit of using, to imagine that they are entitled in all circumstances to certain incomes proportioned to their estates, which must be raised at other people's expense, if the amount cannot be otherwise obtained. Enough has been said already to point out the absurdity of such a notion. The only portion of the annual returns from his land, which the proprietor ought to expect, is what remains after the expenses of cultivation have been fully paid. The husbandman and farmer should first be satisfied, and what they leave (if they leave any thing) may be taken by the landlord,—and very thankful he ought to be for it. However small the amount, "'tis an honest portion," as Bishop Latimer says, "to have *gratis* of another man's sweat and labour." But to insist that people perfectly independent of him shall buy the produce of his fields dearer than they can buy similar articles elsewhere, merely that out of the enhanced price he may appropriate a larger sum to his own use, is a pretension so preposterous, that shouts of laughter would be the only fitting reply to it, if dire experience had not proved it to be any thing but a laughing matter.

A plea sometimes set up for monopoly is, that, however unjust in itself, it cannot be subverted without injury to the interests that have been permitted to grow up under its shelter. Much of the land in this country, for example, has been bought by the present owners or their predecessors during the existence of high prices, and larger sums have been given for it in consequence; a fall of prices would diminish its value, and would thus be prejudicial to the last purchasers. It is a droll thing to say, however, that because injustice has already lasted long, it should be suffered to last longer; it should seem, on the contrary, that the longer it has continued the sooner it ought to be redressed: if it would be a hardship to the few to receive lower rents than usual, it would be a still greater hardship to the many to be prevented from receiving as much food as is offered for their money. The unwitting purchaser of stolen goods may grumble at having the property taken from him by the rightful owner; but the latter would have still more cause to complain, if he might not seize upon his own wherever he found it.

Apprehensions as to the effect which the establishment of free trade might have on the interests of landowners, would not then, even if well founded, afford, except to landowners themselves, any motive for opposing that measure. The propriety of redressing a grievance does not depend upon the certainty that those with whom the injustice originated will not suffer from the loss of their usurped privileges; it is sufficient that those who are labouring under oppression will be relieved by its removal. The present question is not whether the unrestricted importation of food would diminish the incomes of landlords, but whether the cheapness which would result from it would be really beneficial to the rest of the community. The only class about which there can be any doubt, is that of agricultural labourers. This class would gain more perhaps than any other from the low price of provisions, provided the rate of wages remained unaltered, and wages could not fall unless the demand for labour were diminished. But it has been supposed that if British agriculture were deprived of legislative protection, a good deal of land would be thrown out of cultivation, and that the amount of employment and the rate of wages would thus be reduced. Now it is no answer to this argument, that although the demand for labour might be diminished in agriculture, it would be augmented in manufactures, and that those who were dismissed from one occupation might betake themselves to the other.  Carters and ploughmen are not easily converted into spinners and weavers, and experience has shown that they are not in general to be starved into taking up a business so incompatible with their tastes and habits ; husbandry is almost the only occupation suitable for husbandmen : if they lose this, they commonly lose their only livelihood; so that if it could be proved that the repeal of the provision laws would lessen the demand for agricultural labour, the objection would perhaps be fatal to free trade.  It is not, however, pretended that this effect could take place unless land were thrown out of cultivation, and it is obvious that no land would be suffered to become waste for which any amount of rent, however small, was obtainable. Now it has been shown that the probable reduction in the rent of land of average quality would be less than one-third ; and there is no reason to think that the reduction on inferior land would exceed this proportion ; on the contrary, as poor lands require an extra quantity of manure, the price of which would fall with the price of agricultural produce, the decrease of the cost of cultivation would probably be greater than elsewhere, and would more forcibly counteract the fall of prices.  No land, therefore, would become wholly incapable of paying rent, or be abandoned as worthless.  Even the poorest would continue to be let, though at a reduced rent, and would be employed in some sort of production. The important question is, to what particular purpose it would be applied. Grain would most likely cease to be grown upon it, and would be cultivated only on the more fertile soils, but tillage would not be contracted in consequence. Poor land, upon which corn could not be profitably grown, would be found still less adapted for pasture, and would in fact be almost unproductive in such a state. The only way to obtain valuable returns from it, would be to make it bear green crops, such as turnips, clover, or mangel-wurzel; but for this purpose as much human labour would be required as when a crop of grain was obtained every other year. It thus appears certain, that neither the amount of employment for agricultural labourers, nor their money wages, would be at all diminished by free trade in food. It is very probable that both one and the other would be increased; it is very probable that a change would take place in the practice of agriculture, which would not only afford the labourer more work and better remuneration, but would also effectually protect the landlord against a reduction of rent.

The terms upon which land is let in this country, depend very much upon the tenant's social position: the holder of a thousand acres pays only twenty shillings for land for which the holder of fifty acres would have to pay thirty, and of which a cottager would be unable to obtain the smallest portion at a lower rate than forty shillings an acre. As large farmers are perpetually exclaiming, and very justly too, of the great difficulty they have in paying their rents, while no rents are more punctually paid than those of cottage allotments, it is pretty clear that land is able to pay better when divided among several occupiers, than when united into one extensive holding. Nevertheless landlords are generally partial to the system of large farms, which gives them least trouble, and offers them the security of considerable capitalists; but these considerations would scarcely reconcile them to a further reduction of rent. Rather than submit to this, which might be ruinous to such as were themselves bound to large periodical payments, they would not hesitate to split their farms. The repeal of the corn laws might thus cause the race of large capitalists to disappear from the occupation of the soil, and to be replaced by small farmers, holding on an average, perhaps, not more than fifty acres each. Very eminent writers contend that a change like this would be highly detrimental to agriculture: by these, large farms and large capitals are held to be essential to good farming, without which it is said there cannot be effectual drainage, nor sufficient manure, nor judicious rotation of crops, nor can expensive implements be procured, or labour properly husbanded. Now, without stopping to controvert these assertions, let it be asked, In what does the value of improved agricultural processes consist? Are they esteemed for some intrinsic merit of their own, for some pleasure which is found in adopting them, or solely for the effect they produce? The one thing needful is obviously to make land yield the largest possible

surplus, after adequately remunerating the cultivator; and that small farms can afford a larger
surplus than similar portions of a large one, is
evident from the fact of their paying higher rents.
Further proof may be found in Flanders and
Lombardy, where the densest populations in Europe,
and those in a large proportion *town* populations,
are maintained in comfort by land divided amongst
small farmers. How this end is attained, is surely
of comparatively little importance: even if it were
true that the implements and methods of small
farmers are clumsy and defective, that they disdain
the aid of science, and require twice as much
labour as would suffice under a different system, it
would still be manifest that they possess some advantage which more than compensates for all these
drawbacks. In spite of their adherence to old
practices, they manage to get more from the land
than the large capitalist with all his improvements,
and after reserving sufficient for their own consumption, they have a larger residue left for sale.
They might, perhaps, do better still by imitating
some of the methods of the large capitalist; but even
as it is, they do better than he does, and their plan
must, on the whole, be preferable to his. Nothing
can be more unjust, however, than to stigmatise the
culture of small farms, as necessarily rude and in-
artificial. The small holdings of the Flemish
peasantry not only bear heavier crops than land of
the same quality in the best farmed districts of
England or Scotland, but the land is kept much
cleaner, is much better drained, and much more

abundantly manured. It may be true that in Great
Britain large farmers are almost the only improvers;
but this is because few, except large farmers, have
leases, and consequently any motive for improvement. Where small farmers have a firmer hold
upon the land, as in Norway, Belgium, Switzerland, and France, they combine to raise funds
for any project that promises to be generally beneficial. In this way channels many miles in length
are made for irrigation or drainage; and a
dozen owners of three or four cows, or occupiers
of as many acres, contrive to make cheeses as large
and fine as any that Cheshire can produce; and
even to establish a beet-root sugar manufacture, the
most extensive and scientific of all modern agricultural operations. Mutual co-operation thus places
within the reach of small farmers almost every advantage possessed by their wealthy rivals. The
principal difference in their modes of procedure is,
that the former being less able to purchase extensive machinery, employ a larger relative quantity of
human labour. This, however, is the reverse of
disadvantageous, either to themselves or to the
public. The agricultural class constitutes the
nerves and sinews of a nation, and its increase, so
generally deprecated by political economists, only
becomes an evil when it encroaches on the nourishment which might be reserved for other classes. If
additional agricultural labourers can procure subsistence without detracting from that of other
people, their existence is a national advantage. If
by the labour of two men the produce of a piece of

ground can be so much augmented as to furnish ample subsistence for both, and yet to leave as great a surplus as when only one cultivator was employed, the double application of labour increases both the strength and the wealth of the country. If the surplus be greater than before, it increases also the income of the proprietor of the land. Now this, and much more than this takes place on small farms. Labour there is much more productive than on large ones. Most of the work is done under the master's eye, and much of it by his own hands, or those of his family. All the labourers have motives for exertion unknown to hired servants, or at least are subject to a vigilant supervision which a large landholder cannot exercise. They bestow on their work a care, patience, and assiduity, which cannot be purchased at any price; and these qualities much more than compensate for any waste of labour occasioned by bad tools or injudicious arrangement. The produce of the soil is so much increased in consequence, as not only to provide for the consumption of the additional cultivators, but to leave a larger quantity remaining, than if fewer labourers, without the same motives for industry, had been employed. If then the merits of a system may be judged of from its results, the subdivision of farms would be favourable instead of injurious to agriculture. It would certainly occasion a change of practice, and would cause more labour to be employed, but it would increase the produce of labour in a much greater degree. A larger proportion would thus become applicable to the payment of rent, and to the consumption of the non-agricultural part of the community; provisions would grow cheaper, but landlords, notwithstanding, would receive incomes as large, if not larger, than at present.

The principal benefit, however, would accrue to the agricultural labourer. With the increased demand for his services, his wages would of course rise, and he would have more money to spend, as well as be able to buy more food, &c. with the same money. A great improvement would also take place in his relations towards his employer. The wide gulf which now separates the holder of a thousand acres from the workpeople in his pay would no longer exist. The occupier of a farm, not a twentieth part that size, would associate familiarly with his servants, and would not scruple to dine with them at the same table, or to lodge them under his roof. He would rather prefer doing so, because he could so both keep them at less expense, and would have them always at hand to assist in the minute and garden-like cultivation, on which the extraordinary productiveness of small farms mainly depends. Single labourers would in general be permitted to live in the farm-house, and in such comfortable quarters would be content to wait, until they could marry without imprudence. When that time arrived, the intimate connexion and kindly feelings subsisting between themselves and their employers would not be broken off. On every farm of moderate size, it would be convenient to have one or more cottages, and when one of these became vacant, the master would naturally offer it to some expectant couple among his servants, whose union had been postponed for the occurrence of such an opportunity.  He might also allot to them in part payment of wages, a small plot of land, and perhaps likewise grass for a cow. By so doing, he would confer a signal favour on them without any loss to himself, and would, at the same time, attach them firmly to his service; for the use of a bit of ground is invaluable to a day labourer.  Its cultivation costs him nothing, but serves rather as an amusement for the leisure of himself and his family, enabling all but the very youngest to make themselves useful.  Abundance of manure is found in the refuse and scraps of all kinds, that would otherwise be thrown away.  Nothing is wasted, and habits of thrift and industry are formed.  The produce being proportioned less to the extent of the ground, than to the care and attention bestowed upon it, is infinitely greater than a larger occupier could have obtained from the same space; and besides the direct addition which it makes to the labourer's means of subsistence, enables him to keep pigs, poultry, &c. at little or no expense.  He enjoys a variety, as well as an abundance of articles of diet, which, even if he possessed their value in money, it would be scarcely possible for him to buy, and he has besides a resource on which he may rely when other means of livelihood temporarily fail.  A day labourer is always liable to be thrown out of work by a number of causes, when, if he be entirely dependent on wages, he may become involved in inextricable difficulties, whereas with the help of a stock of food of his own raising, he might easily struggle through his embarrassment. The occupancy of a little land does away with much of the precariousness, which is the worst feature in the labourer's condition ; and this is particularly the case when the land is the labourer's own property, as it would not improbably become, in circumstances such as those supposed, when he might often be able to save a little money. He then feels himself sufficiently independent not to be over-anxious about the future; but not so much so as to grow careless of obtaining work, or of satisfying his employer. On the contrary, finding that he has been admitted into a higher order of society, he uses every exertion to maintain his new position. Men of this class are commonly the most diligent and trustworthy, as well as the most respectful servants.

In opposition to these assertions, the misery of the Irish peasantry will probably be urged. The example of Ireland is very commonly cited as a decisive proof that small farms and the possession of land by labourers powerfully promote over-population, and that this in turn occasions a further partition of the land, until the smallness of the separate portions equally prevents the wretched cultivators from growing sufficient food on their own land, and from obtaining it in the service of larger occupiers. In reply, it might be sufficient to refer once more to those districts on the continent of Europe, in which the most thriving peasantry in

the world have subsisted for ages on farms not
much larger than the generality of Irish holdings.
The inhabitants of those districts have not multiplied beyond the means of subsistence; their
farms are not continually decreasing in size, or
divided into patches too small for the comfortable
maintenance of a family.   Directly opposite effects
cannot spring from precisely the same cause.   The
subdivision of the soil, from which so much happiness
arises in Flanders and Switzerland, cannot of itself
have produced misery in Ireland.   In an earlier
portion of this Essay, however, the over-population
of Ireland has already been traced to the universal
poverty which existed while the whole country was
still in the hands of an inconsiderable number of
occupiers : having been antecedent to, it cannot
have proceeded from, the subdivision of farms.
The keen competition for land which it has occasioned, has indeed been the sole reason why the
subdivision of farms has not been beneficial to the
present tenants.   An Irish cottier is not miserable
because he has two or three acres of land attached
to his dwelling, but because he has to pay for this
land three or four times as much as it would be let
for in England.   How is it possible that, after paying
six pounds an acre, he should have more than
enough left to keep body and soul together, more
especially as his poverty prevents his adopting any
but the rudest and most defective modes of culture?
It is not the occupation of land, but the landlords'
exactions which make and keep him poor.   The
Irish peasantry have always been grievously over-

rented. The farmer of forty or fifty acres never, except in rare instances, was able to live in any thing like comfort, and his children commonly grew up as regardless as savages of the conveniences and decencies of life. On their father's death, the law permitted them to divide his farm amongst them, and, provided the share of each individual were sufficient to supply him with all he had been accustomed to, viz., potatoes enough to fill his stomach, they did not hesitate to do so. Their example was followed by their successors, until at last the whole island became parcelled out amongst the present multitude of petty tenants. Such a phenomenon could scarcely occur, except in a country prepared for it by a combination of circumstances, such as is rarely to be found, and which certainly does not exist in England. When free trade shall have given the English labourer high wages and cheap food, he will be little disposed to pay more for the use of land than it is worth. Instead of being, like the Irish cottier, absolutely dependent upon it for subsistence, he will desire it only as a means of employing his leisure profitably, and will not offer a rent that will deprive him of any part of the just reward of his industry. To him therefore, and to others who obtain land under similar circumstances, the possession will be decidedly beneficial, and they will be able to live more comfortably in consequence. To the children of these first occupiers, however, the consequences, it is feared, might be very different. Reliance upon the produce of the paternal domain might perhaps seduce

them into premature marriages, for in it they might
fancy they possessed a certain, although a scanty
source of income.  Or on their father's death, they
might divide his tenement amongst them, and
trusting to their separate portions for security
against starvation, might thereupon venture to
marry forthwith; whereas, without land they would
have to wait, at least until they got into some kind
of service.  A somewhat similar opinion has been
recently advanced by a distinguished political
writer, who maintains that the allotment of land to
labourers would lead inevitably to a reduction of
wages.   " Every shilling," he says, " which it
bestows as a supplement to wages, it subtracts
from the wages themselves. . . . By giving labourers an extra means of support in addition to
wages, you merely enable them to exist upon still
lower wages than before.  Wherever there is already an excess of labourers above employment the
reduction of wages will be immediate; wherever
there is not, a surplus will speedily grow up."*
This argument, if valid, is equally applicable to
every increase of a labourer's income from whencesoever derived. Its meaning is, that by augmenting
the resources of the poor, you only enable them to
bring up more children, whose competition soon
reduces them to the poverty from which their
parents had emerged.   It is hoped that there is no
necessity for entering in this place into a lengthened
opposition to this conclusion, since it is the very

* Edinburgh Review, No. 164. pp. 523, 524.

reverse of that, which much of the reasoning of the present volume has been designed to establish. Like the objection first mentioned, it is based upon the assumption that persons of the lower orders are unrestrained by prudential considerations, and require only the prospect of a bare subsistence to induce them to marry. But this is true only of the very poor. If, by augmenting their incomes, you raise them from poverty, you cure them also of improvidence. The more they have to lose, the more afraid they become of losing it. It is admitted that a high standard of comfort is really a most effectual preventive of thoughtless marriages, and that labourers are not more disposed than other people to forfeit by their rashness, advantages to which they have been accustomed. Now the standard of comfort would, *cæteris paribus*, be much higher in a family possessing the produce of an allotment in addition to its earnings, than in one subsisting on wages alone. In the former case, therefore, a young man would be least likely to marry early. He would wait until he could do so without altering his style of living for the worse. He would see clearly that the same income which sufficed for the support of the family to which he belonged, could not maintain half a dozen additional members in equal comfort, and he would not presume to bring a wife into his father's house without bringing likewise a corresponding accession of revenue. Neither would he seek a habitation elsewhere until he could afford to live there as comfortably as he had been accustomed to

do in his former home.   As for the partition of a labourer's tenement after his death,
this could only take place if the land were the
labourer's own; for in England landlords have
always been careful to retain the power (which,
with the fear of increasing pauperism and poor's
rates before their eyes, they would not fail to
exercise) of preventing the division of land by
lessees.   Supposing, however, a labourer to be a
small landowner, he might if he pleased bequeath
his estate to all his children indiscriminately, and
it is important to ascertain how the latter would
dispose of their inheritance.   Would they divide
it into portions too small to contribute materially
towards the maintenance of a family, or would
they hold it in common, or sell or let it, and divide
the proceeds?   Mr. M'Culloch thinks that the
former alternative would be most commonly
adopted.   " The strong predilection," he says, " entertained by the great bulk of the children of persons engaged in the business of agriculture for
the pursuits of their fathers, has been remarked
by every one in any degree familiar with rural
affairs," and it is obvious " that the equal division
of an estate among the proprietor's children must
afford the greatest facilities for gratifying this
natural inclination.   It will give them the power
of continuing in that line of life for which they
have been educated, and which must in consequence be endeared to them by all those early
associations which exercise so strong an influence
over future conduct.   The possession of a small

piece of ground gives a feeling of independence to a poor man that he cannot otherwise experience. It is very rare, indeed, that a possession of this sort will afford him the means of becoming comfortable in his circumstances, but it gives him a security against want. It furnishes him with a cottage, and unless it be unusually small it will enable him to raise such a supply of potatoes as will go far to support himself and his family. In no way, therefore, can a poor man be so independent. The possession of a piece of ground renders him in some measure his own master. It exempts him from the necessity of severe labour and unremitting application, though it condemns him to perpetual poverty, and extinguishes every hope of rising in the world." Consequently, " in the great majority of cases," the children of petty landowners " will continue to reside on the little properties they have obtained from their ancestors, and the process of division and subdivision will continue until the whole land has been parcelled out into patches, and filled with an agricultural population equally destitute of the means and the desire of rising in the world." *

Without altogether denying the force of these observations, it may be permitted to refuse assent to the conclusion involved in them. Fondness for rural pursuits, and the desire of independence, may induce a labourer's sons to keep their patrimony in their own hands, but cannot cause them to divide

* M‘Culloch's edition of the Wealth of Nations, vol. iv. pp. 462—464.

it. Unless any of them wish to sell their shares, they cannot, in general, have any motive for making a partition of their common property until they are about to marry. Until then, it would be much better for them to live together in the family cottage, subsisting, as before, partly on the joint wages of their hired labour, and partly on the produce of their own field, than to form separate establishments. But young men who had enjoyed ease and plenty in their father's lifetime, and who, if they remained single, might still live as comfortably as ever, would seldom sacrifice these advantages by marrying without any other certainty than that of having potatoes enough to eat. They would wait until they could hope to keep a wife and children in the style in which they had been brought up themselves, that is to say, until the death of a relation or neighbour either increased their property, or promoted them to a better paid situation in another man's service. They would then be guided by circumstances in the disposal of their hereditary plots of ground; but these, whether retained or sold by them, would, in general, be annexed to other plots, so that properties would continue to be of the same average size. This representation is not merely conjectural, but is confirmed by almost universal experience. Wherever small landholders, whether owners or tenants, are in the enjoyment of a fair measure of comfort, the average size of their tenements undergoes little variation, the agricultural population retains the same proportion to the means of subsistence, and poverty is almost unknown. In Belgium, Switzerland, Tuscany, or, to take examples nearer home, in Guernsey and Jersey, a peasant does not think of marrying until he finds himself in as good a situation as was occupied by his father before him. If only a part of the latter's property have descended to him, he may, perhaps, sell his share, and establish himself in some business with the proceeds, or he may leave it in the hands of his brothers, receiving some consideration from them in return; or if he be himself strongly bent on a rural life, he may reside with them in their common habitation until some favourable change takes place in his circumstances. It is only in Ireland that people marry the moment they get a scrap of land to settle upon, and they do so there, not because they are landholders, for if they had more land, or derived a better income from it, they would be more prudent, but simply because they are poor. It is misery that makes them reckless, and no inference drawn from their habits can be applicable to a race of substantial yeomanry.

Happily the question at issue need not be decided by theoretical reasoning, nor by an appeal to analogous conditions in other countries. We have the results of experiments tried before our own eyes, to assist in guiding us to a right conclusion. England, as we have seen, was once a country of landholders, and although the connexion of the great body of agricultural labourers with the soil has long been severed, there are still some districts in which the labourers have always been occupiers

of land, and others in which the practice of granting them allotments has of late been revived.  In
many parishes of Rutland and Lincolnshire, especially, the cottagers have never been dispossessed
of their little tenements.  What has been the consequence ?  Have their fields been divided into
minute patches by never ceasing partition ?  Has
population become excessive, or has pauperism
extended more rapidly than elsewhere ?  On the
contrary, the peasantry of these counties stand out
in most pleasing relief from the melancholy picture
which must be drawn of the generality of their
brethren.  So comfortable, contented, and well-
conducted a race can scarcely be found in any
other part of the kingdom.  The quantity of land
occupied by a family is, in general, as large as that
of its predecessors centuries ago, and enables it to
keep a cow or two, as well as pigs and poultry, and
sometimes a few sheep.  The paupers, instead of
being extraordinarily numerous, were maintained
by a poor's rate averaging about $9d.$ in the pound,
at a time when in some of the southern counties,
where the labourers had nothing beside their wages,
the poor's rates absorbed more than half the rent.
So far, indeed, is the " allotment system " from
encouraging the growth of pauperism, that its
abolition has invariably been followed by a great
increase of poor's rates.  There are instances on
record of parishes in which until the cottagers
were deprived of their plots of land, it was scarcely
possible to find any one who would deign to accept
parochial relief, in order to protect his birthplace

from the obligation of contributing to the support
of the poor of neighbouring villages. One of these
parishes came by purchase into the hands of a
single proprietor, who took away the cottagers'
gardens, and annexed them either to the adjoining
farms, or to his own pleasure-grounds. Before
another generation had passed away, a poor's rate of
3s. in the pound had come into existence. In
another parish, the rates were raised by similar
means, in seven years, from 1s. 9d. to 3s. in the
pound, and in a few years more to 6s. In a third
parish, containing fifty-eight landholders, of whom
twenty-two were cottagers, the poor's rates were
6d. in the pound. Forty years afterwards, the
cottagers had lost their land, and the rates had
risen to 4s. in the pound.* Nay, the introduction
of the allotment system, when properly conducted,
has been found almost a specific for the cure of
parishes already infected with pauperism. Nor
can this be wondered at, when the value of a field
or garden to a poor man is duly estimated. It has
been mentioned that a small farm, properly cultivated, is much more productive than an equal
quantity of land in the hands of a large farmer;
but few persons are aware how vast the difference
is in a farm small enough to be entirely cultivated
by the occupier's family. Three hundred bushels
of potatoes per acre are commonly considered a
very good crop; but a cottager will obtain, at
least, one hundred bushels from a quarter of an

* Quarterly Review, No. 81., Article ix., on the Condition
of the English Peasantry.

acre, besides turnips and cabbages enough to pay his rent. Eight quarters of wheat would be thought a very large quantity for a farmer to get from an acre, but fourteen quarters an acre have been got from land dug with the spade. The average profit derived from cottage allotments is at the rate of 20*l.* per acre, and an instance has occurred of a man growing a crop worth 5*l.* on the eighth part of an acre of very indifferent land.* Equal quantities of produce are obtained year after year from the same ground, which is never suffered to lie fallow. Even wheat and potatoes, the most exhausting of crops, and which would soon impoverish the land of an ordinary farmer, have been grown alternately for twenty years together on cottage allotments, without any diminution of the returns. These results are owing, in a great measure, to the unremitting industry and attention of the cultivators, but still more to the use of the spade, a much more efficient instrument, at least on heavy soils, than the plough, and to the abundance of manure which a cottager can collect for his patch of ground. Rent is the only deduction to be made from the value of the crop; all the rest is clear profit, for the cultivation costs absolutely nothing. It does not draw the labourer from work for which he is paid, nor does it even cause him to tire himself before he sets about his employer's business. It is performed partly by his wife and children, who would other-

---

* Evidence before Committee on Allotments of Land, 1843.

wise be idle, and partly by himself, but only in the evening, when his daily task is done, or on whole days, not exceeding two or three in the year, when he is either not wanted for his master's work, or gets leave to stay at home. Thus nine-tenths of what he raises are clear profit to him, and a single rood of land will yield him a supply of vegetables worth an additional income of 2s. a week, besides enabling him to keep a pig or two, worth, perhaps, one half as much. His home-raised provisions are, indeed, worth to him far more than their market value, for they come into use principally in the winter, when work is slack, and when, but for them, he might be thrown upon parish assistance. But an accession of comfort is only one of many advantages which the possession of an allotment affords. Its moral effects are not less important. It gives the labourer a feeling of independence and self-respect, and at the same time the strongest incentives to diligence. It makes him prudent and thrifty, and assists him in instilling similar habits into his children, and in training them for the particular calling for which they are destined. Thus, while it raises the labourer's social position, it endows him with the very qualities most requisite to keep him in his new station. It draws him also from the temptation to debauchery and crime; teaches him to respect the rights of property; interests him in the preservation of order, and checks his disposition to regard his wealthy neighbours with envy and animosity. In a word, it contributes more than any other single cause whatsoever, to his physical and moral improvement, and to convert him from a burden and a pest both to himself and others, into a contented, upright, and useful member of society.

# CHAPTER VIII.

REMEDIES FOR OVER-POPULATION IN ENGLAND AND WALES —
(*continued*).

Certainty of the early Repeal of the Provision Laws. — Importance of the subsequent Conduct of Landowners, in determining how Rent and the Remuneration of Labour will be affected. — Certainty of considerable Benefit to Agricultural Labourers from the establishment of Free Trade. — Ability of Landlords to improve their Condition forthwith. — Expediency of their preparing for the approaching Change in their own Position. — Identity of the Means of promoting the Interests both of themselves and their Dependents. — Peculiar Obligation of Landowners to provide for their Poor Neighbours. — Recent Movements of Parliament in behalf of the Peasantry. — Mr. Cowper's "Field-Gardens'" Bill, and Lord Lincoln's "Commons' Enclosure" Act. — Objectionable Provisions of the latter. — Advantages obtainable from it. — Suggestion of other Expedients for the Extension of the "Allotment System." — Estimate of the Amount of Benefit derivable by Agricultural Labourers from Free Trade and Cottage Allotments. — Probable Permanence of the Improvement in their Condition. — Auxiliary Means of promoting their Welfare. — Payment to Farm Servants of fixed Proportions of the Crop. — Location of them on the Farm Premises. — Education. — Its general Advantages. — Inapplicability to the Labouring Classes of the ordinary Modes of Teaching. — Oral Instruction. — Sorts of Knowledge most useful to the Poor. — Expediency of a National Provision for Education. — Obstacles to its Establishment in England. — Secondary Importance of Scholastic Education. — Improvement of the Habitations of the Peasantry. — Retardation of the Progress of Population consequent on Improvement of the Condition of the People. — Moderation of the necessary Restraints upon Marriage. — Means of ameliorating the Situ-

ation of Town Labourers. — Insufficiency of High Wages
alone to render them comfortable. — Paramount Importance
of Education, — and of proper Lodgings. — Limitation of the
Labour of Females and Young Persons. — Probable Consequences of Legislative Interference.

THE distribution of land among our agricultural
labourers seems to be not only entirely free from
the dangerous consequences with which many
writers imagine it to be fraught; it is, perhaps,
indispensable to the restoration of that noble
yeomanry, the strength and honour of England, of
that bold peasantry, their country's pride, whose
decay was so feelingly described by Ascham and
Goldsmith, and whose almost utter extinction is
now the subject of such frequent lamentation. It
appears to be the only means by which an adequate body of farm-servants can be maintained in
comfort. Wages alone can scarcely suffice for
the purpose. The nature of husbandry requires
the employment of many more labourers at some
seasons than at others, but a farmer cannot be
expected to keep a number of persons throughout
the year whose assistance he needs only in spring
and harvest. Though he cannot keep them himself, however, he may enable them to keep themselves by assigning to them small portions of land
which yield little to him, but from which their
labour can extract plentiful supplies.

This course must be adopted almost necessarily
if the repeal of the provision laws do really lead
to the subdivision of farms. The demand for labour
being then much increased, the market will be so

far from overstocked, that farmers, in order to have a sufficient quantity constantly at command, will find it expedient to attach labourers to their service by giving them solid reasons for remaining in it. Besides the unmarried servants who will be lodged in the farm-house, two or three cottagers will probably be permitted, and even invited to settle on the farm, in order that the assistance of their families may be obtainable when required in busy seasons. Whether these agricultural arrangements will result from the repeal of the provision laws, will depend entirely on the landlords, and on the choice they may make between an increase of trouble and a decrease of income. If they attempt to maintain the present system of large farms, rents must inevitably fall; but if they will let their land in portions not exceeding fifty acres, rents will certainly not recede, and will very possibly advance. If they choose the latter alternative, free trade in food will be deprived of all its terrors for their particular class, and will prove an un- alloyed national blessing. Its immediate effect, — cheapness of the first necessaries of life, from which all men, without exception, will benefit as consum- ers, — will result less, perhaps, from importation from abroad, than from increased productiveness at home; and this circumstance will create a new fund, from which both labourers and landowners, without taking a penny from any other class, will derive an accession of revenue. Free trade, unaided and alone, will then have safely delivered the labouring portion of the peasantry from their slough of despondency.

Heads of families will subsist in comfort, partly on the produce of their little domains, and partly on the high wages of their labour, raised still higher in effect by the fall of prices. Their children, when old enough to leave home, will be distributed amongst the houses of the neighbouring farmers, until they succeed by inheritance to the possession of the cottages of their seniors. All will have been placed in circumstances in which happiness may in general be secured by good conduct, and it must be admitted in favour of human nature, that men seldom require any other encouragement.

That all these consequences will flow from the repeal of the provision laws seems but little doubtful; but it would be rash to indulge in predictions which a few months may not improbably afford the means of testing. No one is now so blind as not to see that the days of the landlords' monopoly are numbered. When even the landowners' chosen champion imitates the policy of King Stork, and seeks to maintain his political strength by pecking at his devoted constituents, the latter can scarcely hope for protection from any other quarter. The legal meshes in which they have long kept the rest of their countrymen entangled, are already grievously rent, and only a few vigorous efforts are wanting to tear them completely away. Sir Robert Peel is the mouse that is now nibbling at the net; but he must ply his teeth more vigorously, unless he would have the Anti-Corn-Law League forestall him in his task. By whatsoever party effected, the establishment of free trade cannot be

much longer delayed, and it will then be decided
whether cheapness of provisions will be the only
advantage which the labourer will derive from it,
or whether the same cause will not likewise create
an additional demand for his services, and restore
his ancient connexion with the soil. To a greater
or less extent he will unquestionably be benefited;
but although the prospect of early relief be encouraging, the prolongation of his distress, even
for a limited period, cannot be regarded without
anxiety. It is in the power either of farmers or landlords to do much at once towards palliating the
evil; and it would be well, both for their own sake,
and for that of their unfortunate dependents, if
they would universally avail themselves of the
means they possess for so good a purpose. It is
not unusual for farmers to let potato gardens to
their labourers; but the exorbitant rent charged
for them renders the possession a curse instead of
a blessing. Eight pounds an acre is a common
rate of charge for land underlet in this manner, for
which the real proprietor receives about thirty
shillings. Lust of gain is of course the farmer's
sole motive in such a transaction, which, so far
from affecting to have the labourer's welfare in
view, is the best course that could be taken for
reducing him to the level of the Irish cottier. If
instead of grinding the faces of the poor, the
farmer would be content to receive for his labourer's
allotment the same sum which he himself pays, he
might lose a few pounds in the first instance, but
he would be abundantly repaid. A saving equal

to his loss would in most cases be effected merely by the reduction of poor's rates, when able-bodied men were furnished with the means of maintaining themselves, and a positive gain of much greater amount would result from the conversion of idle desperadoes into cheerful and industrious servants, too busy and too happy in their own gardens to think of setting fire to his barns. In all the advantages arising from this change, the landlord would have a principal share, and it is for his interest to provide allotments for labourers who cannot obtain them on equitable conditions from their employers. Farmers, for the most part, are strongly prejudiced against the allotment system; and if they were favourable to it, it would still be very preferable that the poor man should hold land directly of the proprietor, rather than of the farmer. In the former case he has a degree of independence which it is ridiculous to suppose he will venture to abuse, but which is necessary to protect him against a sordid and narrow-minded master. The apportionment of a field or two for the poor demands not the smallest sacrifice from the proprietor, for it is not requisite, — nay, it is exceedingly undesirable that labourers should hold land on easier terms than farmers. The only personal objection that the proprietor can have is to the additional trouble which a number of small occupiers may occasion. This additional trouble, it may be observed, is purely imaginary, for allot-ment-tenants are the most punctual of rent payers, not falling into arrear once in a hundred times, and rarely waiting even to be called upon for what they owe. Some personal inconvenience, besides, might well be borne for the sake of cancelling one half of the poor's rates and of making some dozens of fellow-creatures happy. If these considerations are unavailing, still in every English village may be found at least one just person, who from love to God and man will voluntarily take upon himself the duties of property, and make himself responsible for the obligations of the poor. Let but a land-holder announce his willingness to set apart ground for allotments, and either the clergyman of the parish, or some other benevolent individual or as·sociation, will become security for the whole rent, and will gratuitously undertake the superintendence of the land and of the sub-tenants. Offers of this kind have already been made in many instances, and the little attention which has been paid to them, and the consequently slow progress of a system which has been proved by experience to be admirably calculated to benefit the labouring class, evince an extraordinary indifference on the part of the owners of the soil to the welfare of their inferiors.

The same apathy, it must be owned, makes land-lords negligent of their own interests also. If they were wise, they would prepare betimes for the change in their circumstances which will be occa-sioned by free trade. As leases fell in, they would detach portions of fifty acres or thereabouts from their overgrown farms, and let them separately on lease and at corn-rents. In return for conditions so advantageous to the farmers, increased rents

might be obtained, which, when the prices of agricultural produce fell, would admit of considerable
reduction without sinking below their present
amount. Practical knowledge of the working of
small farms would also be acquired, and the resource offered by them would be estimated at its
true value. If landlords refuse to try this experiment, and persist in keeping their extensive farms
intact, it is the more expedient for them to consider how the cost of cultivation may be lessened.
The extension of the allotment system, by lowering
the poor rates, would have some effect in diminishing the farmer's expenses ; but in spite of all
that could be done with this view, it would be
scarcely possible to evade the necessity of sooner
or later reducing the rent of large farms. The
sooner this is done, indeed, the better ; for an immediate abatement of the landlord's claim might
prevent the reduction from becoming permanent.
One cause of the defectiveness of English farming
is the deficiency of farming capital. Even the
modes of tillage actually practised require for
their successful prosecution more labour than is
commonly bestowed upon them. Almost every
farmer would employ more men if he could afford
to do so, but the money with which he would have
paid them has already gone for rent. The consequence is, that the land is not sufficiently attended
to, and the produce is proportionably small. In
this way avarice defeats itself, and the landlord
(to use a rustic proverb) kills the calf in the cow's
belly. If his claim were limited to what the

farmer could satisfy without detriment to his business, his income would at first, of course, be
smaller, but the difference in his receipts would
not be a permanent loss. It would be a loan re-
payable with enormous interest — money entrusted
to the farmer's care to *fructify* for the owner's use.
Of the increased produce arising from increased
expenditure upon the soil, the largest portion
would eventually be taken by the landlord; his
rent would rise above the point from which it had
fallen, and would abundantly recompense him for
his temporary sacrifice. This would be the case
even if the practice of agriculture remained
unaltered. But farmers who had noticed the extraordinary crops of cottage allotments would
naturally be desirous of trying the same mode of
culture, if they could spare the necessary outlay.
This is quite out of their power at present. An
acre of land, when dug, will often produce twice as
much as if ploughed; but it costs about fifty shillings to dig it, and not more than six or eight to
plough it, and a farmer who can scarcely contrive
to pay for one man's work, cannot venture to hire
half a dozen merely to do the same job more effectually. If by an abatement of his landlord's claim
upon him he were enabled to try the experiment,
the result would soon give him the means of paying
a higher rent than before.

Whichever of the courses here indicated were
adopted with the view of enabling agriculture to
make head against foreign competition, the effects
would be not less beneficial to labourers than to

landlords. Neither the subdivision of farms nor the temporary reduction of rent can occasion an increase of produce, except through the employment of additional labour, which must be attended by a rise of wages. The fortunes of agricultural labourers for some time to come are in fact in the hands of the owners and occupiers of the soil, and particularly of the former. Free trade, in spite of all opposition, must bring them relief at last; but landlords have it in their power to restore them at once to a position not inferior to that occupied by their forefathers four centuries ago. Landlords can do this, too, without the smallest sacrifice. They are not called upon to *give* any thing. It is only requisite that they should condescend to deal with the poor, and suffer them, as well as the rich, to hire land. They are quite at liberty to exact from allotment-holders payment at the highest rates which they can obtain from any other class of tenants, — higher rates, that is, than are commonly paid by large farmers. Their own revenues would be augmented instead of being diminished by the very measures best adapted to promote the welfare of their inferiors. Even if, besides letting allotments to cottagers, they consented to reduce the present rents of extensive farms, the loss would be only temporary. Agriculture, relieved for a while from the burthens which now impede its growth, would soon gather strength enough to support still heavier burthens.

Lords of the soil, who imagine they have nothing more to do with its cultivators than to live in idle-

ness on the fruits of their industry, are little aware
how wide a field of enjoyment their selfishness ex-
cludes them from. They might see happiness take
the place of misery, and know that they were its
authors, and without trying, they really cannot
appreciate the exquisite luxury of doing good.
Smiles would then greet them instead of scowls,
and blessings instead of muttered curses. If they
have eyes and ears, to say nothing of hearts, the
change could not be otherwise than pleasant. A
good conscience would cheer them by day and lull
them to sleep at night. Wine and down beds are
not half so efficacious. True wealth, according to
that most original of moralists, Mr. Carlyle, consists
in those things only in which the owner takes an
interest. Country gentlemen could not then hit
upon a much better way of growing rich than by
surrounding themselves with a happy and contented
peasantry. Many of them take great delight in
experimenting on live stock. Improving the breed
of men would apparently be quite as interesting an
occupation. How to make a pig too heavy to bear
its own weight, and to spoil good wholesome beef by
overloading it with fat, are possibly very fitting subjects for philosophical investigation, but it would be
quite as gratifying, one would think, to efface the
famine lines from a poor man's face, to rekindle
cheerfulness in his downcast eyes, and to restore
the vigour of his muscles. Amateur graziers are
fond of making visiters go the round of their cow-
houses and piggeries, to remark the neatness and
order that prevail there. Did it never occur to

them that a visit to their labourers' cottages would be equally satisfactory to themselves, if they were sure of finding there the same admirable arrangements for drainage, ventilation, and warmth, equally clean and comfortable beds, and inmates as well fed and thriving ?

It is not intended by these remarks to cast a stigma on landowners as a class, or to deny that many of them make a worthy use of the vast power placed in their hands. Still it is indisputable that too many are utterly regardless of the duties of their position, and incapable of being awakened to a proper sense of them by any considerations of benevolence or justice, or even of self-interest. For the neglect of such as these, the legislature alone can make adequate provision, and it has of late shown some disposition to exert itself for the purpose.

The extension of the allotment system was a professed object of two bills proposed during the last session of parliament — those, viz., respecting Field Gardens and Commons' Inclosure. The first of these, if enacted, would have been chiefly valuable as a monument of the genuine philanthropy of its author ; for, except in so far as it authorised " field wardens " to assume, for allotment purposes, the tenancy of land held by parish authorities, it would have enabled the friends of the poor to do little or nothing, which they could not do equally well without its aid. Lord Lincoln's bill has become law, and is calculated to produce results of much greater moment. While affording extraordinary facilities for the inclosure of common land, it provides for the appropriation in every parish in which it may come into operation, of a space, not less than four, nor more than ten, acres in extent, for the exercise and recreation of the inhabitants, and for the investiture of trustees (to be styled " allotment wardens ") with a further space sufficiently large to allow of one quarter of an acre being allotted to every poor householder. Very valuable advantages are by this means promised to the poor. Wherever there is any waste land worth inclosing, the landowners will take care to lose no time in giving effect to the law ; and every cottager who desires to have an allotment will be enabled to procure one. Moreover, the tract set apart for the benefit of the poor will be incapable of being diverted to any other purpose. The improvidence or misfortunes of the actual tenants will not afford to their wealthy neighbours opportunities of buying up their little tenements. The property will be placed inalienably in trust for a special purpose, and the same extent of ground will always remain available for distribution among successive generations of labourers. Good management alone will be requisite to make this a most useful auxiliary in the repression of pauperism, and in the formation and maintenance of a thriving and contented peasantry. Considered by itself, therefore, and without reference to the conditions annexed, the boon accorded to the poor by Lord Lincoln's Act is one of great value. Whether it might not have been granted on easier terms is a very different question. The whole quantity of waste and common land still existing in England and Wales is

estimated at about eight millions of acres, of which
at least one half is supposed to be reclaimable.
It is barely possible that so many as two hundred
thousand acres may be set apart for play-grounds
and gardens for the poor, and every inch of the
remaining 3,800,000 acres may be seized upon by
the neighbouring landowners for their own exclusive use. They may fence round every heath
and moor where the untravelled Englishman can
still catch a glimpse of nature, may bid the grum-
bling tourist keep the road, even among the Welsh
mountains and the Cumberland lakes, and may
leave the landless multitude without a scrap of
turf to set their feet upon, except in city parks and
village greens. They may totally extinguish any
still surviving rights of common, and pound the
unfortunate goose or donkey that may venture
back to its old feeding place ; they may forbid boys
to gather nuts or blackberries in the woods, and
confiscate stray cricket-balls struck beyond the
prescribed four acres. Nevertheless, the act which
enables them to do all this originated, as the
framer assures us, in a sincere regard for the poor.
It is from purely generous motives that landlords
have consented to the addition of one-seventh to
the size of their estates. Excess of conscientious-
ness, no doubt, a punctilious sense of justice to
themselves, prevented their abandoning their useless rights over a few acres of waste land without
abundant compensation. Then, at least, the transfer to the poor is made absolutely, and without
reservation. No benefit surely is derived by the

landlord from the tracts entrusted to allotment wardens? Not so. The latter may be required to pay rent equal to the full annual value of the land at the time of its occupation; so that landlords may positively draw larger profit from cottage allotments than they did before resigning their common rights over the site. No additional compensation, therefore, can really have been wanting to reconcile them to the sacrifice they have made. In order to induce them to let small portions of waste for their full actual value, it was not necessary to permit them to appropriate nearly twenty times as much for themselves, to seize upon what the rapacity of ages has spared, and to exclude the public from what have always in effect been national domains and public pleasure-grounds. The poor man might have had his garden without losing his right of pasture, and the power of walking a mile or two straight on end without being stopped by a hedge.

It is too late now, however, to complain of what has been done. The bargain is struck, and nothing remains but to make the best of it. In every parish containing any considerable quantity of common land, we may expect speedily to see the cottagers in possession of gardens; but whether they will derive therefrom all the benefit expected, or any benefit at all, will depend greatly on the position and size of the gardens, and on the rent for which they are let. Experience has shown that a labourer may be greatly benefited by an allotment of land to which he has to walk three or four miles;

but in order perfectly to answer the intended purpose — to afford profitable occupation for his own
and his family's leisure, the allotment should be
near his dwelling, and, if possible, close to it. No
time will then be lost in passing backwards and
forwards; every spare minute may be usefully spent
in weeding, watering, or something of the sort, and
a good deal of work may thus be got through
without an effort, and as a pastime instead of a
task. With respect to the size of cottage gardens, allotment wardens, according to the original
bill, were to have been prohibited from forming any
larger than half an acre, and as this is probably as
much on an average as a labourer in full employment has time to manage, the limitation might have
been proper. By the act, as it now stands, the size
of allotments is restricted to one quarter of an acre,
which is certainly too little. At any rate it is of
as much consequence that the gardens should not
contain less than a quarter of an acre each, as that
they should not contain more; and it is of still
greater importance, that having once been made of
a certain size, they should not afterwards be diminished, in order to accommodate a larger number
of applicants. An allotment cannot do much to
improve the tenant's condition, unless it is large
enough to yield him a considerable supply of food;
and there can be no fear of over-population resulting from the minute partition of land, if the land
distributed among the first generation of tenants is
not allowed to be subdivided afterwards. Again,
as it is ordained that the rent demanded by the

wardens for the allotments let by them shall not be less than the annual value of the land for farming purposes, so assuredly it ought not to be more. It may be right to make the labourer pay for his garden at the rate at which land of the same quality is usually let in the neighbourhood, but not a farthing more can be exacted from him consistently with the object for which allotments are designed.

If these considerations be properly attended to, every objection to the allotment system will disappear. Farmers will soon discover that a labourer, assisted by his wife and children, can easily cultivate a rood of land without neglecting his master's work; and it is obvious that gardens of that size let at rents worth not a fourth part of the crops, and indivisible, cannot have any tendency to reduce their tenants to the condition of Irish cottiers, to whom the landlord leaves nothing but the bare means of subsistence. As for the danger of farmers making the profits of allotments a pretext for reducing wages, it is clear that they can do so only where the supply of labour exceeds the demand, and where the employer is able in consequence to dictate his own terms. But allotments would give labourers a resource independent of the hire of their services, and enable them to resist the depreciation of their labour. With a stock of provisions of their own raising, they would be able to hold out for better wages, instead of being obliged to accept whatever was offered.

It is only, however, in places containing much waste land that legislative interference has as yet provided for the formation of allotments. In parishes already completely inclosed, the matter is still left entirely to the pleasure of the landowners, and it deserves to be inquired whether some artificial stimulus ought not to be applied to the sluggish sympathies of persons of that class. To compel them to let land in any particular manner would seem an unjust, and would certainly be an injudicious invasion of the pretensions of property. But although the compulsory formation of cottage gardens on private estates cannot be recommended, a less objectionable method may be mentioned of producing the same effect indirectly. By an act passed in the reign of Henry the Seventh, and not repealed till the middle of the last century, it was provided, that no cottage should be built without at least four acres of ground attached; and such a precedent would amply justify the enactment of a new law, ordaining that in parishes not containing any waste land available for allotment purposes, no cottage should be built in future without having at least half an acre unalienably annexed to it. The operation of such a law would be slow, but it would be sure. In the course of time it would (to use Lord Bacon's language respecting an act of a somewhat similar character) "amortise a great part of the lands of the kingdom unto the hold and occupation" of the peasantry, very much to their advantage. For "houses being kept up, *would* of necessity enforce a dweller; and the proportion of land for occupation being kept up, *would* of necessity enforce that dweller not to be a beggar, but a man of some substance." * All cottages would at last have their gardens, and the number of the latter being made equal to the demand for them, they could not be let except on fair and moderate terms. Every cottager would be a small landholder, and would be able to keep the greater part of his produce for his own use. Further than this it is not, perhaps, desirable for the legislature to interfere. In consequence either of the inclosure of commons, or of the building of new cottages, there would very soon be few villages without a sufficient number of cottage allotments to demonstrate their good effects, and the example of forming them, when once set, would no doubt be voluntarily imitated.

The reader has by this time discovered that the measures chiefly relied on for improving the condition of the peasantry are two : — the repeal of the Corn Laws and of all other restrictions on the importation of foreign provisions, and the general adoption of cottage allotments. The first, by making food and other necessaries cheap, would raise the value of the labourer's actual earnings, and it would probably increase the demand for labour, and with it the rate of wages; and the second would supply the labourer with a considerable stock of food, in addition to what he might be able to buy. By the two together, it seems certain that the means of every labouring family in rural districts might be increased one-half at least, and, in many instances, they would more probably be doubled. Poor creatures who are now pining on

* Bacon's Hist. of Hen. VII. : Works, vol. v. p: 62. edit. 1824.

seven shillings a-week, would, independently of any increase of money wages, be as well off as if their present pittance could be immediately raised to eleven or twelve shillings; and the fortunate few who earn as much as fourteen shillings a-week, would enjoy an annual income worth as much as fifty pounds at the present moment. If in this manner adequate relief were afforded to the privations of the labouring class, not only would the symptoms of over-population be removed—the disease itself might also be regarded as radically cured. When the question of cottage allotments was discussed just now, it was not proposed that they should ever be more numerous than the applicants for them, at the time of their first institution. Not only was no mention made of a provision for a subsequently increased number of claimants; it was even declared that the first allotments should on no account be divided to satisfy future claims. It must not, however, be supposed that allotment holders would, after a while, become a favoured class, and that, as population advanced, there would necessarily rise up labouring families desirous of obtaining land, but unable to procure any. The probability is, that unless some peculiar causes intervened, population would not advance at all. If all the labourers now living in any place were to be raised to a prosperous condition, their children also would become used to new comforts, and would not marry until they could keep their families as well as they had been brought up themselves. If an allotment were needed to assist a man in doing

this, he would remain single, living most likely
either with his relations or in his master's house
until the death of one of his elders left an allotment
vacant for him. The number of families would
thus continue to correspond with the number of
allotments, unless, from some rise in the price of
labour, a man's earnings became sufficient for the
comfortable maintenance of a family without the
aid of a piece of ground. Population might then
advance without lowering the condition of the people, but otherwise it would remain stationary for
ages without any permanent increase. In either
case successive generations would inherit at least
the same proportional amount of wealth from their
immediate predecessors; subsistence would retain
at least the same relation to the number of consumers. In short, as was observed in a preceding
Chapter, nothing more is wanting to cure over-
population than to make people comfortable, and
to make the continuance of their comforts dependent
on themselves. They will then take care not to let
their numbers increase beyond their means of livelihood. Their happy lot will not be forfeited by
any act of their own. If their numbers again become excessive, it will be owing to some extraneous
circumstance, over which they have no control,
such, for example, as a decrease of the demand for
labour, which has absolutely diminished their resources.

The expedients for the cure of over-population
which seem most worthy of confidence have now
been pointed out; but there are other means, sup-

plementary and auxiliary, which ought not to be neglected. The obligation of landowners to assist in providing additional employment for the poor has already been discussed ; but farmers have it in their power, without aid from their landlords, and without resorting to the allotment system, to improve the condition of their labourers most materially, not only without any loss, but with immense benefit to themselves. One principal cause of the extraordinary productiveness of land under the management of small occupiers, is, that all or most of the cultivators are directly interested in the success of their labour: they work for themselves, and consequently work with an ardour which cannot be expected from hired labourers. Every farmer might, however, make his servants almost equally zealous in his cause, by altering the mode of remunerating them. If, instead of being paid at a fixed rate of wages, they were entitled to a certain proportion of the crops, they would strive to make the crops as abundant as possible. They would be engaged as partners in their master's business, and would look upon his interests as their own. Knowing that their reward depended on their exertions, they would exert themselves accordingly. From increased diligence corresponding results would doubtless proceed, and something like the fertility of gardens would be exhibited in extensive farms. Part of the increased produce would of course be appropriated by the labourers ; but they would draw their recompence out of a new fund of their own creation, which, after supplying them with a plentiful subsistence, would leave an ample residue to be added to the ordinary profits of their employers. Here is another method in which the peasantry might be raised from poverty, not only without subjecting any other class to expense, but even admitting others to participation in their gains. The pecuniary advantage, too, which farmers would obtain by taking their labourers into partnership, is only one among many good consequences of such an arrangement. Nothing else would tend so much to repair the rents so visible in the framework of society, and to substitute affection and esteem for the jealous mistrust and malignancy with which the poor have long regarded their superiors in station.

Another expedient which farmers would do well to adopt is, that of again taking their unmarried labourers as inmates into their own dwellings. "Gentlemen farmers" — men of cultivated minds and refined feelings, cannot indeed be expected to resume the obsolete patriarchal familiarity of olden times, and to treat their rude unlettered dependents as messmates and companions; but they might, without any sacrifice of gentility, provide comfortable lodgings and a plentiful table for their servants, either in or immediately adjoining the farm-house. The duties of superintendence would not be onerous, and might be performed by deputy, and the expense might be defrayed by a deduction from the wages of the labourers, smaller than what they would have to pay elsewhere for the most wretched shelter, and the coarsest and scantiest food. They would palpably benefit by the arrangement; and

besides the obvious advantages of better quarters
and diet, an enlightened and benevolent master
might easily furnish them with the means of spending their leisure time both agreeably and profitably.
The desire of retaining so comfortable a situation
would very generally preserve them from early
marriages; and the same motive would make them
anxious to please their master, and act as a powerful incentive to good conduct.

Much stress is laid by many persons upon the
efficacy of education to arrest the progress of population. Habits of foresight and self-restraint may,
it is supposed, be communicated by precept and
direct mental instruction. In the largest sense of
the word, every one of the measures already recommended in these pages for the advancement of the
labouring class, may be regarded as contributing to
education; for it is only by its influence on the
mind, that an accession of comfort can tend to dissuade people from premature marriages. Even
mere schooling, however, is calculated to have
some effect of the same kind. Whatever exercises
the mind, develops its powers: mental power can
only be expended in thought; and a man who
thinks at all, is never so likely to think as when he
is about to act. To whatever sort of culture, therefore, the mind be subjected, there is every probability that more or less of forethought will be
among the products. The same result may be
looked for more certainly, and in larger measure,
if pains be taken not only to employ the mind, but
to awaken its thirst for knowledge, to store it with

information, and with materials for investigation and comparison. The habit as well as the power of reflection will then be created, and will naturally lead to conclusions which will be adopted as rules of conduct. Still better security for the practice of self-government will be taken, if the pupil's attention be particularly directed to the evil consequences of vice and folly, — if he learn to appreciate the peace and satisfaction which virtue ensures to her votaries, — and if he be made acquainted with the duty of subduing his passions, and keeping his inclinations in check.

To dwell longer on the importance of mental culture in the formation of character, would be waste of time; for it is denied by none, and none are now opposed to the extension of the blessings of education to people of all ranks. In order, however, that much good should arise from the instruction of members of the labouring class, a peculiar method should be adopted. As almost any kind of intellectual exercise is better than none at all, it is no doubt better that the poor should be taught the elements of reading, writing, and reckoning, than that they should be taught nothing. As even the alphabet cannot be learned without some application and exertion, a child who has got to the end of his A B C is probably a trifle more intelligent than before he began it; but the difference is so mere a trifle, that the sagacious Mr. Weller was perfectly warranted in questioning whether it is worth any one's while to go through so much to gain so little. Nevertheless, very little more proficiency is at-

tained by the majority of pupils at dame and
charity schools. Few, after passing through the
usual course of study at such seminaries, can do
more than spell through a page of easy words, at
the rate of a line in two minutes, and scratch a few
shapeless hieroglyphics on the false pretence of
signing their names. Even those extraordinary
geniuses who can read pretty fluently, have, in
general, only learnt to do so like parrots, without
understanding much more of the meaning of the
sounds they utter. The art so painfully acquired
is rarely afterwards of any use to its possessors.
Their faculties may have been somewhat sharpened
in pursuit; but the prize itself, when caught, turns
out to be of little or no value. An opinion very
prevalent among worthy persons of more benevolence than discernment, is, that when the poor have
been taught to read, they will enter voluntarily
upon studies which must make them intelligent,
moral, and religious. It is forgotten that, in general, they have neither inclination nor time to do
any thing of the sort. They have indeed the key
of the temple of knowledge, but they have no curiosity to enter; so the key soon becomes rusty from
disuse. This can scarcely be wondered at. The
man of business or pleasure, who has been sitting
in his office or counting-house from ten till four, or
who has spent the day in hunting or shooting, or
paying visits, feels himself too much exhausted
after dinner for any harder reading than a novel
or a newspaper, though the mere act of reading
does not cost him an effort : yet the poor hus-

bandman, who, from dawn till dusk, has been trudging in the mire of a ploughed field, or mowing under a blazing sun, is expected, after all his toil, to be ready, not simply for reading, but for poring over a book, syllable by syllable, with more difficulty than a tolerable scholar would find in translating Pindar, or solving a proposition of Euclid. It is all very well for children of the middle and upper ranks to commence their education by learning to read, for they have plenty of time left for reading, after they have learnt the art. But the children of the poor are no sooner strong enough to be of use, than they are set to work. The few vacant years which intervene between infancy and labour, are all that they can spend at school. The interval is too precious to be wasted upon an acquirement of which they do not perceive the value, and of which they will have little leisure to avail themselves. Instead of being employed in teaching them to read — in giving them the means of obtaining knowledge, it should be spent in giving them the knowledge itself, and a desire to procure more. Their minds should be filled and expanded with useful and interesting information; their curiosity awakened, their reasoning powers animated and assisted, and their taste cultivated. Is it asked how this can be done for children who do not even know their letters? By the same means as were practised before printing made books cheap, and when a single volume sold for the price of an estate, — by the method which taught an Athenian mob to appreciate the sublimity of Æschylus and the eloquence of Demosthenes, which made thousands of indigent scholars competent to discuss the subtleties of Thomas Aquinas and Duns Scotus, and which is even now successfully employed by Faraday to communicate a smattering of chemistry to fashionable audiences. In a word, by oral instruction. A national schoolmaster's proper business is that of a lecturer. Instead of merely teaching his boys the arbitrary symbols of unmeaning sounds, and disgusting them with study by confining them to so dry a subject, he should strive to imbue them with ideas at once. He should tell them stories of the world and its inhabitants, of the different customs of different nations, and of the habits of animals; he should relate to them the most striking events in the history of their own and other countries, and the actions of illustrious persons; he should reveal to them the structure of the universe; and, if permitted, he should, above all, instruct them in the principles of morality, and the truths of religion. Pupils made to commit to memory interesting facts, would have gained something of real value at school. The difference between them and children who had merely learnt to read, would be the same as that between a person who had just enjoyed a hearty draught, and another who stood parched with thirst beside a concealed spring. Even if they made no addition to their knowledge after leaving school, the stock already accumulated would serve permanently to occupy and enlarge the mind, to exercise and assist the judgment, and to please the fancy. But intellectual wealth can scarcely remain without variation in amount. The appetite for knowledge, when once awakened, grows by what it feeds on. A peasant, who had once listened with interest to tales of the Laplander and his reindeer sledge, whose enthusiasm had been kindled by the mention of Thermopylæ or the Spanish Armada, or who had been initiated into the sublime mysteries of the celestial mechanism, would not rest satisfied without seeking further acquaintance with such attractive topics. Books would be looked upon as the most agreeable resource for his spare time. For it must not be supposed, that because he had learned much by catechism and conversation, he might not also have learned to read. The education of the poor, though based upon oral instruction, should not be restricted to it alone. Reading and writing need not be neglected because other things, of more immediate value, are first taught. There is ample time for all. In fact, the quickest way of teaching children to read, would be to begin by teaching them how much delight reading is capable of affording. They would then apply themselves with voluntary ardour as well as with quickened faculties, and might certainly learn to read as fluently in two years as they now do in the five or six commonly spent at national schools.

Further, the matter taught is of as much consequence in the education of the poor as the method of teaching. It is not sufficient to communicate information,— it is also important that a portion of the information should be of a particular kind. The object of education is not merely to improve the mind of the pupil, but also to qualify him for the situation which he is destined to fill, and the nature of the instruction should vary accordingly. If it be good to be well informed on almost any subject, it is particularly desirable to understand thoroughly one's own business. It may be thought that an agricultural labourer can learn enough of his occupation after he begins to practise it; but his services would certainly be of greater value if he were acquainted with the theory of husbandry — if he understood the mode of nutrition of plants, and the qualities of different soils and manures. It would be very possible, without plunging him into the mysteries of physiology and chemistry, to give him such a knowledge of this subject, as, if it did not procure for him better wages, would enable him to manage his own garden more skilfully and profitably. As peasant boys should be instructed in the principles of horticulture, so girls should be taught to sew and to cook. A knowledge of these arts would be of more practical advantage to them in the ordinary business of life than any mere book learning. It would even tend more to promote their moral improvement, for it would assist them in making home comfortable, and a comfortable home is still more essential to morality than mental culture. Both boys and girls should be carefully impressed with the necessity for foresight and self-restraint, and no pains should be spared to convince them that upon their exercise of these qualities their future welfare mainly depends. No more valuable lesson can be taught to the poor than that their condition is regulated principally by their own behaviour, and that, without exertion on their part, it cannot be permanently ameliorated.

Education of the superior character alluded to cannot, it need scarcely be said, be afforded by schools supported solely by the working classes. Illiterate parents seldom appreciate duly the advantages of learning; and even when they do, those who cannot supply their children with food enough for the body, are still less able to purchase any for the mind. Many, too, may be far enough raised above material want, without having the means of procuring suitable instruction for their families. A tutor capable of communicating the rudiments of geography, history, and natural philosophy, would not be satisfied with such fees as the ordinary patrons of a hedge school can afford to pay. If he is to teach the poor, he must derive his recompence principally from the rich. The latter, it must be owned, are not backward in contributing to the education of the poor; but an object so important ought not to depend entirely upon voluntary aid. It is a matter in which all ranks of the community are interested, and for which national provision ought to be made. So far there is no difference of opinion. No one now denies that proper schools for the lower orders of people ought to be founded and maintained at the cost of the state. The expense no doubt would be considerable, but it would scarcely be so great as that already incurred for prisons, hulks, and convict ships; and it is certainly better economy to spend money in training up people to conduct themselves properly, than in punishing them for their misdeeds. Still, although all men are agreed as to the expediency of adopting a scheme of national education, nothing is done towards its establishment. Our miserable religious dissensions are allowed to stand in the way. Conflicting sects differ as to the nature and amount of the religious instruction which ought to be administered; churchmen, for the most part, contending, that in schools established by the *state*, the *state* religion only should be taught; while their opponents plead that children of *all* sects should be allowed to share in the advantages of *national* education, without having doctrines instilled into them from which their natural guardians conscientiously dissent. Unanimity upon such a subject is not to be hoped for, so long at least as the prolonged agitation of the question continues to exasperate existing prejudices. In the mean time, because it cannot be settled how religion shall be taught, no arrangements are made for teaching any thing; and but for the exertions of individuals, the mass of the people would be suffered to remain in utter ignorance. Is not this the extreme of absurdity? The great truths of Christianity are held in common by all Christians. The most bigoted churchman can scarcely suppose that the peculiar tenets by which the Church of England is distinguished are essential to salvation. He will at least admit that men are the better for understanding the doctrine of the atonement, even if they understand nothing else. Might he not, therefore, allow them to be instructed in universally admitted articles of faith, without requiring, as a condition of their receiving this measure of enlightenment, their assent to the spiritual supremacy of the sovereign, and to the divine origin of bishops? If, however, no plan for religious instruction can meet with general approbation, why should not opportunities be offered to the poor of obtaining the elements of human learning at least? Is there anything startling in this proposition? Is education from which religion is excluded necessarily godless? Is all learning impious which does not conduce to piety? Of the two great branches of knowledge which it is the business of education to teach, religious and secular — the first is no doubt immeasurably the most important. To say this, is nothing more than to say that the soul is superior to the body, or that eternity is more lasting than time. But it does not follow that the second also may not possess great value. Surely, even pagans and atheists are all the better for being well informed. The great business of life is to prepare for futurity; but few persons think it possible to take too much pains to make even this life comfortable; and since secular education tends to promote men's temporal happiness, and to make them useful, moral, and orderly members of society, it would be worth while to establish schools even of secular education. Undoubtedly the matter of most moment is to make men pious; but if this primary object cannot be attained, must all secondary ones be voluntarily relinquished ? If the spiritual instruction of the poor be obstructed, must they therefore be left in total ignorance ? Must they remain savages because they cannot be made saints ?

From the way in which this subject is sometimes discussed, one might almost suppose that children attending schools where religion is not taught, must be in consequence deprived of opportunities of spiritual instruction which they would otherwise have enjoyed. But they may still be sent to church or chapel quite as much as if they did not go to school; their parents may teach them what they know of religion, and their pastor may converse with and catechise them. All the knowledge of divine things acquired in these ways may be miserably insufficient, but its amount will not be lessened because the children are taught something of worldly matters also. It is certainly not necessary that the teachers of every art and science should be teachers of religion. People in easy circumstances find it useful to place themselves and their children under a variety of tutors, and, without requiring their classical and mathematical masters, their professors of music or drawing, to be doctors of divinity, are content to learn from each what he is competent to teach, and apply to other quarters for spiritual advice. Let equal facilities be granted to the poor. Let national schools be established for supplying them with the knowledge essential to their temporal welfare, and if it be impracticable to afford religious instruction in the same establishments, let the pupils be left in spiritual matters to the guidance of instructors selected by their natural guardians.

Nothing, it is to be hoped, need be added to these remarks, to guard them from misconstruction. Their object is, not to recommend the exclusion of religious instruction from national schools, but merely to show, that if some plan of communicating that instruction cannot be agreed upon, the establishment of schools to teach human learning alone would not only be far better than total neglect of popular education, but would be productive of public advantages that cannot be too highly estimated. Their substance is simply this: Educate the poor, religiously, if you can, but at all events educate them: if you are permitted, make them pious, — prepare them for eternity; but if you are prevented from doing this, do not sullenly refuse to do any thing whatever; do not withhold the knowledge calculated to make them happy in this life, because you are not at liberty to assist in making them happy hereafter.

The advantages of education, however, are very apt to be over-rated. It is not, as its advocates too often fondly imagine, all-sufficient for social and moral regeneration. As an auxiliary, indeed, it is invaluable, but of itself it avails little. By making people more intelligent, it enables them to make the most of their resources, but it cannot rescue from destitution those whose means of living are positively inadequate. The one thing needful is to cure the poverty of the poor. Then, and not till then, are they in a fit state to benefit by mental culture; but as long as they suffer from want, increased intelligence is quite as likely to make them dangerous rebels against their ill fortune as patient endurers of it. If knowledge is to bring forth good fruit in them, they must be well lodged, clothed, and fed first, and taught afterwards.

Another observation remains to be made before this part of our subject is dismissed. It is absurd to inculcate maxims which circumstances render it impossible to practise, and to talk of cleanliness, neatness, and decency to persons condemned to live in places little better than pigstyes. Civilisation cannot be expected among people who are very badly housed. Inhabitants of hovels with floors ankle-deep in mud, who have no water but what they bring from a distance, nor any receptacle for refuse but the dungheap beside the door, and who are obliged by want of space to sleep half a dozen in one room, cannot but become filthy and coarse-minded. In such circumstances it is likewise impossible for them to have very exalted ideas of comfort. They cannot be very apprehensive of forfeiting a position that has so little to recommend it, nor is such fear likely to make them combat strong temptation. This is a source of evil which landowners alone can remove, and those who will not do so voluntarily, ought to be compelled by legislative interference. A Building Act is nearly as much wanted in the country as in towns. No cottages ought to be built without proper arrangements for drainage and for the supply of water, or without accommodation for the separation of the sexes. With untaxed bricks and timber a commodious dwelling might be built for a sum of money upon which the average rent paid by a Dorsetshire peasant for his miserable hut would be very liberal interest.

At the risk of being made to smile, the reader must now be reminded, that the final purpose for which free trade, the allotment system, education, and sundry other expedients, have been so strongly recommended, is neither more nor less than to diminish the frequency of marriage. The immediate object is indeed to improve the condition of the poor; but the improvement would be very short-lived, if it did not serve to check the progress of population. No community can long remain prosperous, if marriage does more than preserve the proportion between the numbers of the people and their means of subsistence, — if the former increase more rapidly than the latter, — or if the former increase at all, when the latter are stationary. In this last case, population should altogether cease to advance, and ought only to be prevented from receding. The poor are therefore to be placed in a situation of comfort, in order that they may abstain from marrying until they can do so without imprudence. So hard a condition may seem perhaps to destroy the value of the boon. That may appear a very dull, prosaic state of existence, in which marriages are only permissible in order to prevent depopulation; in which youths and maidens can only gaze at each other " through the grate of

the preventive check*;" and no one can succeed to
the privilege of matrimony, except by the death of
another.    Such, however, is the inevitable fate reserved for mankind; for, if they do not voluntarily
restrain their power of multiplication, the time
must at last come when the earth will be unable to
maintain more than the actual number of inhabitants, and when some must die before room can
be made for any new comers.  We should long ago
have been reduced to this necessity, if men had
always blindly obeyed their natural appetites.  Five
hundred, instead of six thousand years, would have
sufficed to stock the world with eight hundred
millions of human creatures, if Noah and his descendants for twenty or thirty generations had
done their utmost for the propagation of the
species.  So, likewise, to take our own country as
an example, England, supposing her to have contained two millions of inhabitants before the Norman invasion, would have become, at the accession
of Edward the First, as well peopled as at present,
if population had advanced as rapidly during the
two centuries immediately succeeding the Conquest
as it has done during the last fifty years.  It is
clear then, that, in every part of the world, population must often have remained nearly stationary
for ages together; and that our own ancestors, at
certain epochs, were as rigid practical Malthusians
as the rest.  What man has borne, man may bear.

* This expression is Colonel Perronet Thompson's.  See his
Political Exercises, vol. iii. p. 164.

We cannot be less able to practise moderation in matrimony than our forefathers. The restraints to which they submitted cheerfully cannot, after all, be so very intolerable. History tells us of no period in which marriage was confined to the elderly and middle-aged, and in which youth was forbidden to indulge in dreams of love; and England would certainly never have obtained the name of merry England, if the bonds of celibacy had sate very heavily upon her people. General abstinence from marriage is not required to keep population stationary. After submitting to every needful delay, a fair proportion of couples might annually reach the altar long before the light of romance was extinguished by the cold realities of life, and quite as soon as they had acquired experience and steadiness enough to manage a house and a family. The truth of this assertion will become manifest on closer examination. The necessity for greater moderation in connubial affairs has been represented as applicable to the poor only; not because the wealthy are entitled to greater indulgence, but because they are already sufficiently subject to self-control. People in the enjoyment of competence are found by experience not to multiply beyond the means of subsistence. Over-population does not originate with them. It is even believed, with apparently good reason, that the rich do not keep up their own numbers; and that, unless recruited from the lower grades of society, their ranks would gradually fall off.* Yet most mem-

* See ante, p. 121.

bers of the upper and middle classes, who desire to marry, find the means of doing so some time or other, and seldom have to wait till they have past the age of thirty, or thereabout. No doubt a good many of them die bachelors or old maids ; but the former are generally such from choice, and the latter, though possibly without an invincible aversion to marriage, would prefer remaining single to losing their position in society. It is then at least clear, that, by the most intelligent part of the community, the deficiencies of single-blessedness are less dreaded than the consequences of imprudent unions, and nothing more is sought than to persuade all to take the same view of the matter. It is not desired to deprive the poor of the privilege of matrimony, but merely that, for their own sakes, they should not avail themselves of it more freely than the rich, who can so much better afford the expense. The most ardent Anti-Malthusian may be safely challenged to show upon what grounds such an object can be stigmatised as unnatural and odious.

In the consideration of remedies for over-population, attention has hitherto been directed almost exclusively to the condition of the peasantry. The reason for this has been stated in a preceding Chapter, in which the opinion was hazarded, that the natural increase of the species never proceeds too rapidly except in rural districts, and that the redundant population of towns consists almost entirely of overflowings from the country. If this view be correct, it is clear that it is only necessary to confine the population of the latter within due bounds, in order to make that of the former return to its proper level. Make the country people happy, and they will not flock in to partake of the misery of towns. Although, however, in the treatment of a malady, the removal of its causes principally demand our care, the alleviation of its symptoms must not be neglected. Among the inhabitants of almost every considerable town, are to be found numbers without adequate means of livelihood, ill fed and clothed, and worse lodged, who pass the day in a vain search for work, and take shelter at night in wretched cellars and garrets, crowded, filthy, and noisome, — very hotbeds of vice and disease. It is not sufficient to take measures for preventing future generations from being placed in such circumstances: no exertion should be spared to extricate those who are already subject to so much misery. To this end some of the measures suggested for the benefit of the peasantry would largely contribute. Free trade would supply poor townsfolk with cheap food, and by creating an increased demand for manufactures to be exchanged for foreign provisions, would likewise furnish them with additional employment. The high value of land in the neighbourhood of large towns seems to forbid the adoption of the allotment system in such situations, except as a means of amusement rather than of profit to the tenants, but great numbers of hand-loom weavers, stocking makers, and operatives of some other classes, reside in the villages of the manufacturing districts, and there is no body of men to whom the possession of moderate portions of land would prove of such signal service. A very important distinction between the country-bred and the town-bred workman must here be pointed out. To the former, high wages are almost always an unalloyed advantage. Their effect is commonly to enable him to live and to bring up his family in greater comfort than before. His business, especially if he be an agricultural labourer, fills up his time so completely and so agreeably, that he has not much leisure or desire for any other relaxation. Unless he were previously a man of dissolute habits, he is not seduced into intemperance and debauchery merely because he has greater means of indulging his appetites. Instead of spending his surplus earnings at the alehouse, he prefers buying some piece of furniture for his cottage, or a Sunday coat or gown for himself or his wife, and he is too happy in his little garden, or by his fireside, with his children about him, to seek any other diversion for his evenings. With the townsman the case is different. After several hours' close application to a dull monotonous task, he is naturally eager for recreation. Home possesses no attraction for him, for in the crowded neighbourhood in which he is obliged to live, the only habitation he can afford to hire is probably a dark, close apartment in a narrow alley, infested by thieves and prostitutes. Without water or other conveniences for cleanliness, and in a murky pestilential atmosphere, no pains could make such a dwelling comfortable, and there is often no one to take any pains about the matter, for if the man be married, his wife as well as himself is probably engaged all day in a factory. From such a home then he flies to the tavern and the theatre, and the more money he has to spend at such places, of course the more welcome he is there. Thus, high wages, instead of contributing to his happiness, may only serve to promote his moral debasement, by enabling him to revel more freely in sensual excesses. To withdraw him from these allurements, education, which is highly useful to the countryman, is absolutely indispensable to the town labourer. A person in his situation cannot be expected to resist the temptations that surround him, unless he have been early imbued with a taste for intellectual pleasures, and with sentiments of piety and virtue. In every town, schools ought to be founded, at which education should be so far compulsory, that all the inhabitants who did not otherwise provide for the instruction of their children should be required to send them there. The most careful mental culture, however, could not by itself, nor even in conjunction with high wages, do much to improve the condition of the poorer inhabitants of towns. Whatever their inclinations may be, if they are forced into daily contact with vice and misery, they must suffer from the intercourse. No one can touch pitch without being defiled, or live in a filthy den, with the vilest of the vile for fellow lodgers, without acquiring something of the habits and character of his associates. Of all the expedients suggested for the benefit of the poor, one of the most urgent is to

furnish them with decent habitations. Until they
have homes capable of being made comfortable, it
is impossible for them to practise the domestic
virtues, or acquire a taste for domestic happiness.
But, as the working classes in large cities are necessarily confined within bounds very disproportioned
to their numbers, it is impossible that they can be
accommodated there, except in buildings of a peculiar plan. Families cannot be furnished each with
a separate house, nor yet with a separate suite
of rooms in houses of the present construction.
Adequate space can be obtained for them only in
large edifices, occupying altogether no more ground
than their present habitations, but raised to a much
greater height, — if necessary, to that of seven or
eight stories, and divided internally into separate
lodgings, of various sizes, suitable for families and
single persons. In mansions of this sort, if proper
arrangements were made for sewerage, and for the
supply of water, the crowds who are now huddled
together in close courts and alleys might be admitted to the privilege of breathing a comparatively
pure air, and find means of practising cleanliness
and neatness, and attending to the decencies of life.
These blessings might, moreover, be afforded to
them gratuitously. The rents actually paid, in the
worst quarters of a large city, for the most wretched
abodes, are monopoly rents, and would amply re-
munerate a speculator for whatever extra expense
might be necessary to provide suitable habitations
for the poor. But although town labourers are well
able to pay for good houses, no rich builder is anxious

to have the poor for his tenants: he dislikes the harsh measures he must employ, or at least the trouble it will cost him, to recover his dues. As a matter of profit and speculation, then, the project is not very likely to be undertaken, nor can individuals be prompted to works of such magnitude by motives of philanthropy only; and charitable associations, which might be moved by such considerations, are pretty sure to fail whenever they attempt any thing of the sort. There is, however, a class of persons — the master manufacturers — whose benevolence and self-interest may be equally appealed to. Men, whose yearly gains are counted by thousands and tens of thousands of pounds, cannot but acknowledge that their operatives have a special claim to their sympathy. The enjoyment of their wealth must be disturbed by the reflection, that those by whose toil they are enriched, are exposed to evils and perils from which a little exertion of theirs would deliver them. It would be easy for the iron kings and cotton lords of Birmingham and Manchester to provide comfortable habitations for their workpeople; and in so doing, they would be only very imperfectly imitating the example set to them on the other side of the Atlantic, by persons of much smaller means. When the founders of Lowell had determined to erect factories, they thought themselves bound to provide dwellings for the factory girls. Every firm has consequently constructed upon its premises a number of boarding-houses, appropriated entirely to their use. There they are placed under the protection of ma-

trons, who are answerable for their boarders, and
who are themselves subject to a very strict control
in every thing that concerns the management of
their little community.*   A plentiful table is provided, and the utmost neatness and regularity pervade every part of each establishment.   Nor is the
physical comfort of the inmates alone considered;
equal attention is paid to their moral and intellectual welfare.   The outward observances of religion
are strictly enforced; no indecorum and still less
any immorality is tolerated; and literature is cultivated with a success of which English readers are
enabled to judge by the recent publication of the
" Lowell Offering."  Many of the regulations adopted
at Lowell might be inapplicable to the operatives
of Great Britain, but the employers of the latter
might at least endeavour to place them in habitations
fit for human beings.   Any trouble which they
might take for this purpose would be abundantly
rewarded.   What the admirers of past ages most
affect to regret, in the abrogation of feudalism, is
the separation of the affectionate tie which once
connected the peasant with his lord; and what is
found to be the greatest practical inconvenience of
the modern factory system, is the total absence of
any such bond between the manufacturer and his
operatives.   If the former imagine that his duty to
his workmen is amply discharged when he has paid
them their wages, the latter, whenever a prospect
offers of obtaining better pay, do not fail to show

* Chevalier, Léttres sur l'Amérique, tom. i. p. 212.

that they care as little what becomes of their master as he does about them. For the slightest cause, or for no cause at all, they are ever ready to strike work and to involve themselves and him in one common ruin. No surer method of averting this danger can be adopted, than that of making operatives the tenants as well as the servants of their employer. They would not be so ready to leave the factory, if they could not do without losing their homes at the same time, and had to exchange the quiet and comfort of airy, clean, and roomy apartments, for the disorder and filth of a damp, crowded cellar. Thus, by becoming the benefactors of their dependants, manufacturers would immensely increase their own influence over them, and that by a means to which the most punctilious stickler for liberty could not object.

High wages, education, and commodious dwellings are not, however, all that are necessary to place the working classes of towns in a satisfactory position. Another thing, not less requisite, is to relieve women and young persons from the obligation of excessive labour. In most large towns in Great Britain, textile manufactures furnish occupation to a large portion of the inhabitants. Of the persons so employed, not much less than one half are females, nearly as many are under sixteen years of age, and an eighth part are less than thirteen years old. The labour to which very young children in factories are set is comparatively light, but after completing their thirteenth year, they, as well as adult females, commonly work, for twelve hours

out of the twenty-four, at occupations requiring for
the most part a good deal of bodily exertion.    It
is barely possible that labour so early begun, and
almost incessant, may not, if carried on in spacious
well-ventilated apartments, be seriously detrimental
to health; but it is at least clear, that women who
spend the whole day in a factory can know nothing
of household management, and would have no
time, if they did, to attend to their families.    How
is it possible for them then to discharge their duties
as wives and mothers ?    Besides, the vigilant inspection to which factories are now subject, prevents the same abuses from being committed in
them as are elsewhere perpetrated with impunity.
Children are employed not only in textile, but in
all other manufactures, and in many of the latter
they are not only excessively overtasked, but ill
fed, and otherwise cruelly treated.    From such discipline only the worst consequences can proceed.
The children who survive it grow up more brutal,
if possible, than their oppressors.    These evils cannot perhaps be corrected, except by legislative interference.    It is not always necessity, nor the impossibility of procuring a livelihood otherwise, that
sentences the weakest portion of the working class
to such unnatural exertions.    Even if the means
of subsistence were more easily procurable, the desire of gain would still, no doubt, tempt many
women, as well as men, to overtask themselves, and
selfish parents would still tax the powers of their
children to the uttermost, in order to be able to live
in idleness at their expense.    Nevertheless, although

the evils are undeniable, and although compulsory
measures alone can correct them, there are few
questions on which differences of opinion are more
allowable than on that of the expediency of resorting to compulsion in this case. A shocking
thing it is, most certainly, that children should be
deprived, almost from their birth, of a mother's
care, exposed during their earliest years to all sorts
of malignant influences, and, as soon as they have
acquired a little strength, removed to situations in
which their constitutions are undermined by confinement and toil, or shattered by ill-usage, — that
women should abjure the duties and gentleness of
their sex, and be distinguishable chiefly by their
greater coarseness and shamelessness. The picture
needs not the high colouring which has sometimes
been used for political purposes ; however faintly
drawn, it is sufficiently revolting. But, bad as all
this is, there may still be something worse. Even
slavery will be instinctively preferred to starvation,
and it would be misplaced kindness to those who
must strain every nerve in order to get a living, to
prevent them from working too hard, lest they
should injure their health, or be obliged to neglect
their families. If the hours of labour be contracted,
it is reasonable to expect that the produce of labour
will be proportionately diminished, and it is evident that the employers of labour cannot pay the
same wages for a smaller quantity of work, unless
a corresponding advance take place in the price of
their goods. But a rise in the price of British
manufactures is forbidden at present by foreign

competition, which would immediately cause them to be undersold. If then the daily labour of British operatives were shortened, it is very possible that their wages would fall. If Lord Ashley's proposition, that women and young persons should not be allowed to work more than ten hours a day, had been adopted, it has been calculated that their wages would have fallen about a fourth part. Now, as the wages of operatives, although liberal enough in prosperous times, are certainly little more than adequate for their maintenance, it may fairly be questioned whether the daily enjoyment of two hours' additional leisure would have fully compensated for so great a decrease of income. But although, as an isolated measure, the limitation of the hours of labour is of very doubtful expediency, a simultaneous arrangement might easily be made, which would free it from every objection. A fall of wages would be of no consequence if the price of provisions and other necessaries fell at the same time, so as to enable the operative, notwithstanding the decrease of his earnings, to purchase as much as before of every article required. It has been shown that free trade would reduce prices one-third. Suppose then that wages should fall one quarter, the operative would, notwithstanding, be really better off than before. Besides, it is possible that the unrestricted entry of foreign provisions might serve to prevent the occurrence of a fall of wages. It would give a stimulus to foreign agriculture, which would draw capital to itself, instead of allowing additional quantities to be invested in manufactures, so that if the supply of fabrics from Great Britain were diminished, foreign countries might be unable to supply the deficiency. Prices would then rise, and the British manufacturers would be enabled to continue the old rates of wages, notwithstanding the reduction of the hours of labour. Further, it is not quite certain, that a diminution of produce would result from shortening the duration of labour. Persons who are not obliged to work so long, may work harder than before, and may get through the same quantity of work in a short time as formerly occupied them for a longer period. The business of the eleventh and twelfth hours is most likely very languidly done, and might perhaps, without very great difficulty, be despatched in the preceding ten. If so, the limitation of labour to ten hours daily would not in any circumstances reduce wages, and at all events the reduction might be either prevented or neutralised by the establishment of free trade in food. With this precaution, the adoption of Lord Ashley's plan, or even of one still bolder, would be an experiment of little hazard, which, if successful, would, by partially, at least, reinstating woman in her proper domestic office, contribute more than any other single means to the welfare of the labouring population of large towns.

# CHAPTER IX.

REMEDIES FOR OVER-POPULATION IN SCOTLAND AND IRELAND.

Similarity of the Measures required in England and in the Lowlands of Scotland. — Defects of the Scotch Poor Law. — Inadequacy of the recent Attempt to amend it. — Necessity for an efficient Poor Law in the Highlands. — Restoration of the Class of Crofters. — Probable Advantages of that Course both to Landlords and Tenants. — Little Benefit to Ireland to be expected from the Redress of her political Grievances. — Inapplicability to Ireland of most of the Measures recommended for Adoption in Great Britain. — Necessity of providing additional Employment for the People. — Uncertainty of permanent Results of this kind from Expenditure on public Works or on the Reclamation of waste Land. — Sufficiency of the Land at present under Cultivation for the full Employment of the Peasantry. — Defectiveness of the present Tenure of Land. — Exorbitance of Rents. — Want of Leases. — Profit experienced from the liberal Application of Labour to Agriculture. — Baselessness of Prejudices against Cottier Tenantry. — Necessity for Leases. — Expediency of legislative Interference to enforce the Grant of them. — Location of Poor on waste Land. — Happy Effects already obtained from this Measure. — Possibility of providing for the whole Body of Peasantry by means of a Partition of waste Land. — Duty of Parliament to adopt a Scheme for that Purpose. — Repeal of the Union with Great Britain. — Chances of its being effected. — Speculations on its eventual Consequences.

MOST of the measures which have been recommended for adoption in England would prove equally beneficial in Scotland. In the southern half of that country, the condition of the peasantry is at least tolerable. All who can work have plenty of employment, at wages somewhat above the average rate of England; heads of families have commonly some accessory sources of income, and unmarried farm servants are generally lodged and boarded by their masters. Few who possess health and strength, and a moderate stock of prudence, suffer from want. No very great change is required to make this state of things perfectly satisfactory. Free Trade would most probably bring farmers and their servants into closer connection, and raise the price of labour, and at all events, by cheapening food and other necessaries, would greatly increase the value of present wages. This, and an extension of the allotment system, are perhaps all that are needed to raise agricultural labourers in the Lowlands to an equality in all social respects with the same class in Norway, Belgium, or Switzerland. Intellectually, they are even now superior. The parish schools, which have been in existence nearly a hundred and fifty years, have sharpened the natural shrewdness of the Scottish character, and have assisted largely in giving the lowest orders of people their well-deserved reputation for enlightenment, good sense, and clearheadedness. Undoubtedly, there are serious defects in the existing plan of national education. The teachers are very inadequately remunerated, and are not subject to proper supervision; and the close connection of parish schools with the established church, closes

them against a large portion of the community.
Still, machinery which works so well, and has produced such palpable benefit, cannot be very ill contrived; and although it may be very capable of improvement, is at least quite as deserving of praise
as of censure.

Even in the Lowlands, however, and in the rural
districts too, destitution is not unknown. The able-
bodied are pretty well fed and housed, but worn-
out ploughmen, widows, and orphans, who cannot
maintain themselves, and have no friends to help
them, obtain very little aid from the parish funds.
Eighteen-pence a week is very nearly the largest
allowance ever made to a single person from this
source. In towns, where great numbers of poor
are collected together, the deficiency of public
charity is still more obvious. In only a few of the
largest are there poor-houses; which, moreover,
where they exist, are far too small for one quarter
of the applicants for admission, and the weekly dole
allotted to the majority of out-door paupers, even
with the aid of begging and stealing, only enables
them to struggle hard against starvation. Yet in
the Lowlands, both in town and country, a poor
law, which recognises the right of the poor to
public assistance, and directs the assessment of their
wealthier neighbours for their relief, is in partial
operation. If even there the provision for their
wants is so inadequate, what can be said of districts
in which the same law, though equally applicable,
has never yet exerted the smallest influence? In by
far the greater number of Highland parishes, com

pulsory assessments have never been adopted, and the sums collected at church, and the other funds of every description placed at the disposal of the Kirk Session for charitable purposes, are so insignificant in amount, that two-pence or two-pence half-penny a week is the average allowance made to the "impotent, legally entitled to relief," that is to say, to the bed-ridden, and to widows seventy or eighty years old.

It is unnecessary to repeat, in this place, the reasons which have been already adduced in favour of a public provision for the poor. So far as the aged and infirm are concerned, no novel principles of legislation need be recommended. It is only requisite that existing statutes should be duly enforced. Ever since the year 1579, the Scottish law has acknowledged the right of destitute persons, incapable of labour, to needful sustenance, and has directed that when adequate funds are not otherwise forthcoming, the heritors or landowners, and the householders of the parish, shall be assessed to produce them. No one will have the effrontery to assert, that "needful sustenance" for a human being can be procured with two-pence a week. It is obvious, therefore, that the poor Highlanders are debarred of their legal rights, and that landlords and householders neglect their legal obligations. The law is set at defiance, and a legislature which does not constrain obedience to its decrees, exists to very little purpose.

A tacit acknowledgment of its apathy has at length been forced upon parliament. During the last session, a bill brought in by the Lord Advocate was passed, the professed object of which is to amend the previous law. This it proposes to do in the following manner. The chief subjects of complaint of the Scotch poor are two; first, the difficulty of substantiating a claim to relief, and secondly, the inability to procure sufficient relief when the claim is admitted. It is now enacted, that when a claim is rejected by the Kirk Sessions, to whom it is in the first instance submitted, an appeal may be made to the sheriff of the county, whose decision is binding, pending a further appeal to the supreme court. Whether any good will result from this change, will depend altogether on the personal character of the sheriff. If, like English justices of the peace, he be disposed to be liberal with other people's money, he will be very likely to admit ill-founded claims, and to encourage indolence and pauperism. If, on the other hand, his prejudices are in favour of the rich, he will assist the parish authorities to get rid of their just liabilities. He will be no more infallible than the Kirk Sessions themselves, and he will not have the same means of getting at the facts of a case. At best he can only be guided by appearances, and may frequently be greatly deceived. Still it is doubtful whether a better umpire could be found. What is wanted is an unerring test of destitution, such as a workhouse affords; and if it be, as it very probably may be, inexpedient to incur the expense of building workhouses all over Scotland, there is nothing left for it but to decide according to inferior testimony.

The great grievance, however, is that a claim, even when admitted, is not satisfied. Hitherto, the only means of compelling landowners to provide for the maintenance of their poor neighbours has been by an appeal to the Court of Session; but such a process was too tedious and troublesome, or too little understood, to be often resorted to, and the Highland gentry have very generally evaded the law with complete impunity. A Board of Supervision is now established at Edinburgh, which will receive periodical reports of the treatment of the poor in every parish, and no appeal will be permitted to the Supreme Court without the sanction of the Board. How this limitation of the privilege of appeal can benefit the poor, is not very obvious; but it is perhaps supposed that the Board's recommendation will have great weight with the Court, and that an appeal which it has declared to be well founded, will be rarely unsuccessful. It is further intended that the Board shall publish the reports it receives, and it is expected that the fear of exposure will deter the parish authorities from persisting in neglect of the destitution around them. The publicity attainable by a further annual issue of blue books, is not, however, much to be dreaded; and, moreover, nine-tenths of the Highland lairds are absentees, scattered all over the world, and are not likely to be much affected by the most indignant expression of public opinion. Besides, the information upon which the Board of Supervision must act, is to be furnished by local inspectors, who, being appointed by the authorities of their respective parishes, cannot be expected to take part very zealously against their patrons. Their reports will most probably rather serve to prejudice the Board against the poor, and induce it to put its veto on well-founded appeals. The suspicious character of the testimony by which the Board must be guided, renders the limitation of the powers entrusted to it a matter of less regret. It cannot in any case decide finally, and can only forward an appeal of which it approves to the Court of Session; but, while judgment is pending, it is empowered to award such aliment as it may think proper to the complainant, at the expense of his parish. This, which might have been a really valuable provision, if the Board were well fitted for the investigation of abuses, is likely to prove in actual circumstances as futile as the other clauses of the bill. Whatever may have been the real object of the framers of the latter, it certainly has very much the appearance of an attempt to cheat the poor by a false show of doing something for them. What was really wanted, was the adoption of some means of enforcing obedience to the law, but the new authority set up is calculated to interpose only in order to set aside complaints against evasions of the law. Such a flimsy subterfuge will not, however, be long tolerated. The bill of last session was brought forward in deference to a very generally expressed denunciation of the ill-treatment of the Scottish poor. Should it fail, as there can be little doubt that it will, of its professed ends, the same public opinion which led to its enactment will equally ensure the adoption of a more vigorous measure.

A thorough reform of poor-law administration must be the first step towards a cure of Highland destitution. It will not only relieve existing distress, but, by placing the burden of pauperism upon the rich, it will give the latter a motive which they have never yet had, for assisting the poor to maintain themselves. Among the expedients which may be suggested with this view, emigration has already been tried with success. One at least of the islands on the western coast, the nominal rental of which twenty years ago was 300*l.*, has been converted into an estate worth 800*l.* a year, by means of an expenditure of only 600*l.* for conveying the surplus population to America.* There can be no doubt that the emigrants have profited quite as much as their quondam landlord by this change, but it is perhaps unnecessary to resort to such means to produce equally or much more beneficial results. To provide employment as hired labourers for the multitudes collected in particular parishes, is indeed out of the question. Their only wealthy neighbours are sheep farmers, who do not require more than a score or two of shepherds for the management of twenty thousand acres. But it is not necessary that agricultural labourers should serve any other master than themselves. There is land enough in the Highlands to allow of every family being furnished with a portion large enough for its maintenance in comfort. Four or five acres of moss or heath would be quite sufficient, with proper

* Evidence before Highland Emigration Committee, 1841, p. 71.

management. It is true that, at present, occupiers
of crofts of this extent are scarcely able to get
a living, but this arises from their not daring to
make the most of their resources. They are heavily
rented tenants-at-will, who fear to make any improvement, lest their rents should be raised or they
themselves ejected. The poorness of the soil is not
the cause of their poverty. How poor soever the
land may be, it cannot be worse than the original
soil of the Pays de Waes, in which, while his
carriage wheels sink axle deep, the traveller looks
over the hedge upon fields of the most luxuriant
vegetation that even the Netherlands can boast.
This district has been brought into its present state
of fertility by small-allotment holders working for
themselves ; and Highland crofters, with the same
motives to exertion, would no doubt effect an
equally wonderful metamorphosis. Let it not be
said that Highlanders are "incurably idle," and
that no reward can rouse them into activity. Most
men are naturally indolent, and if the Highlanders
are worse than others, it is because their natural
propensity has been artificially strengthened, and
has become a confirmed habit. What is there at
present to make them industrious ? The cottier
who is driven from the interior to the coast, and
obtains a plot of rock, strewn with moss or heather,
in exchange for the little farm which had been held
by his family for centuries, knows that his new
allotment also will be taken from him as soon as it
is sufficiently reclaimed. He works just so much
therefore as he must do in order to pay his rent and

keep himself alive, and very wisely remains idle the rest of his time, rather than labour for his own ruin. Prolonged inactivity, whether forced or voluntary, seldom fails to beget an aversion to exertion ; and when the poor man, who in general can find no work worth doing, at last gets a job, he will very probably set about it rather lazily. The only way to conquer his antipathy to labour is to continue to hold out incentives to industry. Convert the Highlander from a tenant-at-will into a leaseholder ; assure him that whatever he can add to the annual produce of his croft shall be his own, and he will soon learn to work as hard as the Norwegian bonder, and will obtain an equally abundant recompence for his toil.

Let us now inquire how landlords would be affected by the proposed partition of some small portions of their estates. Their object in creating such immense sheep farms was, of course, an increase of rent. Has this end been attained ? The average rent in Sutherland is at present only sixpence an acre ; about 1000*l.* a year are obtained from a farm of 20,000 or 30,000 acres. The rent paid by the dispossessed crofters of former days was assuredly at least as much as that, and those who are still permitted to exist pay about twenty times as much. In one instance 5*l.* are paid for two acres and a half of land on the hill side, originally covered with moss, and reclaimed by the present tenant ; and in another the rent of between three and four acres of land, likewise reclaimed by the tenant, and consisting chiefly of peat-moss mixed with gravelly loam, and interspersed with stony hillocks, is 5*l.* 4*s.*\* The eighteen families " cleared out " of Glencalvie, in Ross-shire, last spring, paid the almost incredible sum of 55*l.* 10*s.* annually for less than twenty acres of very poor land, dotted over with cairns of stone and rock, and for a right of common on the adjoining hills.† Is it expected that this glen will be worth more as pasture than when it was under the plough ? Why, its value arose principally from cultivation, and will disappear now that cultivation has ceased. In a short time the heather will have crept over it, as it has done over twenty similarly deserted sites of extinct communities ; the arable fields will be covered with bogs and wire grass, and when no longer distinguishable from the neighbouring moor will become equally dear at sixpence an acre.

The truth is, that in making men give way to sheep, Highland lairds have been labouring under a gross delusion, and have sacrificed their own interests not less than the welfare of those whom it should have been their pride to cherish, to a false and not very specious agricultural theory. They were assailed, no doubt, with the usual comparison between the ignorance, indolence, and improvidence of small farmers, and the intelligence, enterprise, and economy of large capitalists. They yielded to arguments which they did not understand ; the results of the policy they adopted are obvious to the meanest capacity. Let them count

---

\* Times, June 13. 1845.   † Ibid. May 20. 1845.

their gains, and be guided by past experience in their future conduct.

"Improvement" in Sutherland began in the year 1811, or thereabouts. Four years later, or in 1815, the rental assessed to the property tax was 33,878*l.* In 1842 it was 35,567*l.*, being an increase of 1700*l.* in 27 years. Thickly-peopled valleys had been made desert, and fertile spots had become barren; but, on the other hand, sheep had been sent to browze on hills beyond the limits to which the cattle of the old crofters were accustomed to stray. The deterioration of the soil in some places has been compensated by its enhanced value in others, and an addition of about 5 per cent. has been made to the gross rental. It is obvious that this increase is in no degree attributable to the expulsion of the crofters, and that, on the contrary, the glens formerly inhabited by them have become comparatively worthless. It is entirely owing to the conversion of barren hills and wastes into sheep pastures, which might have taken place quite as well if the cultivators of the valleys had not been molested. Still, a slight, though only a slight, augmentation of the landlord's revenue has been effected; and this is all that can be set off against the desolation of a territory of 1800 square miles, and the universal misery to which the peasantry have been reduced.

The natural advantages of Caithness, the adjoining county, are not much greater than those of Sutherland. Three-eighths of its surface are barren and mountainous, and the remainder — the best portion, though perfectly flat, is so bleak and exposed that trees will not grow, and though containing a few fertile spots, consists chiefly of moss and moorish soil covered with heath. Instead, however, of being converted into interminable sheep walks, it has been divided amongst a numerous body of small farmers, occupying on an average not more than twenty acres each, which they hold on moderate terms and on lease. What is the consequence? The annual rental assessed to the property-tax, which in 1815 was only about 35,000*l.*, very little more than that of Sutherland, is now about 76,000*l.*, or considerably more than double its former amount. Surely no better proof can be required of the advantages of small farms, so far as landlords are concerned. The evidence respecting their influence on the peasantry is not less satisfactory. Instead of the turf-built, mud-floored, chimneyless hovels of Sutherland, the great plain of Caithness is dotted with good stone cottages, with signs of comfort about them, and frequently with prim little flower gardens in front. The whole land seems to be under cultivation. Instead of dawdling about for want of work, every one is busily employed. Scarcely a field can be seen without men and horses labouring in it, and labour is so well rewarded, that even women can earn sixpence or eight-pence a day, in weeding and stone-picking.* It must be evident from this that

---

* Times, 17th and 23d June, 1845. The readers of the Times will at once perceive the extent of my obligations to the author of the very able reports which lately appeared in that journal,

the best method of promoting the interests of landlord and tenant is the same for both, — that the
unsparing clearance of so many estates has at best
only had the effect of keeping the rent-roll nearly
stationary, while it has utterly ruined the peasantry,
— and that Highland lairds might put an end to
the destitution which surrounds them, and obtain
means at the same time of paying off their own
mortgages, if they could be prevailed upon to detach a few slips of moorland from their favourite
sheep-walks, and re-establish the unfortunate outcasts of the northern and western coasts in their
ancient position of crofters, at equitable rents and
with the security of leases.

Ireland, " the great difficulty " of Sir Robert, is
that also of more humble inquirers, and of the present writer amongst the rest.   If it be no where a
very easy matter to discover an unobjectionable
method of largely increasing the resources of a
community, how much harder must it be to show
how they can be made equal to the wants of the
people in a country in which extreme destitution is
almost universal?   So intricate a subject demands
long and special preparation, and cannot be adequately treated within moderate bounds.   In this
place a detailed discussion of it is impossible, and
little more will be attempted than to point out the

on " the Condition of the Poor in the Highlands of Scotland."
Within the compass of a few newspaper columns he has collected and arranged as large a quantity of valuable information
as can be gleaned from a whole volume of the evidence taken
by the Scotch " Poor Enquiry " Commissioners.

great principles that must be kept in view in every
scheme for relieving the Irish from the reproach of
being the most miserable of free and civilised
nations.

Whatever degree of diffidence, however, may be
proper, in commenting on the evils under which
Ireland labours, one thing at least may be asserted
pretty confidently, viz., that the redress of her political grievances would contribute very little to the
welfare of her people.  If the Established Church
for instance were to be overthrown, and her revenues restored to the Romish Church, from which
they were long since unjustly withdrawn, the
clergy of the latter would be almost the only
gainers.  The poor would not be one farthing the
richer, except in so far as they might be exempted,
in consequence, from their present payments to
their own religious instructors.  The latter, indeed,
when endowed with liberal stipends, and relieved
from dependence on the contributions of their
flocks, would probably become less solicitous in the
discharge of their pastoral duties, and less anxious
to prevent any of their sheep from being lured
away by rival shepherds.  Enlightened Roman
Catholics, too, would no longer be restrained by
considerations of honour from renouncing an erroneous creed, after it had ceased to be persecuted,
and so the very endowment of Popery might hasten
its downfall.  The priests, besides, would certainly
value their own ease too much to stir up their followers to acts of violence, and would rather use all
their influence for the maintenance of order.  Too

much importance has, however, been attached to such a change in their dispositions. It is urged, that the want of capital is the great cause of the inadequacy of employment in Ireland, and that capital is prevented from flowing into the country by the insecurity of property. The frequent outrages by which property is endangered, do not, however, originate in priestly instigation, and could not be prevented by priestly authority. Where the requisites for spontaneous combustion exist in such abundance, no torch is wanted to kindle them. The flames of sedition would burst forth quite as freely and as frequently without any such aid. The lawlessness of Ireland is really attributable to the wretchedness and desperation of the great mass of the people. The law is disobeyed because, to the multitudes who have nothing to lose, it can afford no security, while it withholds from them every thing they covet. Self-preservation is the first law of nature, and those that cannot keep their lives by any other means must fight for them. To an Irish cottier a writ of ejectment is equivalent to a sentence of starvation, and he not unnaturally endeavours to keep possession of his land by sending a bullet through the head of every competitor. It is destitution, sheer bodily destitution, that goads the lower orders of Irish on to crime. In such a temper they are no doubt more easily led away by factious demagogues, and morbidly alive to national insults; but as long as they remain miserable, the most persuasive eloquence will fail to keep them quiet. Before Ireland can have peace, her people

must be better fed and better clothed, and this is
not to be done by merely paying the priests, nor
yet by demolishing the detested establishment that
has been built up with the ruins of the national
faith.

But not only would the concession to Ireland of
perfect political equality fail to relieve the misery
of her people,— some of the remedies which would
probably prove specific in most parts of Great Britain, would be found utterly ineffectual in the sister
island.   The repeal of the Corn Laws would make
bread cheap, but the low price of bread would do
no good to people who eat nothing but potatoes of
their own growing.   As little can be hoped from
the mere splitting of farms in a country where
nearly half of them already are of less than five
acres in extent.   As for allotments, the bulk of the
Irish peasantry are already allotment holders, and
nothing else, so that an extension of the particular
" allotment system" with which they are connected
would evidently be merely an extension of human
wretchedness.   One palliative of national distress
has been applied with success to Ireland by the
recent establishment of a poor law, which, in ordinary seasons at least, secures the poorest from
danger of dying of want.   But a poor law can only
relieve distress, and cannot cure poverty; or at
best can only help to do so indirectly, by interesting landowners and other rate-payers to exert
themselves for the poor.   Emigration may be tried
on a small scale, but as its operation, in order to be
effectual, must be partial, it cannot be considered a

national resource, however useful it may prove in small districts. A good deal has been done of late years for the instruction of the young by the Government Education Board, which has now under its control about 3000 schools, attended by about 350,000 children. The good effects of these schools are gradually overcoming the prejudices entertained against them on account of their being open to children of every Christian sect, and affording moral and literary instruction to all without forcing upon them any particular religious doctrines; and it is to be hoped that they will lead, ere long, to the adoption of a more comprehensive and equally liberal scheme of national education. It cannot, however, be too often repeated, that the poor have many wants far more pressing than that of education. Whatever the old adage may affirm, learning is no longer the same thing as house and lands, and the best-taught pupils must have wherewithal to live, if they are to profit by their mental acquirements. As Mr. O'Connell lately exclaimed in the House of Commons, his countrymen are starving, and must be fed before they are educated; and the remark deserves notice as one of the very few statesmanlike notions to which the Irish Cleon ever gave utterance.

Every scheme, in short, for the benefit of Ireland must fail of success, which does not furnish additional remunerative employment for the poor; and the all-important question is, How is this desideratum to be supplied? Many recommend a large expenditure of public money in the formation of

roads, canals, railways, and bridges; in the em-
bankment of rivers, and other similar works. While
these were in progress, they would afford occupation
to great numbers of persons, and would raise wages
and diminish the competition for land; and it is
imagined that their completion would be followed
by a development of the resources of the country,
and by a consequent increase of employment, which
would make the rise in the price of labour permanent. There can be no doubt that the possession
of improved means of internal communication
would be, in many respects, exceedingly beneficial
to Ireland, and it is even possible that the mere
pecuniary results might speedily afford abundant
compensation for the money laid out in procuring
them. If, however, the main object of the formation of public works were, to effect a permanent
improvement in the condition of the poor, the measure would be of very doubtful expediency. Unless
the increase of employment were sufficient to create
an entire change in the habits and ideas of the
people, it would only serve to give a fresh impulse
to population, and however great the rise of wages
might be while roads, &c. were being made, it would
be very unlikely to last after they were finished.
By the creation of convenient means of intercourse
with tracts previously of difficult access, great encouragement might no doubt be given to several
branches of industry; but although individuals
might thus be enriched, it does not follow that any
benefit would accrue to the main body of labourers.
Fisheries, for example, might be carried on more

vigorously when better markets were opened for
their produce, but fisheries cannot afford regular
occupation except to inhabitants of the coast.
Manufactures might spring up in some places, but
manufactures do not seem to draw away the surplus
hands from other occupations, but rather to create
a fresh population for themselves. Farming
would become a more profitable business, and more
capital might be invested in it, but what is commonly termed improvement of agriculture, by no
means implies the employment of additional labourers, but rather the very reverse. The drainage
and inclosure of bogs and wastes, indeed, would
set a good many people to work for a time; but the
land, when reclaimed, would require comparatively
few for its cultivation, in the mode most approved
by modern agricultural authorities. The produce
would, of course, be an addition to the present
annual stock of the country, but the increased
abundance of food would not necessarily benefit the
labouring class. The evil from which Ireland is
suffering is not, properly speaking, scarcity of food.
Quite enough is annually produced for the comfortable maintenance of all the inhabitants; but the
misfortune is, that most of the latter are too poor
to buy what they require, and their share is consequently sent abroad. If an increase of produce
were to take place, unaccompanied by an augmentation of the earnings of the working class, the
principal effect would be, that a larger quantity
would become available for exportation. How little
dependence can be placed on public works and in-

closures for any amelioration of the condition of the poor, has been proved most conclusively, within the present century, in the Scottish Highlands and in England.   During the last forty or fifty years, nearly two millions sterling have been expended in the former on roads and canals, and about four million acres of waste land have been brought into cultivation in the latter; yet, in the mean time, the Highland peasantry have sunk to the lowest state of destitution, and their English brethren, also, have been continually and rapidly declining.

Besides, it is not precisely an *extension* of the field of employment that is most needed.   Large as the number of agricultural families in Ireland may appear, it is not so great but that all might be fully occupied upon the land actually under cultivation — which, if equally divided amongst them, would allow at least fourteen acres to each.   Fourteen acres are certainly quite enough for one family to manage, and one-third of the quantity would enable a family to live comfortably, and to pay an ample rent besides.   It is not want of space, then, that prevents the whole of the peasantry from being comfortably provided for, either as small occupiers or as hired labourers: the true cause is, the defectiveness of the tenure by which land is held.   The greater part of the tenants are tenants-at-will; uncertainty of possession and exorbitant rents cramp the cottier's energy, and rob him of his needful sustenance; and the former cause prevents the larger holder, also, from making improvements, and from employing the labour required for the proper cultivation of his farm.

Nothing but leases, on moderate conditions, is requisite to make the Irish cottage farmers happy. At present they are a most miserable race, but their wretchedness arises entirely from their being rack-rented tenants-at-will. With proper protection for industry, they would become industrious, and would derive a plentiful subsistence from the land on which they are now starving, and all the labourers without land, or without enough for their support, would be almost equally well provided for, if the larger farmers possessed the capital, knowledge, and confidence needful for the proper management of their holdings. Irish landlords, however, are not in general very likely to grant leases, at least to their cottier tenantry. They are, for the most part, strongly impressed with the idea that the clearance of an estate is the first step towards its improvement, and they are much more bent on consolidating than on perpetuating small farms. It is, therefore, satisfactory to know that their favourite policy is by no means incompatible with arrangements for the welfare of the peasantry. When small holdings are united, it does not necessarily follow that the old occupiers must be deprived of the means of livelihood. This must, indeed, happen where the dogmas of the modern school of agriculture are adopted, and economy of human labour is regarded as the test of good farming. But farmers are beginning to discover that human beings are the most productive machines they can use, and such as think so, will employ as many labourers as they can keep constantly at

work and can afford to pay.   It is certain that the
peasantry of Ireland are not at all too numerous
for the cultivation, in the most profitable manner,
of the land already under tillage.    Mr. Thackeray
paid a visit to a gentleman in Kildare, who farms
four hundred acres, upon which he employs no less
than forty families, comprising a hundred and ten
persons.   Every individual member of this agricultural regiment has quite enough to do to keep
the land in its elaborate state of cultivation, which
gives the whole farm the appearance of a well-
ordered garden.   The proprietor led his guest into
a huge field of potatoes, and made him remark that
there was not a weed between the furrows, and
that the whole formed a vast flower bed of a score
of acres.   Every bit of land was fertilised and full
of produce, the space left for the plough having
afterwards been gone over, and yielding its full
proportion of "fruit."   In a turnip field were a
score or more of women and children, who were
marching through the ridges, removing the young
plants where two or three had grown together, and
leaving only the most healthy, so that every individual root in the field was the object of separate
attention.   This minute cultivation is found to be
highly profitable, for the crops resulting from it
are the best that land can produce, and are quite
unequalled in the neighbourhood.   Neither is it
necessary, in order to make the concern profitable,
to drive a hard bargain with the people employed
in it.   On the contrary, the liberality with which
the latter are treated, urges them to exert them-

selves to the utmost for their kind-hearted master, and is a main cause of his prosperity. Mr. Thackeray, after taking a survey of the farm, proceeded to inspect the cottages and gardens of several of the labourers, which were all so neat, that he almost fancied they were pet cottages, erected under the landlord's own superintendence, and ornamented to his order. But his host declared that it was not so, — that the only benefit his labourers got from him was constant work and a house rent-free, and that the neatness of the gardens and dwellings was of their own doing. By making them a present of the house, he said, he made them a present of the pig and live stock, with which almost every Irish cottier pays his rent, so that each of them could taste a bit of meat occasionally. With regard to the neatness of the houses, the best way to ensure this, he said, was for the master constantly to visit them, to awaken as much emulation as he could among the cottagers, so that each should make his place as good as his neighbour's, and to take them good-humouredly to task if they failed in the requisite care.*

Let it be remembered, that the scene here described is in Ireland, — in a country devoted in common estimation to irremediable woe. A few years ago, this smiling oasis was probably undistinguishable from the dreary wastes around, its happy cottagers were as slothful, and ragged, and famished as the rest of their unfortunate country-

* Irish Sketch Book, vol. i. pp. 55–58.

424        ALTERATIONS IN THE

men. The amazing transformation has been effected
by one man. How one envies the power of doing
so much good, yet the power is possessed and neglected by hundreds who might establish similar
colonies around them, with little or no sacrifice,
and often with great advantage to themselves.
Either by the letting of crofts of four or five acres
in extent, on the same terms as would readily be
granted to large occupiers, or by the introduction
of the mode of cultivation practised in the Kildare
farm just mentioned, the most crowded estate in
Ireland might be quickly dispauperised, its wretched
inhabitants raised to comfort and content, and its
value eventually, if not immediately, augmented.
There is nothing to prevent landlords unen-
cumbered by debt from at once adopting the
former of these courses. There is scarcely one so
situated, who would not gladly consent to a considerable deduction from the nominal rental, if by
so doing he could clear his property of its pauper
population, and replace them by a few substantial
tenants. He well knows that the apparent reduction would not really cost him very much, for that,
although lower rents are offered by wealthy farmers than by starving cottiers, nearly as much is
actually paid. The oppressive engagements into
which the latter are compelled to enter, are in fact
such as it is quite impossible for them to fulfil, and
serve chiefly to paralyse their exertions without
adding greatly to the gains of their taskmasters.
It is now admitted that their burthens are too
heavy to be borne, but surely the load might be

lessened without sending adrift those who have so long submitted to it. They might surely be tried with leases of their land on the same terms as others who have not their claims to consideration. They would then, for the first time, be placed on a footing with the small tenant-farmers of Belgium, with whom they are so often invidiously compared, and it is unjust to doubt that they would soon rival them in industry, skill, thrift, and comfort. It is equally foolish and cruel to prate about inferiority of race, and to pronounce the Irishman incapable of amendment, on account of the defects of his mental constitution. We need only open our eyes to see, that man is the creature of circumstances, which mould his character, and more or less rapidly modify all his innate and hereditary qualities. Celt as well as Saxon will work hard with an adequate motive, and neither will exert himself without one. The Irish cottier is listless and apathetic, because he has never had an opportunity of showing what he is capable of, but if his landlord can be persuaded to give him a fair trial, no doubt need be entertained of the result. The case of the landless labourer is not so easily managed. The introduction of an improved mode of cultivation upon large farms does not depend so much on the will of the landlord, but although he cannot compel his tenants to employ as much labour as their business requires, he can remove an obstacle which now prevents them from doing so. He can grant them leases, without which it is vain to expect that, even if they possess capital, they will lay it out at the risk of having their rents raised.

Unfortunately, however, a very large proportion of Irish landlords are absentees, careless of misery which they do not witness ; as many are deeply embarrassed, and hardly able to meet the expenses incidental to their station in society ; and no small number of estates are still in the hands of middle-men, who are only desirous of drawing as much as possible from the land while it remains in their possession. None of these can be expected to surrender any portion of their revenues for the benefit of others; but although they will not lighten the burdens of their poor tenantry, they might at least grant them leases at the same rents as are now paid. Even this concession would be a most valu-able boon, and would benefit the giver as well as the receiver. The cottier or farmer, when assured that every addition to the average produce of his fields would belong to himself, would have a motive for diligence. As practice makes perfect, industry and attention would impart knowledge and skill. The land would be better cultivated, and would make a return proportioned to the pains bestowed upon it. The husbandman would receive a larger reward for his labour, and besides being able to maintain himself in greater comfort, would be better able to pay his landlord's dues.

The general adoption of leases would thus of itself, and without any other alteration in the pre-sent tenure of land, be an important step towards the improvement of Ireland; while without it, or some other measure for giving to the peasantry a firmer hold upon the land, no scheme for their advancement offers much hope of success. It is evident, however, that Irish landowners are not more favourable to leases than their English brethren; and as long as they retain their prejudices on the subject, how shall they be constrained to act against their own judgment? Lord Devon and his colleagues in the recent Occupation of Land Commission, abandoned this question in despair, and while avowing that leases are highly desirable both for landlord and tenant, decided that the adoption of them ought still to be left optional with the former. In fact, instead of considering what facilities might be afforded for obtaining them, they preferred to inquire whether leases might not be dispensed with, and some substitute provided for them. They proposed that tenants should be enabled to recover compensation of any outlay made by them in the permanent improvement of land, and a bill, founded upon their suggestion, was introduced during the last session of parliament. There is little reason to regret that this bill did not pass into a law. The deep-seated defects of the Irish tenure of land are not to be corrected by such pitiful expedients. Whatever effect the security intended to have been offered might have had upon the few wealthy farmers that Ireland can boast, it would have had none on the great body of the peasantry, and would not have persuaded one of them to use an extra wisp of straw in patching his cottage roof, or to upset an extra barrowful of dung on his potatoes. If parliament interfere at all, it should do so in a manner likely to be effectual, — by a positive prohibition, for instance, of the letting of land except on lease. Such a measure might be scarcely warrantable in ordinary circumstances, but the state of Ireland is too critical for gentle treatment, and where the salvation of a whole people is at stake, punctilious deference to forms and ceremonies would be ridiculously out of place. The uncertainty of the tenure of land is the grand cause of the disorders by which Ireland is afflicted, and while this source of mischief is left unabated, it is vain to hope for any sensible improvement. The peasantry are quite right in assuming that some degree of "fixity of tenure," as they call it, is the one thing needful for them, and it would be absurd to withhold the appropriate remedy from any delicacy for the sensitiveness of landlords. Its application would be the reverse of injurious to this class of men. The only compulsion to which they would be subject, would be that of disposing of their property to the best advantage, and if the interference implied an inability on their part to manage their own affairs, a salve for the insult would be found in the growing value of their estates. A far more violent invasion of property established the reputation of one of the most celebrated of Grecian worthies. When the Athenian lawgiver was invited to compose the strife between the nobles and the commonalty, he did not stop to inquire whether the burthens of the latter were legally imposed or not. He merely satisfied himself that they were far too heavy to be borne, and then proceeded forthwith to lighten them, and his "disburthening ordinance," which gave peace to his distracted country, has procured for himself the applause of all succeeding ages.   If such a man were consulted respecting the state of Ireland, he would doubtless recommend an equally summary course.   He would assume as his premises that the people must live, and as they cannot live without land, he would conclude that the use of land ought to be secured to them.   Unluckily, Solon is not archon of the British parliament.

Parliament might, however, bring about an amendment of the tenure of land, and provide abundant means of livelihood for the people, by a method more effectual and still less objectionable than a direct enactment respecting leases.   The present exorbitance of rents and want of leases are owing to the keenness of competition for land, which enables proprietors to dictate their own terms.   Better conditions would of course be obtainable, if the competitors were less numerous; and if those who are unable to procure adequate settlements on the land already occupied were removed to a distance, the rest would no longer have to outbid each other, or to submit to any outrageous demands.   Is it then possible that an asylum can anywhere be found for the crowds who are at present without any certain means of support?   The question is a difficult one, but there is at least one spot in Ireland where a satisfactory answer has already been made to it.   Two miles from the little town of Kilculler, in Kildare, is a

tract of excessively green land, dotted over with
brilliant white cottages, each with its couple of
trim acres of garden, where you see thick potato
ridges covered with blossom, great blue plots of
comfortable cabbages and such pleasant plants of
the poor man's garden.  Two or three years since,
the land was a marshy common, which had never
since the days of the Deluge fed any being bigger
than a snipe, and into which the poor people descended, draining and cultivating and rescuing the
marsh from the water, and raising their cabins, and
setting up their little enclosures of two or three
acres upon the land which they had thus created.
" Many of 'em has passed months in jail for that,"
said the describer's informant; " for it appears
that certain gentlemen in the neighbourhood looked
upon the titles of these new colonists with some
jealousy, and would have been glad to depose them;
but there were some better philosophers among the
surrounding gentry, who advised that, instead of
discouraging the settlers, it would be best to help
them; and the consequence has been, that there are
now two hundred flourishing little homesteads upon
this rescued land, and as many families in comfort
and plenty." *

Now, if two or three acres of reclaimed marsh
can furnish plentiful subsistence to one family,
600,000 acres would do as much for 200,000 families; that is to say, for one-fourth part of the Irish
peasantry, which is as large a proportion as can

* Irish Sketch Book, vol. i. p. 46.

well be supposed unable to procure a competent livelihood. According to the most recent accounts, there are considerably more than six millions of acres of land lying waste in Ireland; of which, about three-fifths are acknowledged to be improvable. These waste lands have long been looked upon as a grand resource for the poor, and almost every one of the numerous parliamentary committees and sets of commissioners successively appointed to deliberate on Irish affairs has strongly recommended their reclamation, as a means of affording occupation for the unemployed, as well as of locating vagrant and destitute families. Instead, however, of promoting the work in the manner proposed, viz., by loans to landowners and ambitious speculators, who would probably be the sole gainers by their operations, it would be a shorter as well as a surer plan to permit the poor to reclaim the land themselves, and to keep it when reclaimed. No doubt need be entertained of their perfect ability to perform the task proposed for them. Mr. Nicholls tells us, that most of the recently recovered bog which he saw in the western counties was reclaimed by small occupiers, who drained and enclosed an acre or two at a time.[*] The improvement of wastes may perhaps be thought to require a good deal of capital, but capital is principally useful for its command of labour, and the Irish peasantry have quite labour enough at their own disposal. Their misfortune is, that they have so much. Their labour would not be the worse

* Nicholl's Three Reports on Irish Poor Laws, p. 18.

applied because they worked for themselves instead of for a paymaster. So far is capital from being indispensable for the cultivation of barren tracts, that schemes of this kind, which could only bring loss to a rich speculator, are successfully achieved by his pennyless rival. A capitalist must have a certain return for the money he lays out, but the poor man expends nothing but his own superabun- dant labour, which would be valueless if not so employed; so that his returns, however small, are all clear profit. No man in his senses would ever have thought of wasting money upon the original sand of the Pays de Waes; but the hard-working boors who settled there two hundred years ago, without any other stock than their industry, con- trived to enrich both themselves and the land, and indeed to make the latter the richest in Europe. There is no soil so worthless that an English la- bourer will not eagerly accept an allotment of it; and while the green valley, from which some High- land community has been driven, is fast relapsing under the superintendence of a wealthy sheep farmer into its primitive wildness, its former te- nants are forming new patches of arable land on the rock-strewn moors along the sea-coast. The waste lands of Ireland present infinitely slighter obstacles to improvement; and it can scarcely be doubted that, if the poor were permitted to have free access to them, they might all be speedily pro- vided for in a thousand such colonies as that of Kilcullen.

It has been said that the colonists ought to be

allowed to retain permanent possession of the spots reclaimed by them. To employ them "as labourers, in bringing the land into a remunerative condition *," in order that it may then be let to some one else, while they are sent to shift for themselves where they can, may be an excellent mode of enriching the landlord, but must eventually aggravate the sufferings of the poor. It is probably because this plan has been generally practised, that the reclamation of waste land has hitherto done nothing for the benefit of the Irish peasantry. If the latter are to derive any advantage from it, such of them as may be located on the waste, should receive perpetual leases of their respective allotments,—should be made freeholders, in fact, or at least perpetual tenants at a quit-rent. Such an appropriation of waste land would of course require that compensation should be made to all who previously possessed any interest in it. But the value of a legal interest in land, which cannot be enclosed or cultivated without permission of the legislature, can only be proportionate to the actual yearly produce ; and as land in a natural state yields little or nothing, all legal claims upon it might be bought up at a trifling expense, or might be commuted for a very small annual payment to be made by the settlers. Of the perfect competence of Parliament to direct some arrangement of this kind, there can be no question. An authority which compels individuals to part with their most valued property on the slightest pretext of public convenience, and permits railway

* See Report of Land Occupation Commissioners.

projectors to throw down family mansions and cut up favourite pleasure grounds, need not be very scrupulous about forcing the sale of boggy meadows or mountain pastures, in order to obtain the means of curing the destitution and misery of an entire people. The distribution of a part of the waste lands of Ireland among 200,000 pauper families, would convert them into a body of yeomanry, and would be scarcely less beneficial to the remainder of the peasantry, by destroying the excessive competition, which at present lowers wages and raises rent. Industry would then be stimulated by the certainty of adequate remuneration. Industry would introduce plenty, and plenty would be accompanied by content. Tranquillity would succeed to desperation and violence, and capital would no longer be prevented from flowing wherever a suitable field was offered for its employment. The resources of the country would be rapidly developed, new wealth would be created for distribution among all classes of the community, and the advance of national prosperity would correspond with that of individual happiness. The whole empire would receive a vast accession of strength, when the galling wound in one of her principal members was at length healed.

A scheme promising such brilliant results may, perhaps, on that account alone be summarily condemned as visionary, and, unfortunately, neither this nor any other plan for remedying the disorders of Ireland can be satisfactorily tested, except upon a scale co-extensive with the island. Piecemeal attempts at improvement would have very little chance of success. The destitute inhabitants of a single district, for example, might be located on suitable allotments of waste land, and a means might thus be obtained of judging of the effects of home colonies, on the persons immediately engaged in them; but the benefit in such a case would probably be confined to the colonists. As soon as the redundant population was thus provided for, immigration would probably set in from all the surrounding districts, and prevent any permanent or general rise in the remuneration of labour. Whatever remedial measures may be resolved upon, ought to be applied simultaneously to every part of the country, and their adoption must be based chiefly upon theoretical reasonings, or upon observation of their effects in other countries, uncorroborated by fresh experiments made on the spot. Perhaps it may not be thought presumptuous to add, that in all essential respects they must resemble the measures which have just been recommended. It is universally admitted that want of employment is the immediate cause of Irish destitution; and it is clear, that little additional employment can be furnished, unless either additional capital be brought into the country, or land be given to the people to cultivate. But capital will not enter without better protection for life and property; and violence and outrage, originating as they do in the desperation of want, will not decrease until the people have better means of livelihood. The only present method, therefore, by which they can be furnished with

additional occupation, is to give them the use of
land. Until this condition be complied with, all
other efforts will be futile. It would be easy for
the legislature to settle this indispensable prelimin-
ary. It might allot to every family not possessing
adequate means of subsistence, a portion of ground
sufficient for their support; and this, not only without doing the smallest injustice to any one, but
with advantage to the whole community, as well as
to individuals, by bringing into cultivation tracts
now lying idle and unprofitable. The legislature
may bestow peace and prosperity on Ireland; but if
it continue to neglect its obvious duty, the only
remaining hope of the Irish people will be in repeal
of the union with Great Britain. That measure
may perhaps be impossible of attainment, (though
who shall say that the demands of an united and
desperate people can be permanently denied,) and
it can scarcely be attained without a more san-
guinary struggle than the world has ever witnessed.
If once effected, however, it is not impossible that
Repeal might eventually prove a real blessing to
Ireland. It would certainly for a time overwhelm
that unhappy country with a series of indescribable
calamities; but when this troubled period was past,
all who had survived the sharp ordeal might find
themselves abundantly supplied with all the materials of physical comfort. The change would indeed be brought about in a manner very different
from that imagined by the ranters of Conciliation
Hall, whose vigorous fancy conjures up visions of
torrents and waterfalls beset with myriads of mills,

and of harbours choked with innumerable ships. Manufactures and commerce flourish only in tranquillity; and anarchy and confusion would be the first-born, and probably not short-lived, daughters of Repeal. But although no increase of the demand for hired labour would take place for a considerable time, it is very possible that the working classes might be rendered independent of that resource. If ever Repeal be effected, it will be effected mainly by the mass of the people, who will not be content to use their newly-discovered power solely for the benefit of their leaders. It will have been their own sufferings that roused them to action, and for these sufferings they will seek a cure. Their misery arises from their inability to procure land, or from the hard terms on which it is granted to them. They will therefore take it by force, and take it too on their own terms. The phrase, fixity of tenure, will receive a new interpretation, and will signify the fixing of land permanently and unconditionally in possession of the actual tenant. These are no random assertions. Even now the Irish farmer, in defiance of the law, acts as if the land were in some measure his own, and destroys his rival's life, and risks his own, rather than give up possession of the means by which he lives. Is it likely that he will be more moderate in his notions, when he can make laws for himself? Can it be doubted that the first act of an Irish parliament really representing the majority of the nation, would be a general confiscation of landed property, and that, even without waiting for such a legal sanction, the occupiers would cease to pay rent as soon as the power of compelling them to do so was removed? In such proceedings, too, there would be no respect of persons. The infatuated demagogues who are labouring so zealously in the work of agitation, imagine, in the fulness of their self-conceit, that they shall be able to rule the spirit they are evoking, — to ride upon the whirlwind and direct the storm; and they will do so even as much as the clods and stones thrown into the funnel of an Icelandic geyser control the angry fountain that spouts them back into the air. It is a likely matter, truly, that the estates of Catholics will be spared when those of Protestants have been seized upon by the peasantry, and that a Repealer's tenants will continue voluntarily to pay him his dues, when they see their brethren on what was lately the property of an Orangeman self-constituted sovereigns of the soil. Whatever sects and parties there may be amongst Irish landed gentry, in one respect they are all exactly alike. The distinctive pretensions of every one of them rest on precisely the same footing; — their tenants pay rent simply because they are compelled to do so, and for no other reason; and the power which upholds them in their station cannot be withdrawn without involving all indiscriminately, O'Connells and O'Briens as well as Beresfords and Jocelyns, in the same irretrievable ruin. 'Tis an ill wind, however, that blows good to none. No native of Britain, and no right-minded

Irishman, can contemplate without dismay the events by which Repeal must be preceded and followed — the horrors of civil war, the dissolution of the empire, the loss of national greatness, and possibly of national independence. But social happiness is still more to be prized than political importance, and so far as Ireland alone is concerned, there may be discovered, through a long and dreary vista, eventual compensation for all the disastrous consequences of Repeal. Of all kinds of pride there is none so excusable as pride of country, and in political freedom is the only perfect security for the continuance of material blessings; but it is simply ridiculous to be proud of a country which does not provide the boaster with the necessaries of life, and the value of that freedom cannot be very great which only leaves its possessor at liberty to starve, and the market price of which would not keep him in potatoes. The mass of the Irish people would certainly have great reason to rejoice, although their country should cease to be a component part of the greatest empire upon earth, and should sink into a dependency of France or some other foreign power, provided at the same time they were themselves raised from their present degraded condition to a level with the peasantry of continental Europe. Such a change is promised by Repeal for a future generation, at the expense, it is true, of incalculable misery to the present one. Peaceful, gentle, easy means of attaining the same end are at the command of the legislature, but if they are still to remain unemployed, a cool speculator would probably decide it to be better for the interests of humanity that the present race should sustain a tenfold weight of affliction rather than that their heritage of woe should descend unmitigated to a remote posterity.

# CHAPTER X.

Concluding Reflections. — Chances of the Stability of National
Prosperity.

SUPPOSING now that the labouring class were effectually extricated from poverty, it remains to consider whether they might not again, after a time,
relapse into it. What security is there that
their numbers would not again grow out of proportion to their resources, or that the latter would
not undergo an absolute diminution? To the first
of these questions, a satisfactory answer, it is to be
hoped, has already been given; for a principal
object of the preceding pages has been to prove,
that when people are once in possession of sufficient
means of livelihood, they will not, through a mere
increase of their numbers, render those means inadequate to their support. There is not, however,
the same certainty that they would not be impoverished by a decrease of their resources. As the
substantial yeomanry of the fourteenth century
were reduced to want by the substitution of sheep
farming for tillage, so it may be easily imagined
that another revolution in industry — such, for
instance, as the extensive application of machinery

to agriculture — might once more diminish the demand for labour, and deprive the peasantry of their main stay. The best way to guard against such a catastrophe is to raise agricultural labourers from entire dependence on the hire of their services, by immediately furnishing them with allotments of land, and by that and other means enabling them to accumulate wherewithal to purchase land for themselves. Proprietors of four or five acres need have no fear of being thrown out of work, as long as they keep their little farms; and if the mass of British husbandmen could be converted into proprietors of this description, their happiness would perhaps rest on as firm a basis as human foresight could suggest for it. Even without such precaution, the chances of their being hereafter deprived of their occupation are too slight to excite any very lively apprehension. Sufficient for the day is the evil thereof; and if we can only make agricultural labourers happy for the present, we need not distress ourselves with doubts about their future welfare, but may wait tranquilly until the morrow brings with it real matter for anxiety.

Many persons probably think that the prospects of the urban population offer far juster reason for uneasiness. It seems to be a very general opinion that the downfall of greatness founded on manufactures, however long delayed, is sooner or later inevitable; and that the day must come when Britain shall descend from her high estate, and sink into a depth of adversity corresponding with the eminence to which she has been raised by the

energy and ingenuity of her sons. Admitting that
other nations will be content to allow her to manufacture for them as long as agriculture affords to
themselves a more profitable employment, it is foreseen that cultivation will at length have been extended to the utmost, and that husbandry will no
longer allow of the investment of additional capital.
It is supposed that capital then must necessarily be
applied to manufactures, and that a foreign manufacturing population will spring up, for whom the
supplies of food formerly sent to Britain will be
retained. At this rate, all the manufactures any
where used will at last be of native workmanship;
the population of every territory will become as
great as the whole produce of its soil will maintain,
and England and other unfortunate countries that
once manufactured for exportation will be left with
silent mills, and deserted factories, and a ghastly
crowd of starving operatives.

Let us hastily examine the grounds for these
gloomy prognostications. It is said that when the
amount of capital exceeds what can be laid out on
land, the surplus will almost of necessity be employed in establishing native manufactures. It
might be replied that this is by no means certain.
England and other manufacturing countries owe
their present superiority to certain peculiar local
advantages. A capitalist desirous of setting up a
rival manufacture in a less favoured land would
therefore find it impossible to make head against
foreign competition, without the protection of high
import duties. But such protection it might per-

haps be impossible to obtain. An agricultural community could not shut out the goods of a people with whom they had been accustomed to deal, without at the same time shutting themselves out of a market for an equal quantity of their own produce; and they would surely not suffer their corn to lie rotting in the granaries, merely in order that they might have the trouble of weaving worse cloth for themselves than they could procure, without any trouble at all, by the sale of their useless grain. The agricultural capitalist, therefore, bent on engaging in manufactures, would find that he could not do so with advantage at home, and would either remove to some other country better fitted for his purpose, or would send his money there, and live at home on the interest or profits.

But before speculating on the mode in which foreign agriculturists would employ their surplus capital, it would have been well first to ascertain whether that surplus capital can ever really come into existence. Capital is but another name for wealth; and the constituents of wealth, with the exception of metals, minerals, and a few other articles, are all originally the produce of the earth's surface. If, therefore, the whole earth were fully peopled,— if the annual produce of its soil were just sufficient for the maintenance of its inhabitants, barely supplying them with food and with the means of making good the annual consumption of manufactures, it is obvious that the growth of wealth would almost entirely cease. What is true of the whole earth is also true of a part. In a single country, isolated and fully peopled, no considerable increase can take place of native produce, nor consequently of capital. Now, an assemblage of countries connected together by commerce may be regarded, for the purpose of our argument, as a single isolated territory ; all the provisions and all the goods of every kind produced within the whole region being also consumed within its limits. In the various countries forming this assemblage, agriculture would not be carried to the utmost extent, — all the land would not be brought under cultivation, until there was a demand for the greatest possible quantity of produce, — until the population of the whole region became large enough to require the utmost quantity that could be raised. Then, and not till then, would agriculture refuse to admit the investment of additional capital ; but precisely at the same moment additional capital would cease to be created. That which had previously existed might consequently continue to be employed in the accustomed occupations without any danger of being disturbed.

There do not then appear to be any causes in operation which must inevitably remove industry from her ancient seats. On the contrary, in spite of the oft-cited examples of Tyre and Carthage, Venice, Genoa, and Holland, and in spite of the eagerness with which her jealous neighbours gloat over every fancied symptom of decay, Britain may yet, for aught that human eye can discern, retain her manufacturing prosperity till the end of time. To assert that circumstances may not arise which shall neutralise all our advantages, would be to invite a chastisement for our presumption ; but, if we do our utmost for the social and moral welfare of the operatives, we shall have taken every precaution that prudence can suggest, and may safely leave their future fate in the hands of Providence.

THE END.

LONDON :
Printed by A. SPOTTISWOODE,
New-Street-Square.